Sketching NATURE

The Beginner's Guide to Keeping a Botanical Sketchbook

Dianne Sutherland

DAVID & CHARLES
—PUBLISHING—

www.davidandcharles.com

Contents

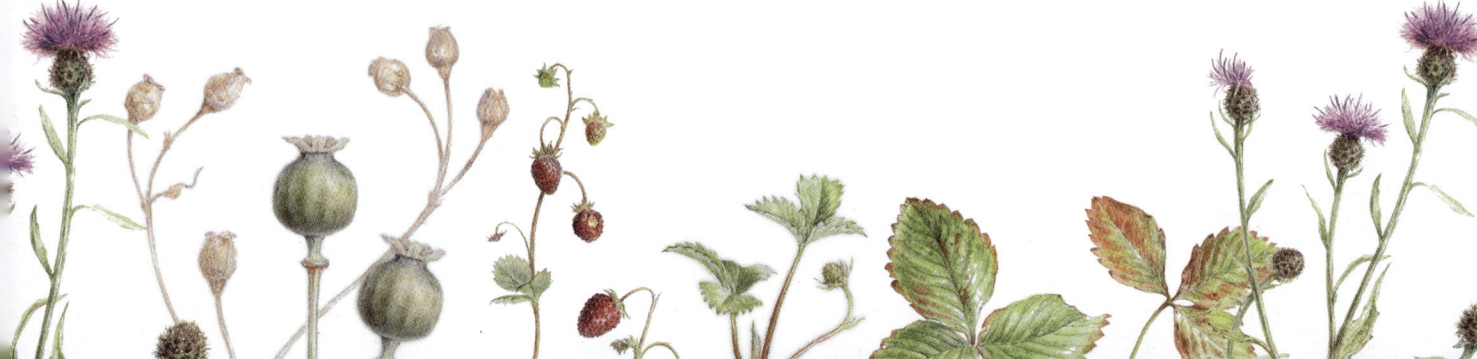

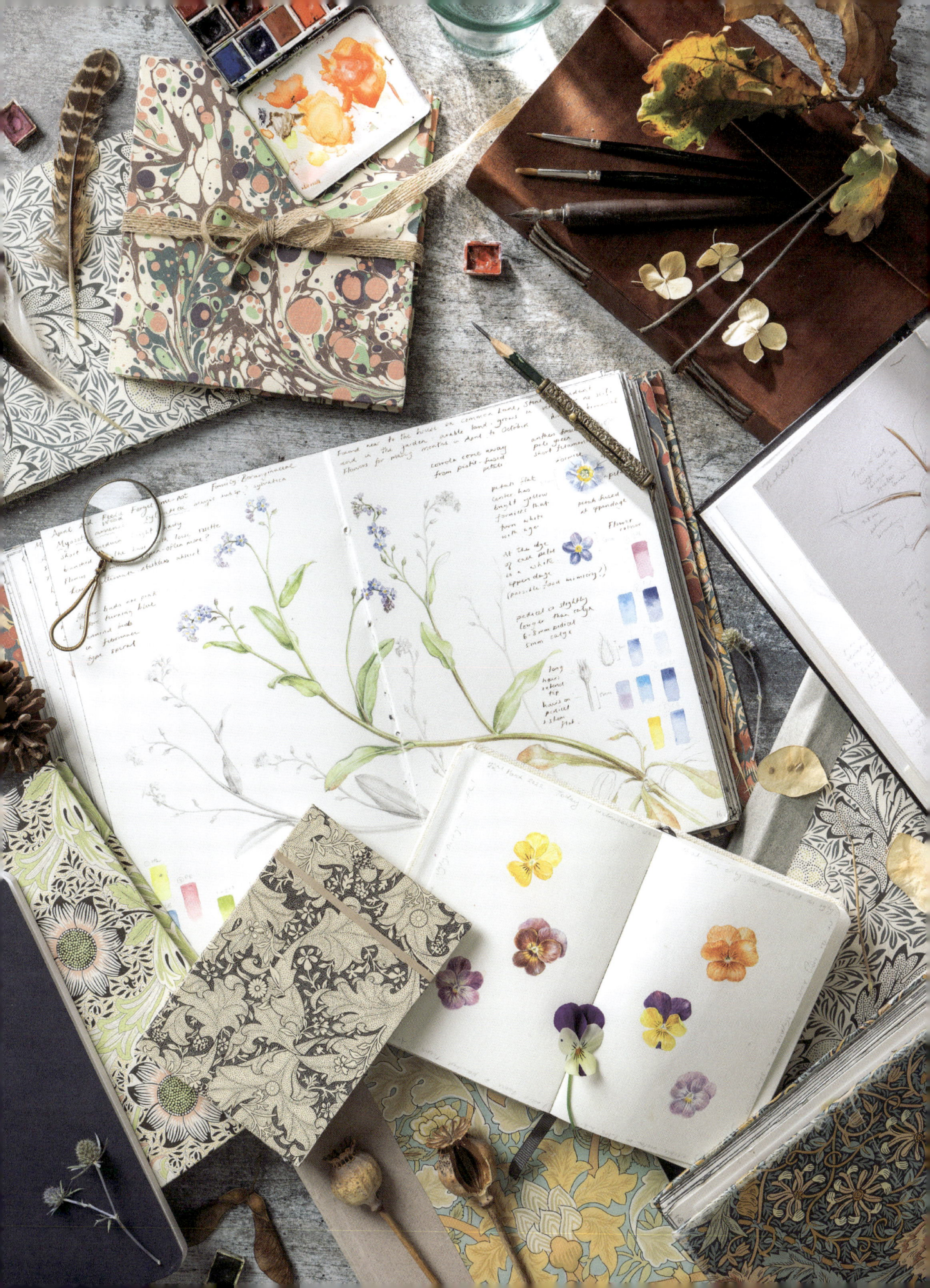

Why Keep a Nature Sketchbook?

Nature-based sketchbooks have long been used by naturalists and artists to document the world. Recently, there's been a renewed interest in botanical art and sketching as people seek to reconnect with nature. In a fast-changing world, sketching offers a mindful way to engage with the environment, encouraging observation and appreciation of the natural beauty around us.

Numerous benefits of connecting with nature through art have been well documented, contributing to the growing popularity of this activity, and here are just a few of them.

CREATIVITY

Engaging with nature through a sketchbook can significantly enhance our observation skills. Documenting our natural surroundings inspires creative thinking through drawing, painting, and writing – all of which improve and develop with practice.

A sketchbook provides a wonderful way to explore nature though art, as seen in this study of a Dandelion, a fascinating and often overlooked plant.

LEARNING

Keeping a sketchbook is an excellent educational tool for fostering curiosity and gaining a deeper understanding of ecological and environmental issues. It's a perfect activity for learning, regardless of your interests or age, and you will quickly learn more about the natural world.

WELL-BEING

Sketching from nature often involves walking or simply being outdoors, whether it's close to home, in the garden, in parks, or in the wild, and that's always beneficial, creating the space and time to relax.

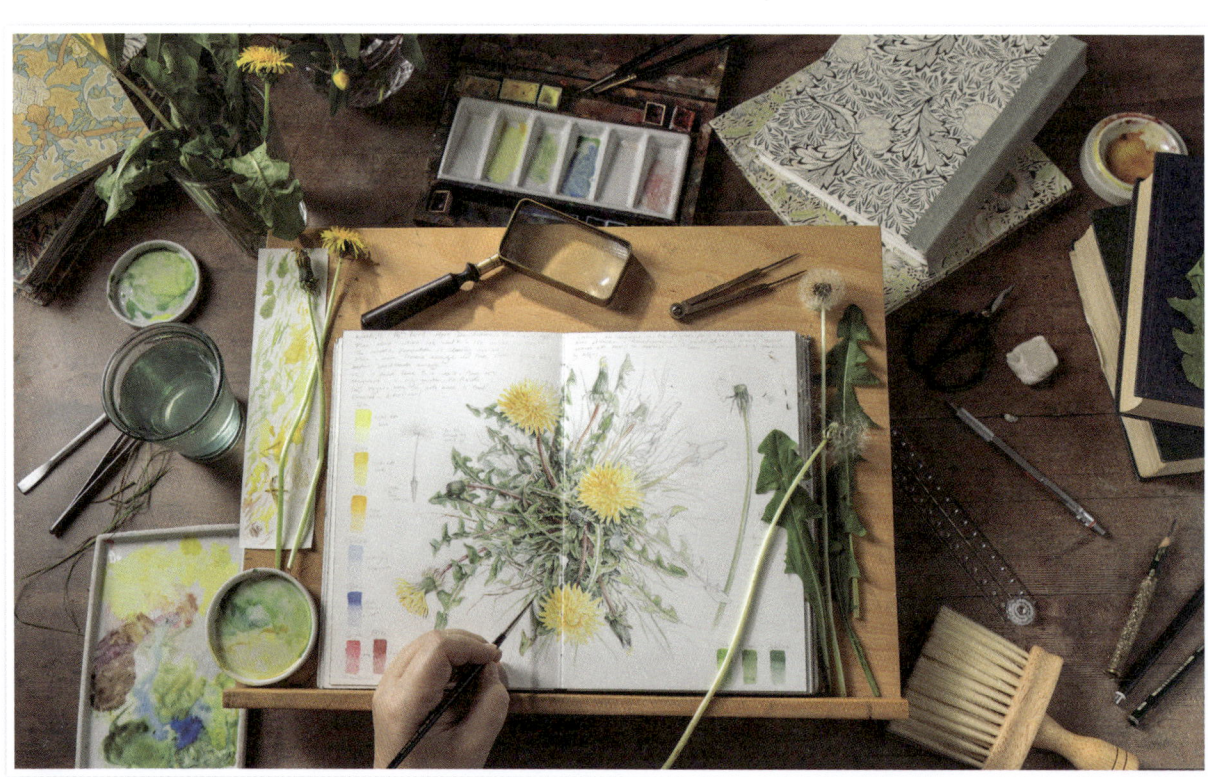

NATURE JOURNALS VS BOTANICAL SKETCHBOOKS

If you're confused about the difference between nature journalling, nature sketchbooks, and botanical sketchbooks, don't worry as there is much overlap.

Essentially, a nature journal is predominantly about being outdoors and recording observations of nature through sketches and writing. It focuses on documenting place and time and the nature within habitats, often with some personal reflections or scientific information.

A nature-based or botanical sketchbook, on the other hand, is a bit more flexible and art-focused. A botanical sketchbook is a visual journal used by artists, botanists, and nature enthusiasts to specifically document plants through detailed drawings, sketches, and notes. It serves both artistic and scientific purposes, capturing the beauty and intricacy of plant life while providing valuable information about plants. A nature sketchbook can include a wider range of nature-based subjects, such as insect pollinators, feathers, shells, and other found items.

A nature-based or botanical sketchbook doesn't have to be completed outdoors but can be, and it can document any nature-based subject. The key concept is to engage with nature by drawing, painting, and exploring natural objects in whatever way works best for you. Whether close to home, in your garden, or something that you do on your holidays, keeping a sketchbook is a personal experience that is a rewarding activity.

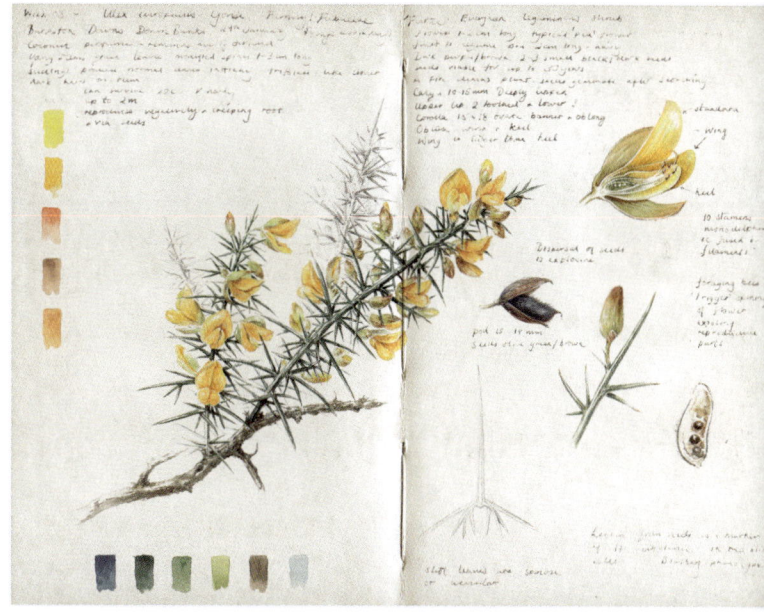

Gorse, *Ulex europaeus*, one of the earliest flowering plants in the year, which goes to show that there's always something to paint in a sketchbook. This could serve the purpose of preparatory work for a painting or could simply be documentation as a personal record.

BE INSPIRED BUT BE YOURSELF

My own inspiration began as a child when my mother bought me a copy of Edith Holden's *The Country Diary of an Edwardian Lady*. Fascinated by this book, I found myself drawn to nature despite growing up in an industrial town. I spent countless hours exploring plants and insects in my grandmother's garden. My interest deepened when I discovered Beatrix Potter's sketches; her first sketchbook, made from stitched and glued scraps of paper, was created when she was just eight years old, in 1875. Later, Janet Marsh's *Nature Diary*, with its exquisite drawings, motivated me to refine my skills further. In my twenties, I discovered the renowned botanical sketchbooks of Georg Dionysius Ehret, which ultimately led me to become a professional botanical artist.

When you start your sketchbook journey, you might not immediately know your preferences, but you'll soon find your own path. Not everyone wants to be a botanical artist, but everyone can enjoy the process of keeping a sketchbook.

Nature sketchbooks can take many forms, and in this book, I share my approach with you. Your style may be similar to mine, or it may be entirely different. The most important thing is to let your sketchbook reflect your unique style and interests. Don't worry too much about what others do, although it's always beneficial to look at other sketchbooks for inspiration.

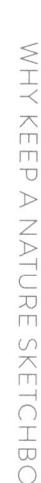

Sketchbook Options

There are a number of different sketchbooks to choose from and I use a combination of home-made and commercially available books for different purposes.

PAPER

The first consideration for me is the quality of the paper; it must be suitable for wet media and have a smooth hot-pressed (HP) surface. This is because botanical subjects can be small but more importantly they require a lot of detail, so smooth paper is best suited to this type of work. A weight of over 190gsm (90lb) is needed unless you only wish to use dry media, such as graphite and coloured pencil, in which case you can work on a less robust paper.

I prefer to use archival-quality and acid-free paper, which ideally is 100% cotton. It's worth investing in good-quality paper for painting because it's actually much more difficult to achieve good results without it; also, it will last longer and will be less likely to discolour over time.

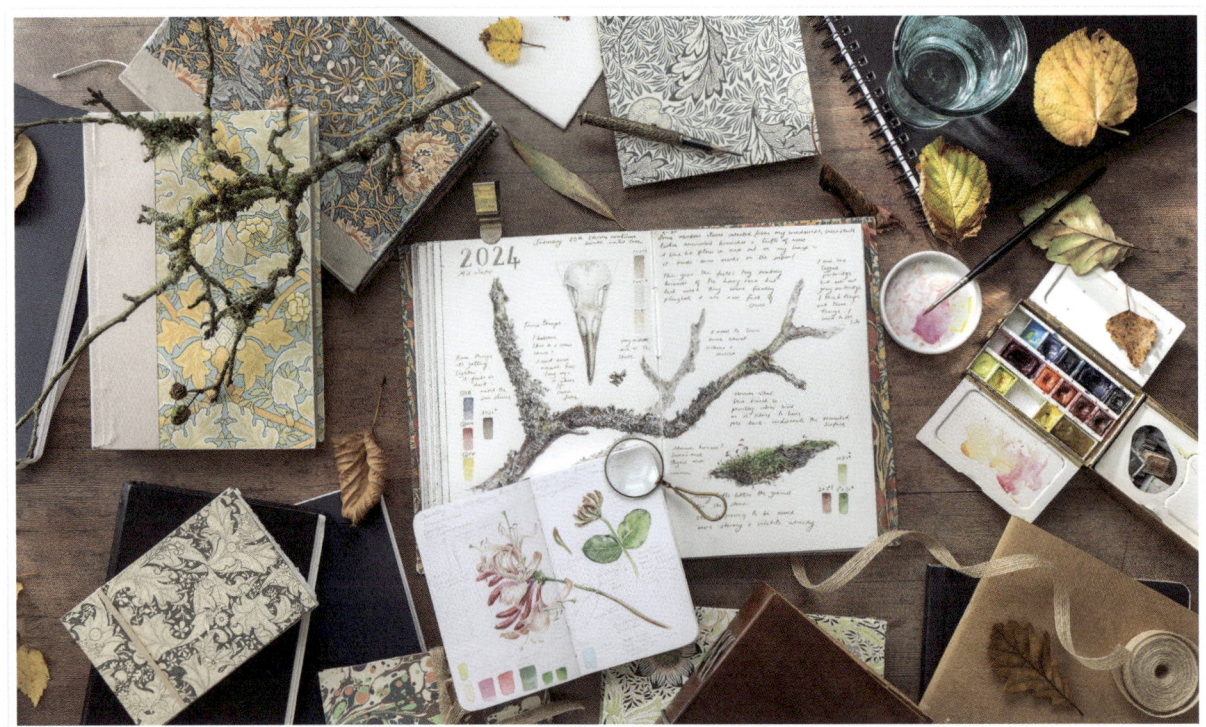

A selection of different sketchbooks used over the years, including my current handmade books.

COMMERCIALLY AVAILABLE SKETCHBOOKS

A wide range of sketchbooks are available to purchase, either in art shops or online. Books can have different papers, binding covers, and orientations, and are available in a range of sizes. Here I discuss a few options.

Pocket-sized Books

Ideal for detail, field work, and notes, pocket-sized books are useful for documenting small subjects such as single flowers and their colours. I like to carry one of these books when travelling or visiting botanic gardens. They are approximately 14 x 9cm (3½ x 5½in) in size.

Bound Books

There are a number of different bindings, including spiral bound, hard bound, and soft bound.

Spiral-bound books sit completely flat, and this is useful, but I prefer to work across the centre of the spread of a stitched book.

Hard-bound books are well protected from knocks and they do look good. My problem with hard covers is that most don't sit very flat, and this can make them difficult to work in.

Soft-bound books are my preference as they sit flatter and are also lighter in weight, making them both easier to work in and less cumbersome.

In terms of size, I prefer a book that's approximately A5, 14 x 21.6cm (5½ x 8½in). This size is easy enough to carry and if it's a stitched book can give a decent-sized double-page spread. Books are either landscape or portrait orientation and portrait is the better option for plants.

A pocket-sized sketchbook is easily transported and ideal for small studies and colour notes.

My first sketchbooks were mostly spiral bound – they are functional and sit completely flat but I find them less appealing than other types of stitched books.

A typical hard-bound book can be more difficult to keep flat, especially near to the middle of the book.

Soft-bound books sit quite flat when open and make it easier for the work to flow across the pages.

HANDMADE BOOKS

Several years ago, I became slightly frustrated by the quality of paper and availability of sketchbooks and decided to experiment with making my own. Fortunately, there are plenty of resources available online that provide great step-by-step information on how to make a sketchbook.

These books can be simple and made as a concertina or accordion sketchbook, or they can be stitched and bound, which is a little more complicated.

HOW TO MAKE YOUR OWN SKETCHBOOK

Making a customized sketchbook is a rewarding experience and you might be surprised to learn that it's not as complicated as you might think. For a beginner, I recommend making a concertina sketchbook first as this is by far the simplest.

A concertina sketchbook is a very versatile book with folded pages that can be used individually or as a continuous project with art that flows across the pages. A hard cover can be added to protect the pages and decorated with decorative paper of your choice.

Follow these steps to make a customized concertina sketchbook with good-quality paper that suits your artistic needs.

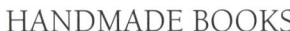

The range of materials and equipment used to make a concertina or accordion sketchbook.

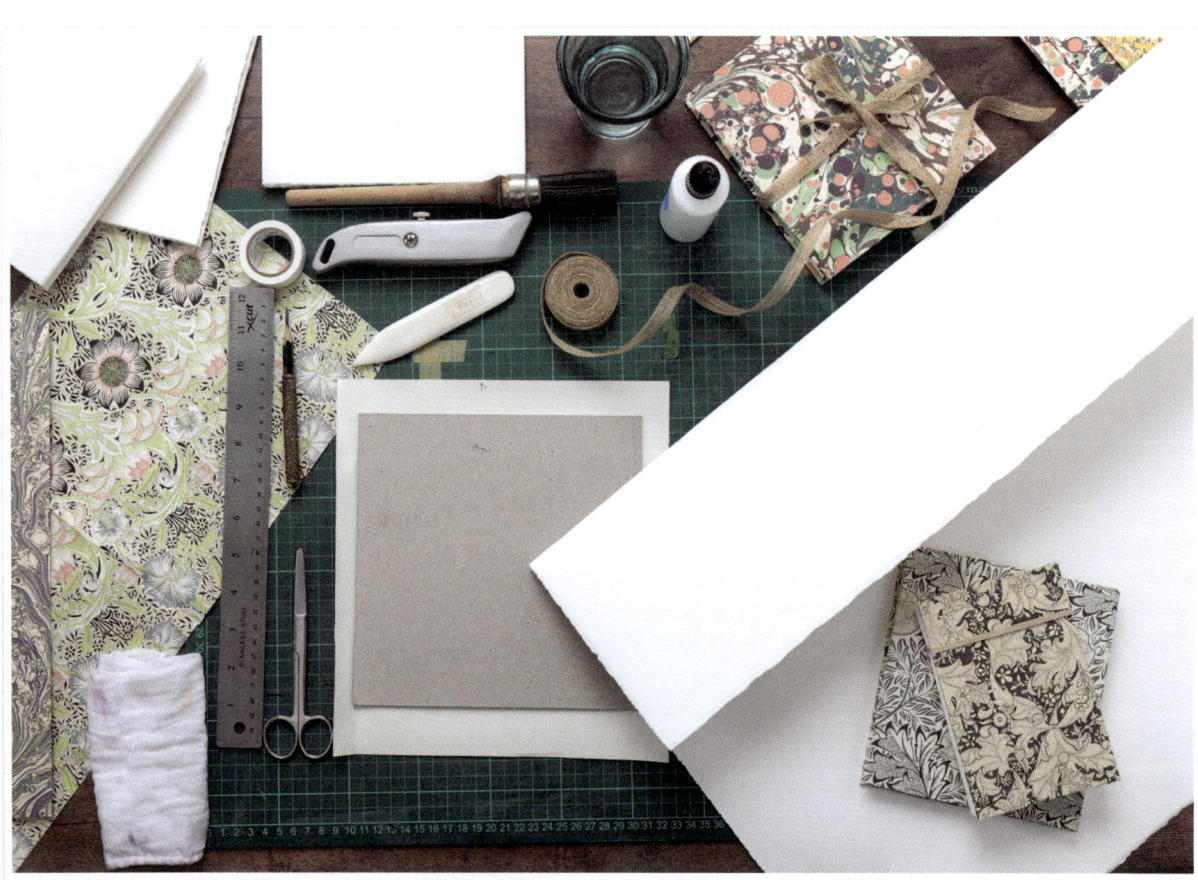

You will need

- Paper: one Imperial-sized (559 x 762mm / 22 x 30in) sheet of smooth surface hot-pressed watercolour paper, 300gsm (140lb)
- Cover material: cardboard, bookbinding board, or thick cardstock
- Decorative paper or fabric: for covering the cardboard covers
- Adhesive: bookbinding glue, PVA glue, or a strong adhesive, and a brush for gluing
- Cutting tools: ruler, pencil, cutting mat, craft knife, or scissors
- Bone folder: for creating sharp folds
- Optional: ribbon or elastic band to hold the sketchbook closed, and washi tape for securing multiple strips together

1. Plan Your Sketchbook

First decide on the format for your sketchbook, which can be portrait, landscape, or square. In the example shown, the book is square and is made from one Imperial sheet of paper torn into three strips.

2. Cut or Tear the Paper

You can cut the paper for a smooth edge, or you can tear it to create a deckled edge (i.e. a ripped edge rather than a neat, cut edge). For tearing, fold back and forth around eight times and then dampen the fold to make tearing easier; then tear it.

The long strips of paper can be joined together later; to make a book with more pages, simply add more strips.

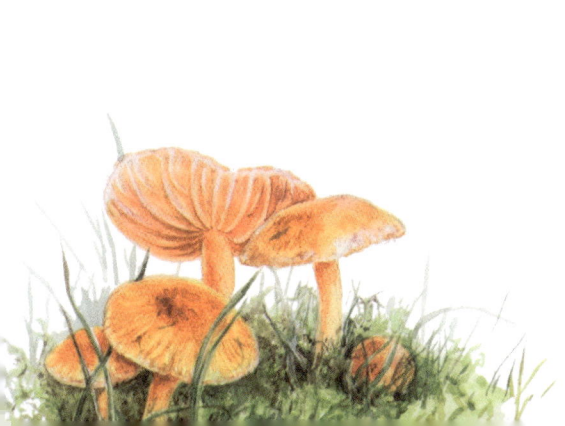

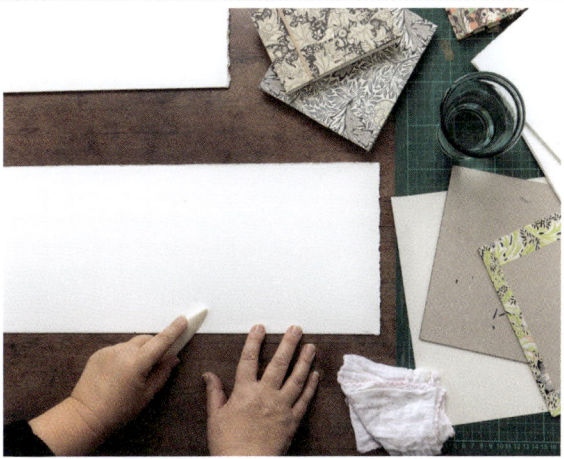

↑ *Start by folding the Imperial sheet of paper into three even strips by bending back and forth to weaken the fibres; then press along the fold with the bone folder.*

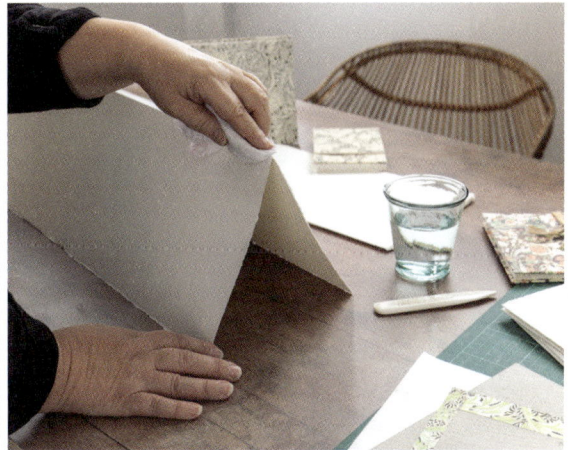

↑ *Next, dampen the fold with a wet cloth to make it easier to tear.*

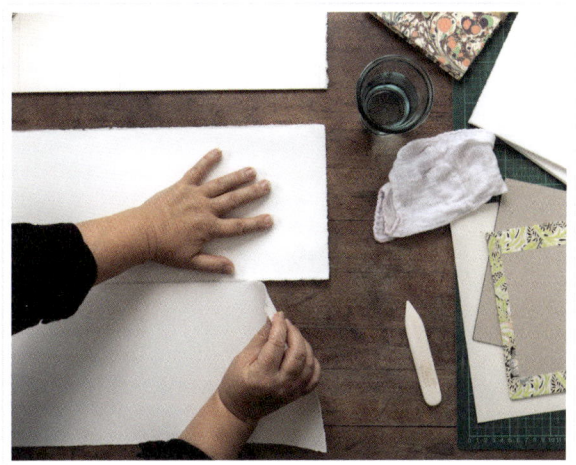

↑ *Lay one hand flat on the paper and tear with the other. This takes a little confidence but it is surprisingly easy.*

3. Fold the Paper

Measure and mark: using a ruler and pencil, measure and mark where each fold will be. This ensures evenly sized pages.

Create the pages: fold the paper back and forth in an accordion style, using a bone folder to crease each fold sharply. Ensure all folds are parallel and even.

Joining strips: if using separate strips of paper, these can be taped together with washi tape on the reverse side.

4. Prepare the Covers

Cut the covers: cut two pieces of cardboard slightly larger than the pages (e.g. a minimum of 3mm (⅛in) larger on each side).

Decorate the covers: wrap the covers with decorative paper (or fabric). Cut the decorative paper slightly larger than the covers, glue it on, and fold the edges over to the inside, securing them with glue.

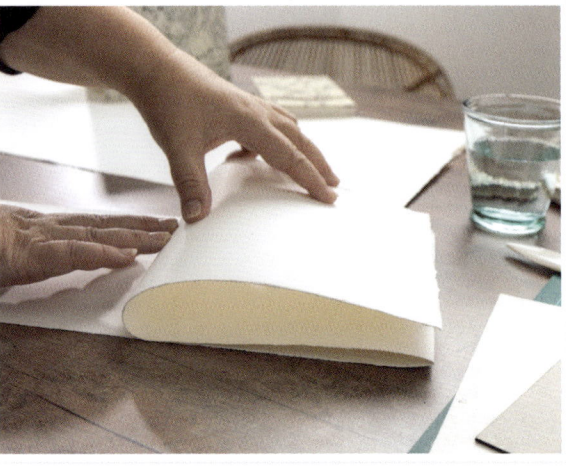

↑ *Fold the paper into the concertina arrangement. It's important to make sure that each page is the same size, or the book won't sit neatly when folded.*

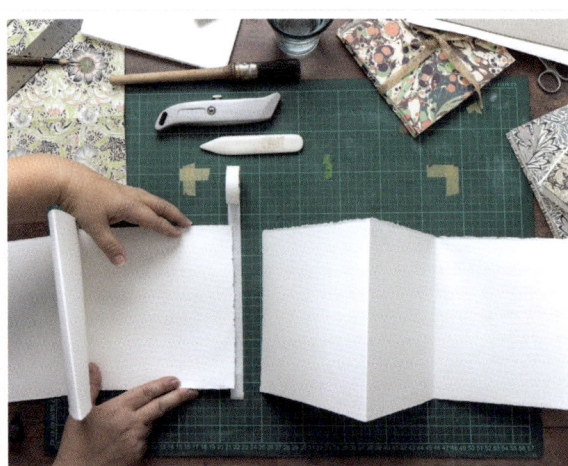

↑ *When using multiple strips, you can tape them together on the reverse side.*

When covering the card, the paper can sometimes bubble, so use a bone folder to smooth out any bubbles and ensure a neat finish. Then, press under a heavy weight, such as a pile of books, and leave overnight to dry.

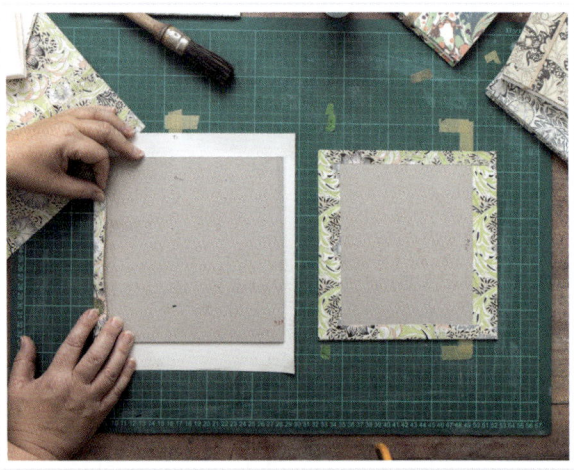

↑ *Cut the front and back covers slightly larger than the paper. You can cover them with paper of your choice and decorate to personalize.*

5. Attach the Paper to the Covers

End papers: glue the first and last pages of the accordion strip to the inside of the covers, aligning them carefully. Ensure the folds are still functional and the book can open and close smoothly.

Press and dry: place the sketchbook under a weight (like a stack of heavy books) and allow the glue to dry completely.

6. Finishing Touches

Add a ribbon or elastic band around the sketchbook to keep it closed when not in use. You can glue or sew a ribbon to the back cover and wrap it around the front.

Now you are ready to begin working in your sketchbook.

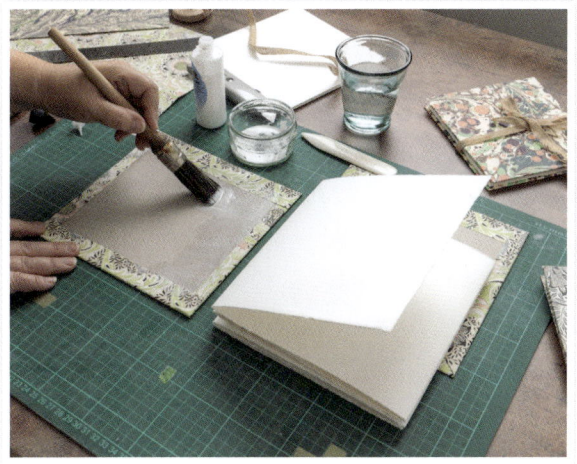

↑ *Glue the card covers to the end papers; this completes the book.*

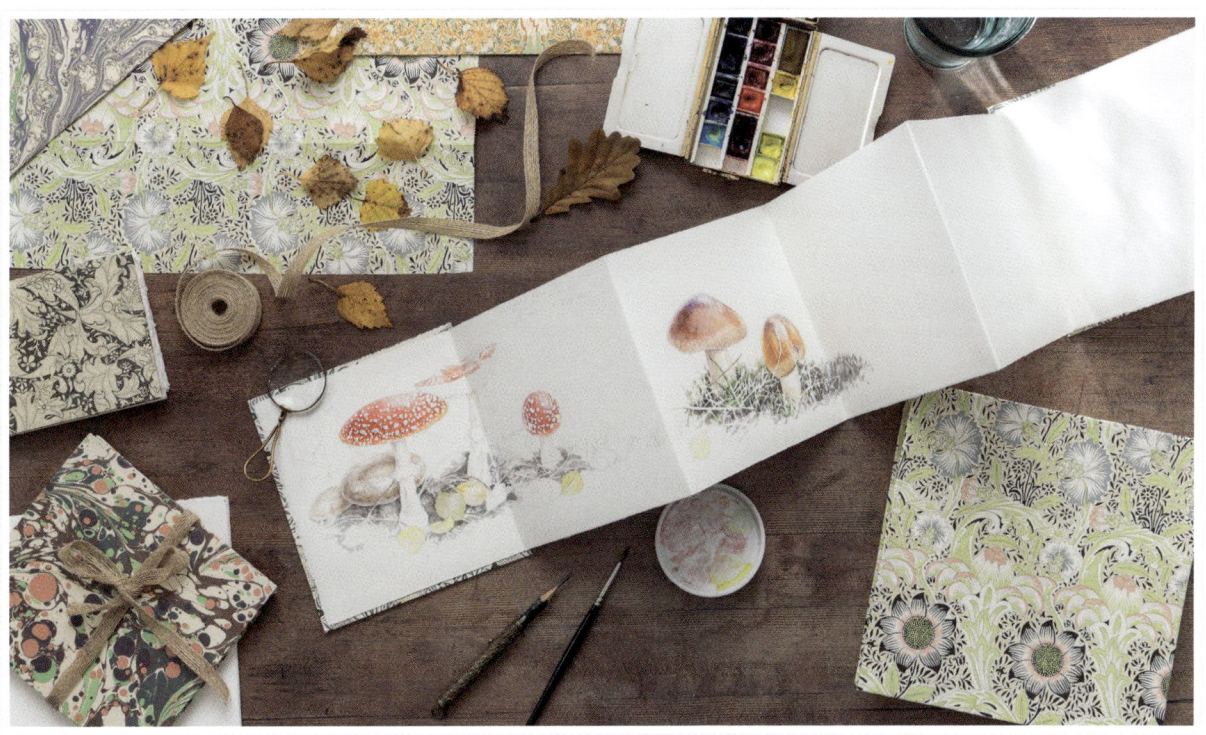

↑ *An open concertina sketchbook showing continuous working across the folded pages.*

Tools and Materials

Drawing and painting in a sketchbook requires a basic kit of materials and equipment and although most artists enjoy trying out different materials, the kit for sketchbook work can be relatively simplified. The first kit discussed here is for work in the studio and the second is a scaled-down version, used for working outdoors.

IN THE STUDIO

In this section, I have outlined the tools and materials that I use in the studio; of course, you can use other brands. Everything is listed for reference: the best approach is to begin with the basics and add later if you feel the need.

Graphite Pencils

Beginning with drawing, there are two approaches: the first is line drawing and the second is tonal drawing, the latter being used to create three-dimensional form with various types of shading.

For line drawing, I mostly use mechanical pencils, including the Faber-Castell TK9713 pencils and Rotring 600 pencils, fitted with either 0.35mm- or 0.5mm-width leads in H and HB grades. These leads create a narrow clean line. I also use wooden pencils if I want to vary the line width.

For tonal sketchbook work, the range of pencils used is relatively simple: Faber-Castell 9000 wooden pencils, grades 4H, 2H, HB, and 2B. See more in Techniques: Tonal Drawing and Painting.

Sharpeners

I use a knife and sanding block but if you find sharpening with a knife difficult, a KUM Masterpiece is a good sharpener that makes the longer leads similar to those made by hand-sharpening. If you decide to use clutch pencils, a tub sharpener is needed.

Erasers

A Winsor & Newton medium putty eraser is the best option. These erasers are gentle on the watercolour paper, and can be gently rolled on paper to remove any unwanted graphite without disturbing the paper surface. Always make sure that the eraser isn't old or dirty as this will mark your paper. A Tombow MONO is a pen-style hard eraser, which is useful for getting into small spaces.

A Dip or Other Ink Pen

In recent years, I began to include text annotations in ink rather than pencil because notes in pencil can be too pale to read, and can rub off the paper. For this purpose, I use a dip pen for writing with Tom Norton's Walnut Drawing Ink, which is a lightfast ink. Alternatively, you can use 'waterproof' fine-liner pens such as the Mitsubishi Uni Pin or Sakura Pigma Micron pens, size 0.1mm. Some pens come in sepia and grey colours.

Measuring Tools

For measuring, you will need dividers and a ruler marked in millimetres. Dividers are used to measure plant parts and distances between plant parts.

Fixative Spray

This can be sprayed on finished graphite work to prevent it from smudging. I use Winsor & Newton Professional Fixative.

Easel

A small desktop easel is useful to elevate the sketchbook; it's better to work this way and easier on your neck.

The range of materials and equipment used for the drawing and writing elements on typical sketchbook pages.

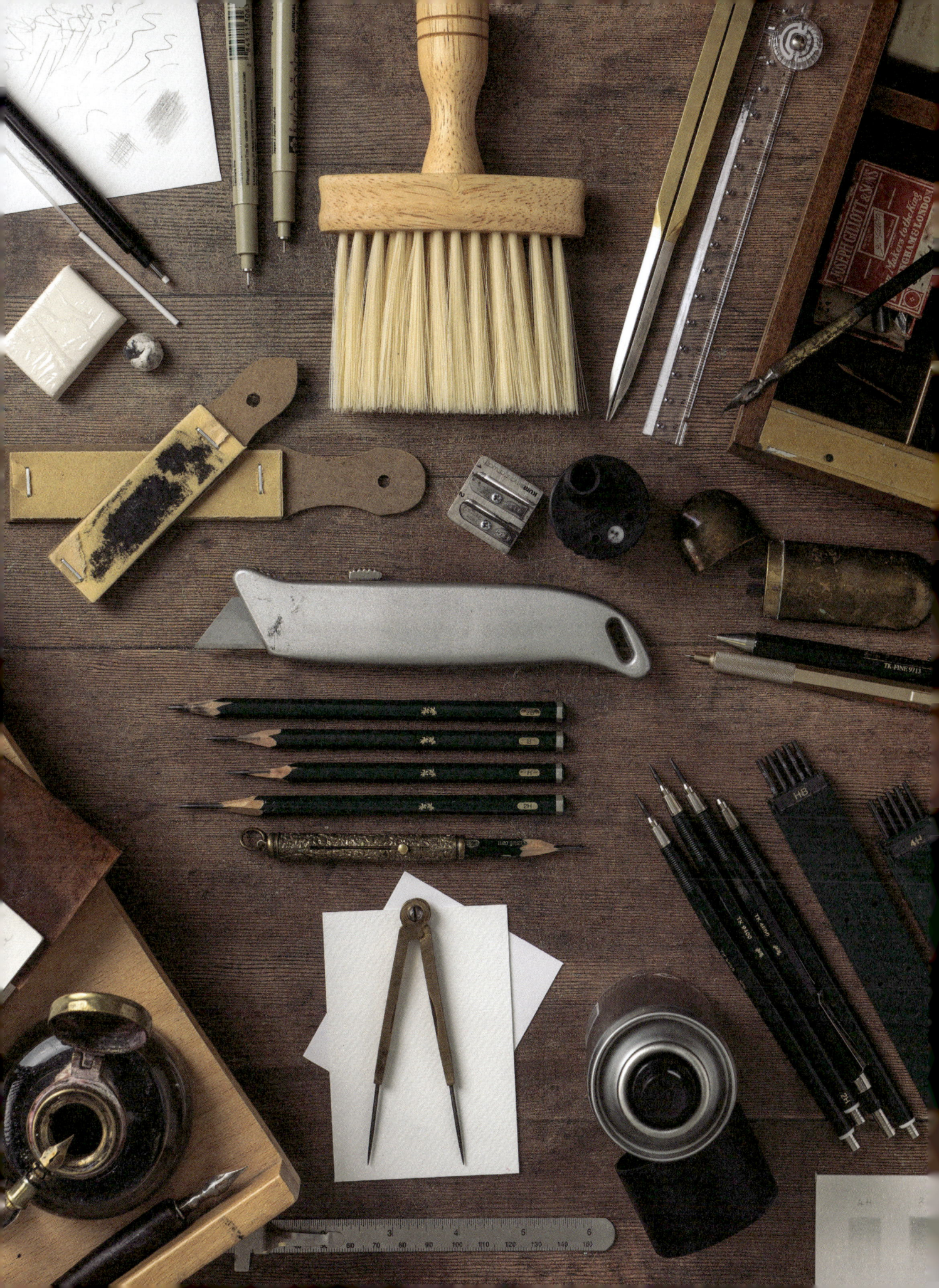

Watercolours

Artist-quality watercolours and good-quality brushes are essential if you want to achieve the best results in your sketchbook. Here are my recommendations, although other brands can be used with a good outcome too.

Paint brushes: you can use any good-quality brush with a decent point and there are plenty to choose from; they can be made from hair or synthetic, ranging from the smaller size 1 and 2 brushes and up to a larger size 4–6 brush. These are sufficient for most botanical subjects and you can add more sizes if needed. I mostly use Winsor & Newton Series 7 Miniatures, sizes 1, 2, and 4, and a Rosemary & Co small eradicator. An eradicator is a flat short-haired brush, usually made from synthetic hair. This brush is quite stiff and allows small repairs and movement of paint, if needed.

Paints: all colours can be mixed from a range of primary colours and I use 14 Winsor & Newton Professional Watercolour paint colours in total. This number is reduced to 10 for my field paintbox (those omitted are indicated by an asterix in the lists below). The range of primaries are as follows:

- **Reds:** Quinacridone Magenta, Permanent Rose*, Quinacridone Red, Scarlet Lake*, and Permanent Carmine
- **Yellows:** Lemon Yellow Nickel Titanate*, Winsor Lemon, Winsor Yellow, and Transparent Yellow
- **Blues:** Cerulean or Manganese Blue, Cobalt Blue, Winsor Blue Green Shade*, French Ultramarine, and Indanthrene Blue.

It's best not to buy a set of paints; instead purchase a separate box and fill it with the suggested colours.

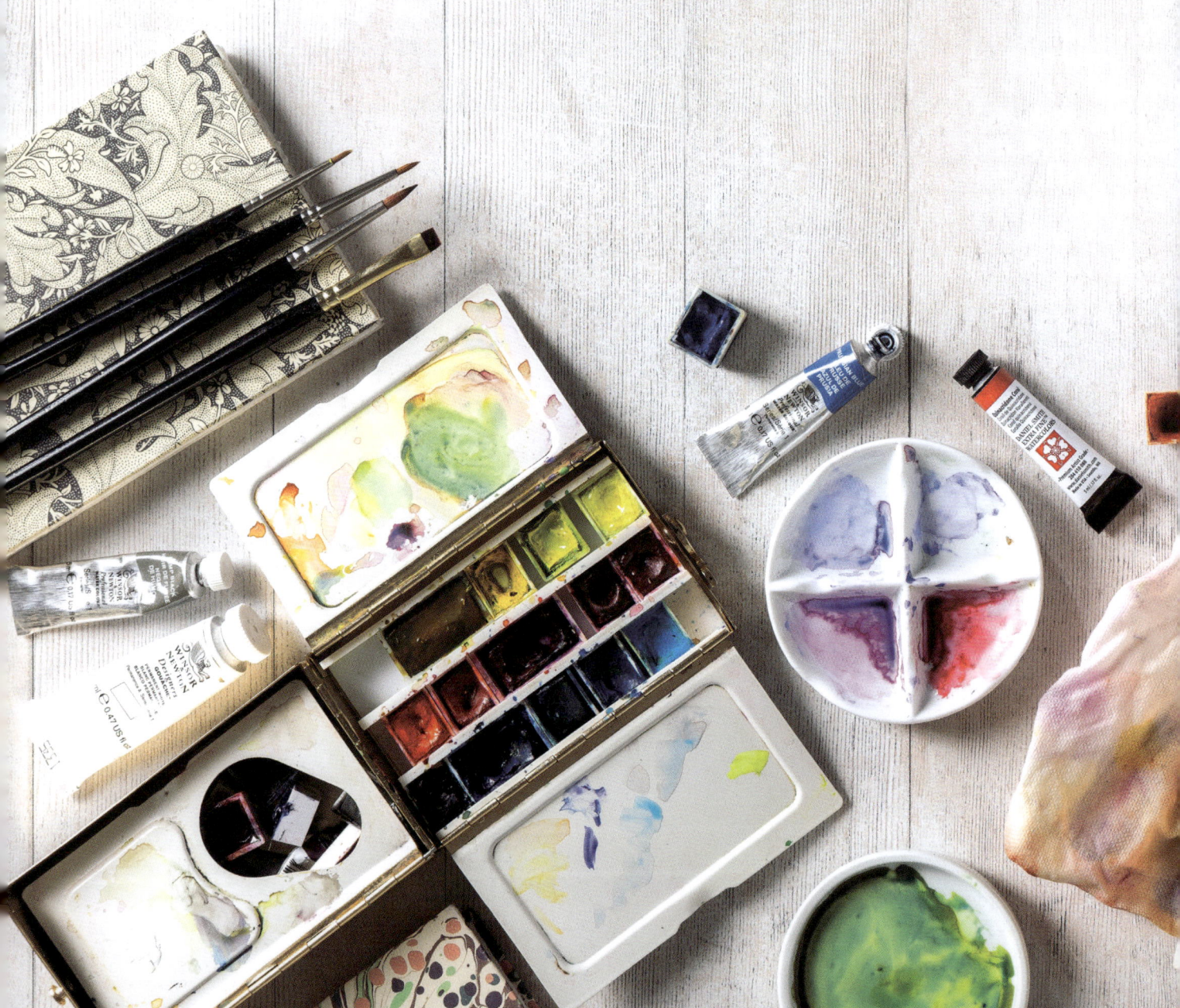

Pans or tubes: I prefer pans over tubes as they are more easily transported and less messy or wasteful. Pans come in whole or half pans and last for a long time. For my most-used colours, I often use the larger whole pans. With some brands of tube paint, you can squeeze paint into empty pans and allow it to dry; however, some tube paints contain significantly more binder than pans (with some using honey), which means that they won't dry and they remain sticky.

Black and white: black is never used for mixing with other colours in watercolour painting but I do use Lamp Black for tonal painting. Black can also easily be mixed from three primaries but a ready-made black is more consistent for tonal painting purposes. I also have a tube of white gouache that is sometimes used for painting hairs. I squeeze a small amount on the inside of the paint lid and leave it to dry, so it's there if needed, which is not very often.

Palettes: in the studio, I use ceramic palettes, and have a range of small stacking palettes, tinting saucers, and flat palettes amongst others.

A burnishing stone: a small agate palm stone is useful for smoothing paper, if you accidentally overwork it.

Painting rags: muslin cloth is useful for wiping the brush or dabbing the paper if there is water on it. Never use kitchen towel on any aspect of your painting – it has many chemicals and is not acid free; it's also very abrasive, which is not good for the brushes.

A selection of watercolours, brushes, and palettes, plus other equipment.

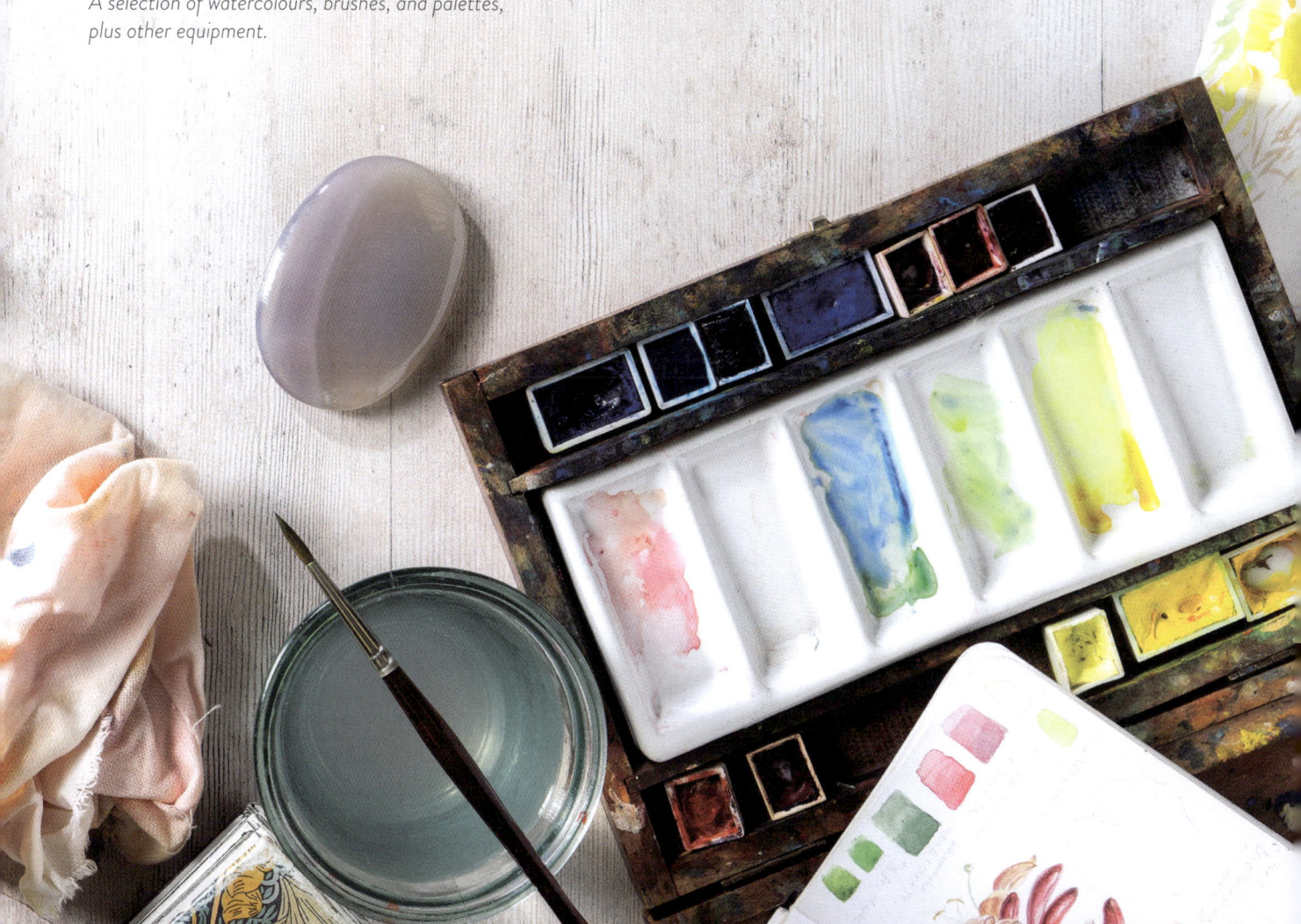

Magnifiers and Microscopes

The following magnifying tools are useful for both investigating plants in more detail, and for checking the accuracy of your work:

- A hand-held magnifying glass with x2 magnification, for checking detail.
- A x10 or x15 field lens, for viewing plants up close.
- A head-mounted loupe or magnifier, useful because it provides hands-free magnification.
- A portable digital microscope can be useful if you want a closer look at plant parts.

Dissection and Cutting Tools

Florist's scissors, a scalpel, and cutting mat are useful if you intend to dissect parts. You can also buy a small dissecting kit, which includes scissors, tweezers, and prods (small plastic tubes that are filled with water; they have a cap that the stem is inserted into, keeping the flower fresh and prolonging the life of the flower).

Tools for Positioning Plants

In the studio, you will no doubt find that plants can be difficult to keep in place, so here are some devices and items that can help:

- A small retort stand can be useful for holding plants into position in the studio.

- Florist's tubes for water help keep the suspended plant alive. When you are not using the plants, store them in a cool place on dampened kitchen towel.
- A florist's frog or pin plant holder is a spiked flower arranging tool that plant stems sit on; this is a good alternative to florist's foam.
- Florist's tape or adhesive tack, string, tape, and long pins can help keep an unruly plant under control.
- There are many more options, such as helping-hand-type clips. You really do have to be quite creative when it comes to setting up plant material in the studio.

Lighting

Good lamps should be used in the studio for lighting both the subject and the workspace. These should be daylight lamps with a colour temperature of 5500 Kelvin and a colour render index (CRI) of over 85CRI.

The lamp above your workspace can run the width of the easel. This should provide even lighting on the working area. The Daylight Company offer several options. Learn more tips for lighting your studio workspace in Techniques: Tonal Drawing and Painting.

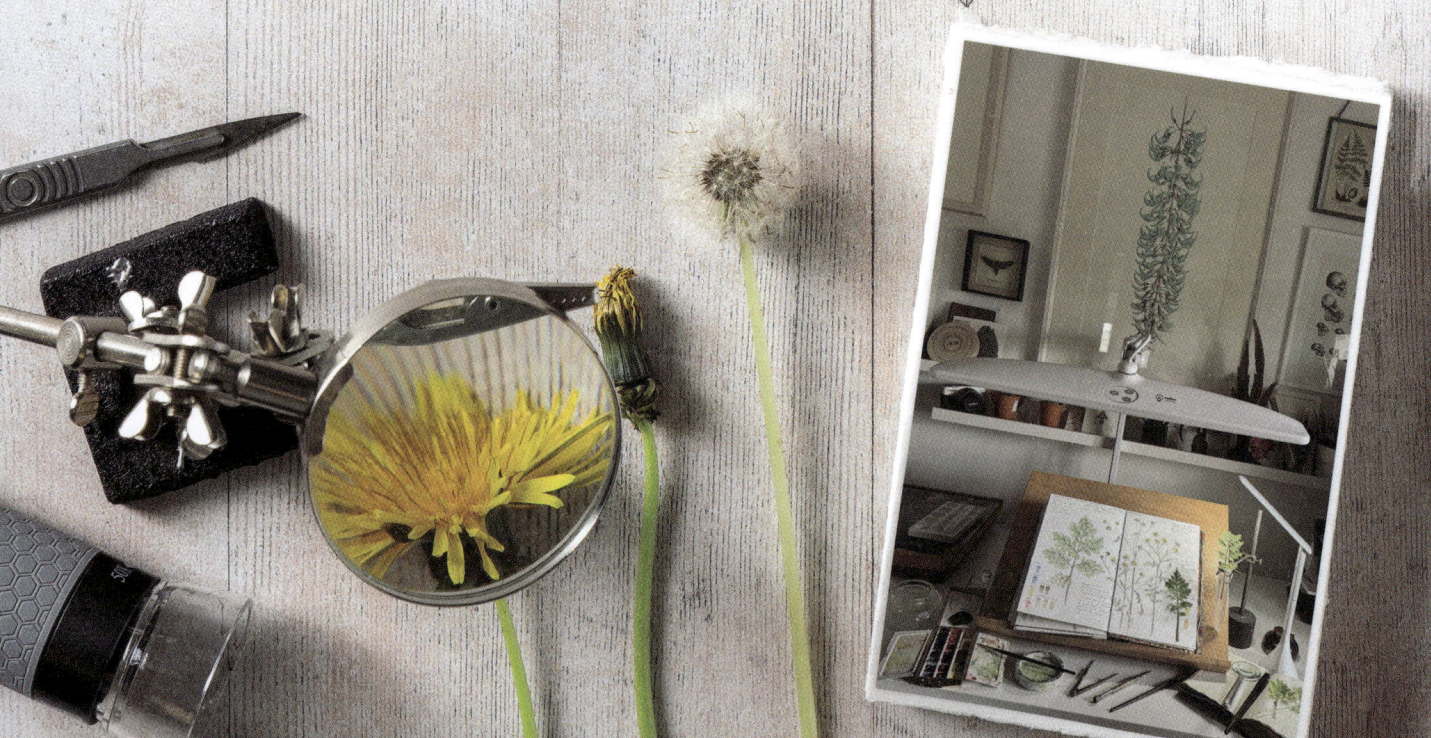

My studio workspace with materials and equipment set up for the left-handed painter. Simply reverse the arrangement if you're right-handed.

TRAVEL KIT OR FIELD-PAINTING KIT

The travel kit is quite small in comparison – there is no desk or equipment, so this makes it much easier. Depending on the weather, you may need a hat to avoid the glare of the sun.

Pencils

Use a HB Staedtler Mars Lumograph clutch pencil, or similar.

Sharpener

Take a Staedtler tub sharpener because it's less messy than other methods.

Eraser

Use a Tombow MONO Eraser or any eraser included in a mechanical pencil.

Watercolour Set

Use a Winsor & Newton box that holds 10 colours (although more can probably be added along the centre). The colours I use are those listed in the previous 'In the Studio' section, minus those marked with an asterisk.

Paint Brushes

Use Winsor & Newton Series 7 Miniatures, sizes 1, 2, and 4, and a Rosemary & Co small eradicator. Take a brush roll or case to protect the brush tips. You can also save the small plastic covers for the brushes and use these.

Palette

The lid of the paintbox can be used as a palette.

Water Pot

An additional collapsible water pot is useful as the water attachment supplied with the box can be very small.

Additional Items

The following items are also invaluable when sketching outdoors:

- A bottle of water
- A waterproof rucksack (because it frees up hands)
- A roll-up plastic sheet or plastic-backed blanket for sitting on
- A hand lens and magnifying glass
- A painting rag
- Easel clips for holding the paper flat
- A sealable plastic bag to protect your sketchbook

For outdoor sketchbook work, it's advisable to reduce the amount of kit.

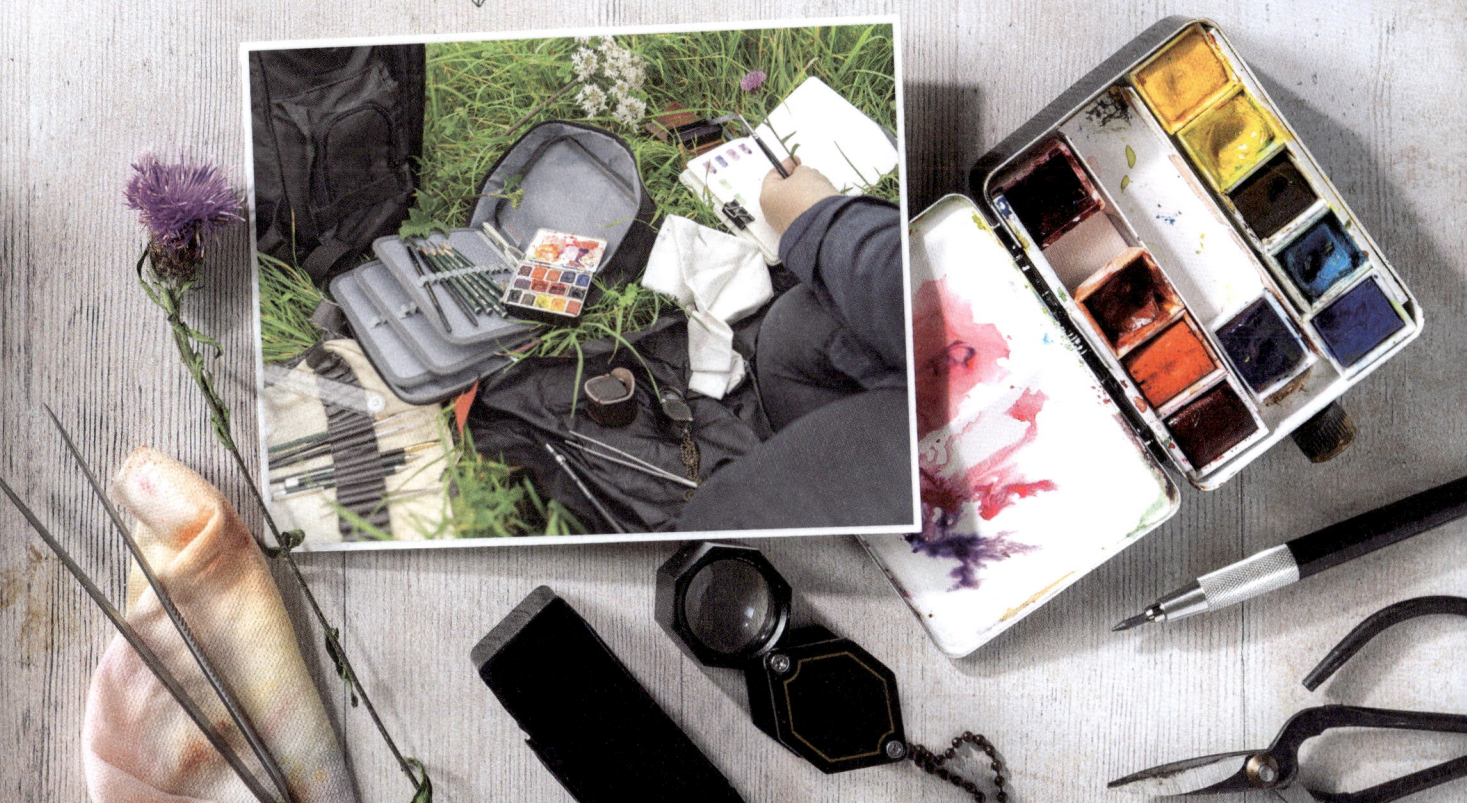

Subject, Place, and Time

Choosing a subject and actually getting started can sometimes be the hardest part of the sketchbook process. Some subjects are definitely more challenging than others, which can make the task feel overwhelming. For beginners, choosing subjects that are manageable and engaging can help to build both confidence and skills, but having the right work environment is important too. Here are a few tips to help you get started and, more importantly, to keep going.

INDOORS OR OUTDOORS?

There's often a misconception that you need to be outside in a wild place, drawing and painting. While this is a wonderful experience, it isn't for everyone and it can be challenging due to the weather conditions – for example, cold and wet, or too bright or hot, making us feel uncomfortable.

Although I do complete some of my subjects outdoors, my approach has been to paint subjects closer to home, including some that I've grown myself. This allows me to bring them indoors, where I can explore them in more detail and paint comfortably, or I can sit in the garden at a comfortable table and paint.

Sometimes, a simple found object collected on a walk, like a lichen-covered branch or small common wildflowers that have grown in the garden, is enough to inspire me to fill a whole spread and there is no need to sit outside to paint them.

While it's important to note that you can't simply pick wildflowers since many are protected and must be painted on-site, there are numerous ways to fill your sketchbook. Remember, it's your book, so fill it with what inspires you.

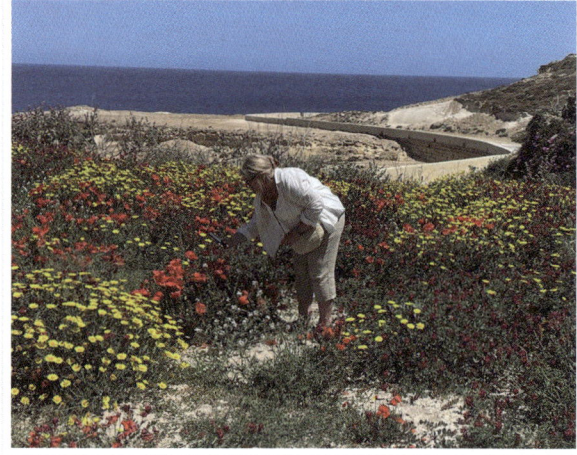

↑ *Out and about in Malta, I'm identifying potential subjects to paint.*

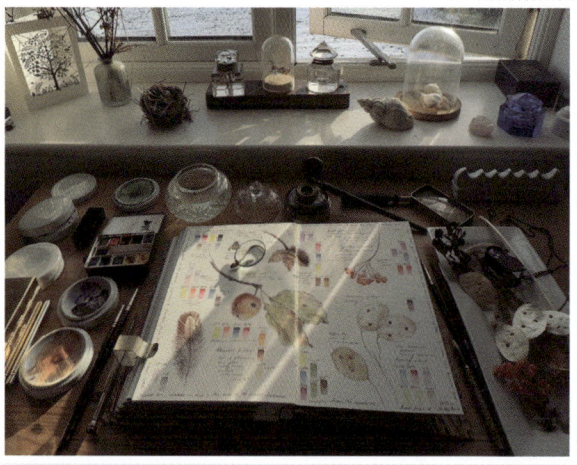

↑ *Taking the outdoors indoors, my small window desk at home provides seasonal inspiration.*

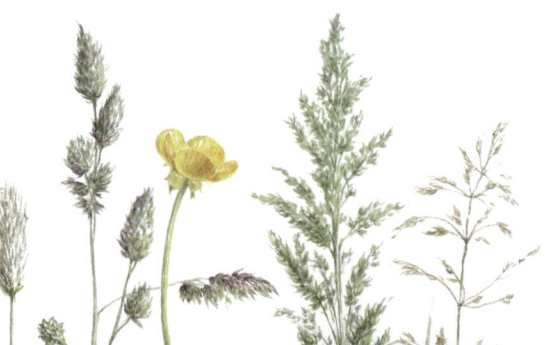

COMPLEX OR SIMPLE?

In the early days, I discovered that being overly ambitious wasn't the best approach for me. Although I wanted to paint every plant, I soon realized that the best approach was slow and steady, and to always complete whatever I chose to illustrate.

For years, I felt my sketchbooks should have more of a complex theme, but I started with simple flowers, fruits, leaves, and seed capsules, and over time, my pages grew more complex with various stages of a plant. I developed strategies to make the pages easier, such as deconstructing a plant into its parts and stages.

I began walking close to home daily, observing the changing seasons and adding to my sketchbook each week. I would return to the same page at a later date to add the next part of the plant's cycle. Before too long, I was telling the story of the plant over time and through the seasons. For some wildflowers, I bought seeds to grow them in my garden so that I could explore them in more detail at home at all stages. Gradually, my book developed its own identity.

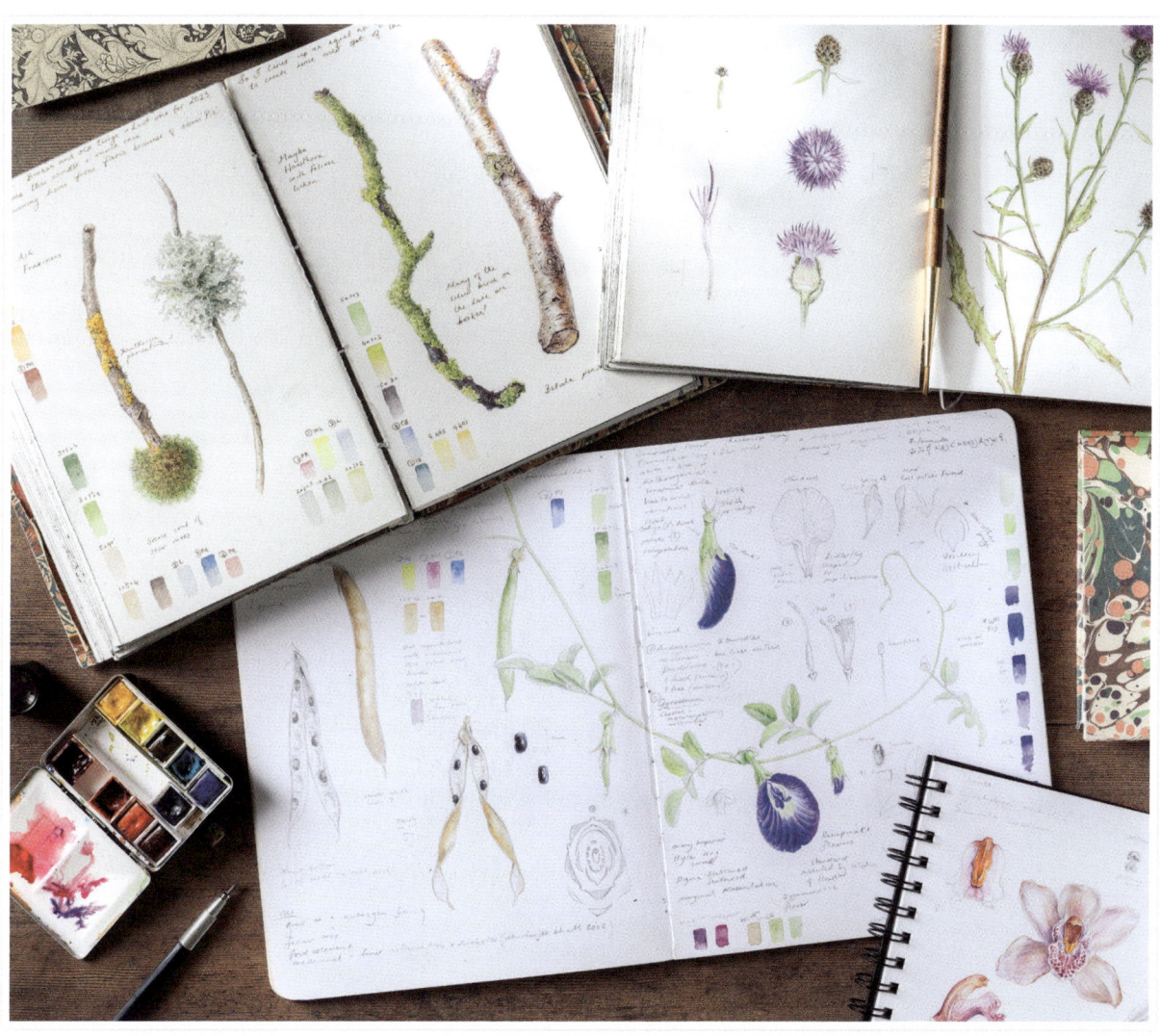

↑ *Overseas work or wildflowers have to be completed on-site, whereas found branches or flowers from the garden can be painted indoors.*

MINI PROJECTS

Small projects are a great idea for beginners, such as drawing individual flowers that you've grown in your garden during the summer or capturing autumnal finds. Holidays offer a perfect opportunity for a sketchbook, as they allow you to draw and paint away from the pressures of work and daily life. Each subject becomes a memory of a place and time, so drawing plants and other elements of nature can be a meaningful way to preserve those experiences. Holiday sketchbooks can also kickstart a more regular habit of working in your sketchbook.

COLLECTIONS

Collections of smaller subjects can be one of the best approaches if you are unsure what to paint. A collection-style page can be very varied. Examples of subjects include autumnal fruits and nuts, seed pods, leaves, fungi, and flowers, either as a mixed selection or of the same type. Additional items, such as feathers, a dead bee or butterfly, a bird's egg found on the ground, lichen, or moss, are all worthy of recording and can keep the sketchbook going through the lean winter months.

The options are fairly limitless and you can gather physical objects while you are out walking and build up a collection. Try working on one small subject at a time, until eventually a whole page is filled.

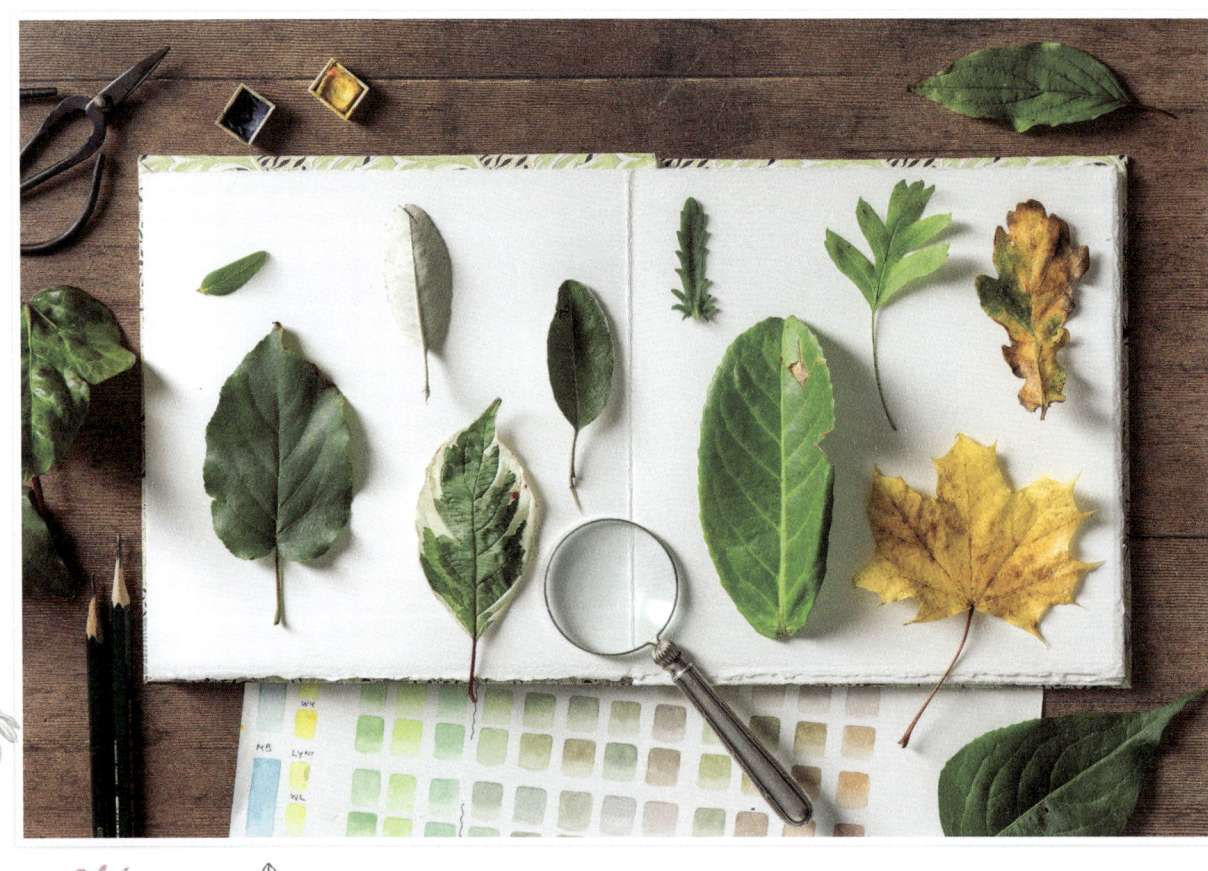

A diverse collection of leaves makes an attractive spread.

MY TIPS FOR CHOOSING SUBJECTS

Here are some tips for choosing initial subjects to study:

- Begin with flowers that are not too small or intricate. Plants such as those in the parsley family that have very small flowers with complex umbels (an umbel has clusters of small flowers on short flower stalks, which rise from a main stem, like an umbrella) are tricky to draw and paint as are those with many petals, such as cultivated roses.

- Don't choose subjects that will wilt too quickly indoors. When not using them, keep them in a cool place.

- White flowers can be very challenging to paint because you are recreating white on white. Although a white flower is really just another colour, with lots of very subtle colours within it, it's easier to begin with more colourful subjects.

- Fruits and seed capsules make great beginner subjects; many will last for a long time and the simple rounded forms are the most basic structures for practice.

- If you find it difficult to paint leaves, why not draw them as an outline or tonal drawing instead. Then gradually introduce simple leaves in watercolour to your work.

- Avoid lots of overlapping leaves initially and later develop strategies to make them easier, such as painting leaves that are further back paler or drawing them as outlines.

- Use a magnifying glass or hand-held lens to observe and understand your subjects in detail.

- Enlarge very small parts by measuring and multiplying the dimensions. This makes it much easier to draw and clearer to see the intricate structures.

- Take reference photographs to help you. Most people have a camera on their phone – don't be afraid to use it. While I advocate drawing from life, it's perfectly acceptable to have additional photographic reference material (as long as they are your own images), especially if you want to illustrate dissections.

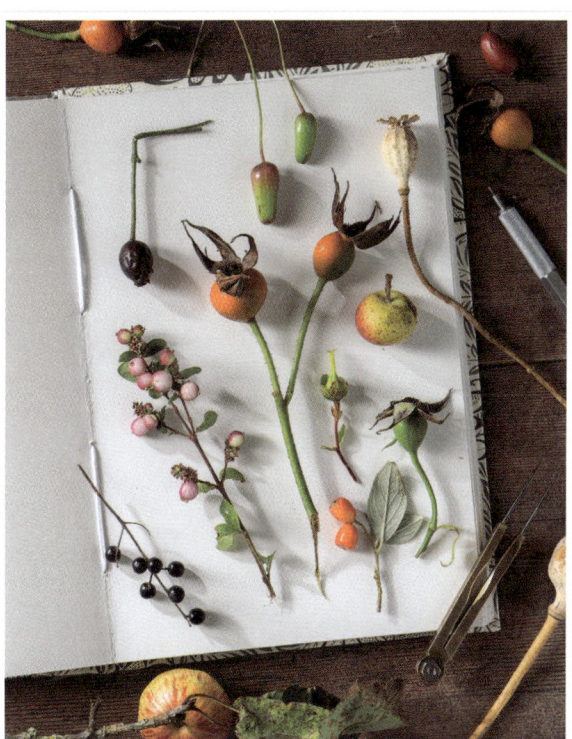

↑ *A collection of autumnal garden finds are positioned on the page, which provides an effortless composition.*

Safety

Always check what the plant is before handling as some plants can cause allergic reactions or may be poisonous. Use a field guide to assist you or carry out research online.

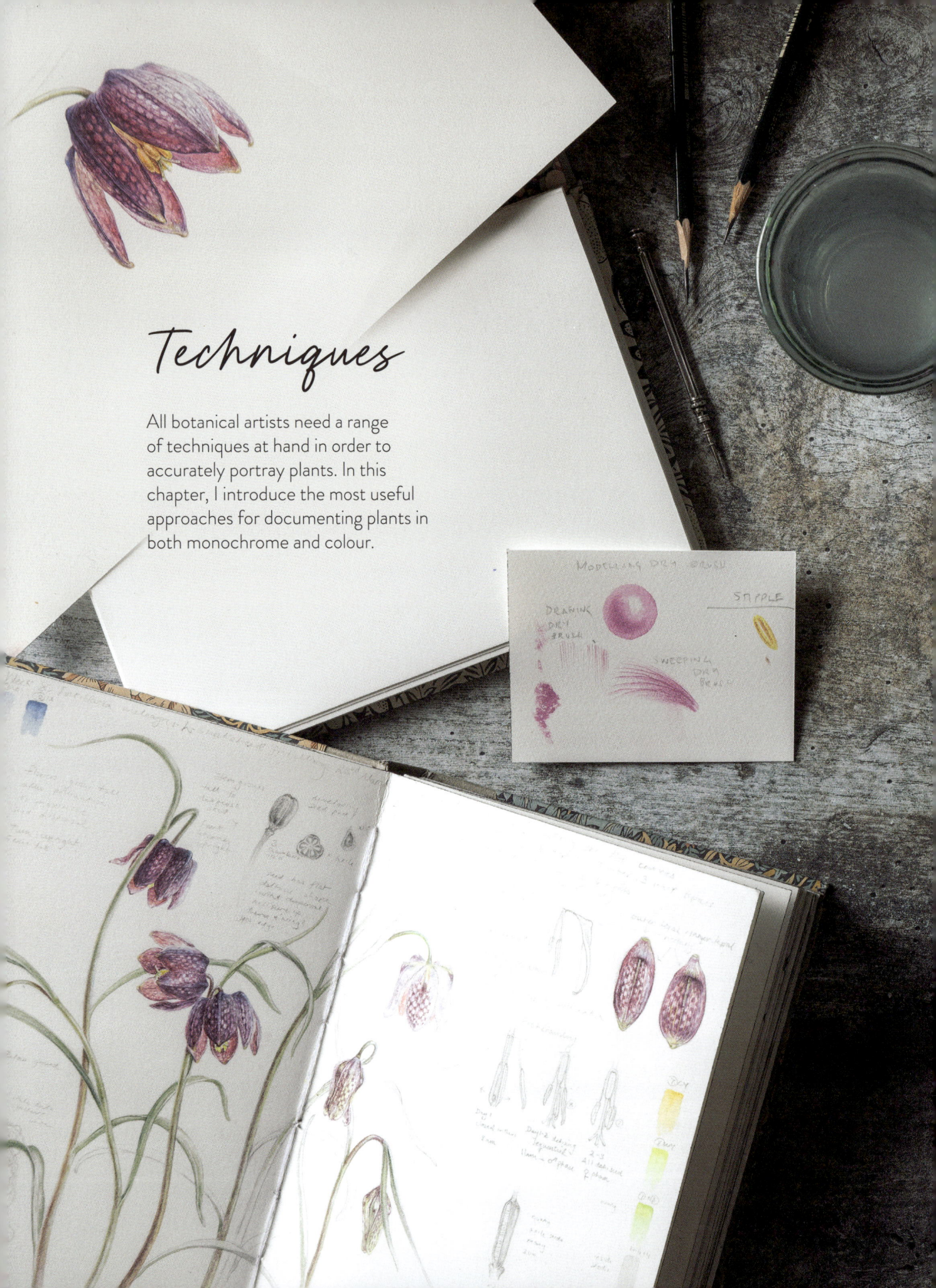

Techniques

All botanical artists need a range of techniques at hand in order to accurately portray plants. In this chapter, I introduce the most useful approaches for documenting plants in both monochrome and colour.

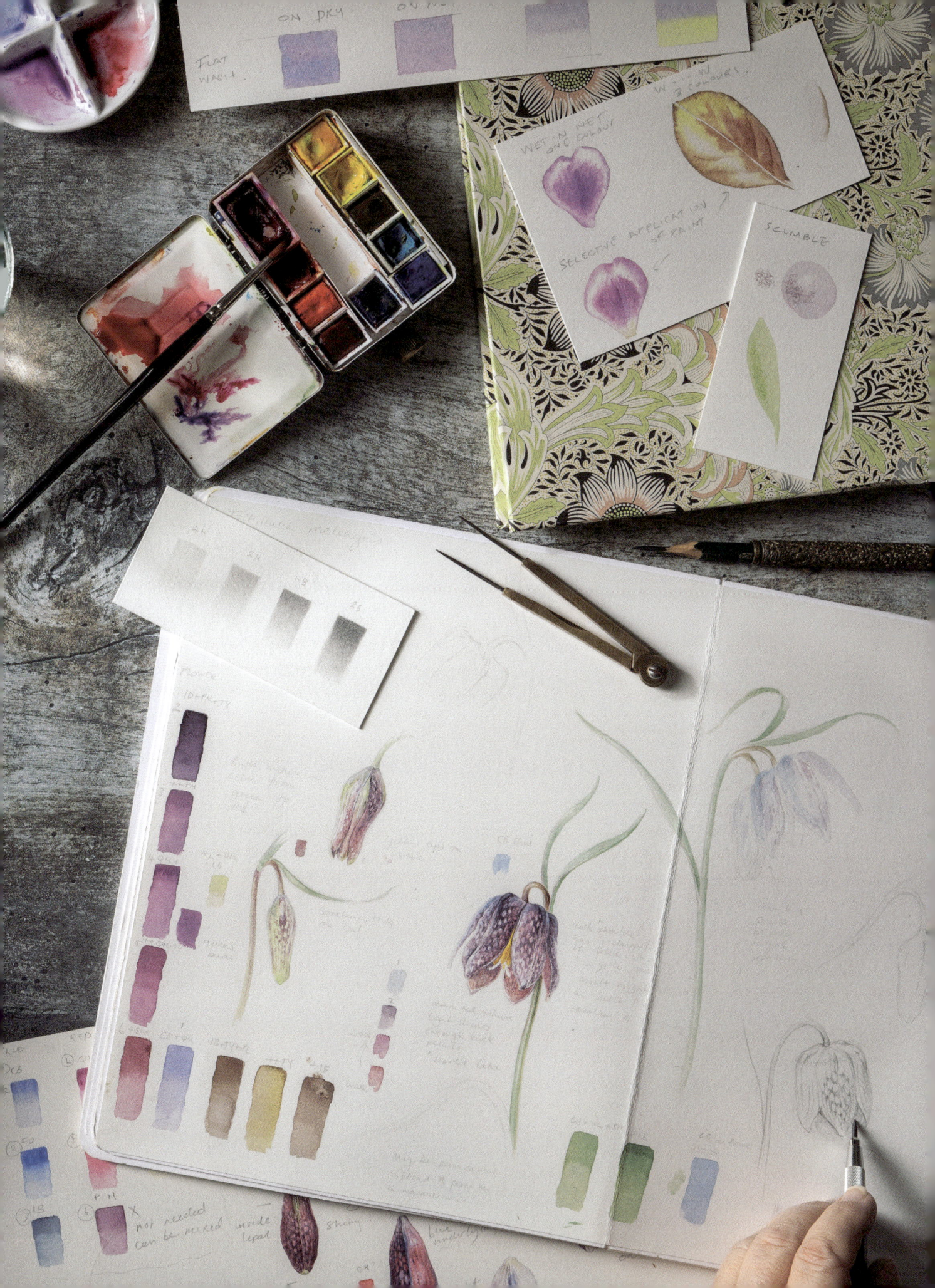

Observational Drawing

Good drawing underpins everything else that will happen on a sketchbook page, and so time spent working on your sketching skills is well worthwhile. Observational drawing may sound a little daunting but, put into simple terms, it means that you simply spend time looking at a plant subject, then try to understand how it all fits together; finally, you draw it as accurately as possible from life by taking some basic measurements.

The best way to get started with this type of drawing is to choose simple subjects, such as flowers, leaves, or fruit, to practise with first. In this section, I include some simple sketches and gradually build to more complex ones. Taking this gradual approach will enable you to build the foundations for accurate drawing and avoid the danger of becoming overwhelmed or not knowing where to start. At first, drawing may seem difficult but with practice, drawing really does become easier.

The first task is to get a feel for your subject, whether it's a leaf, flower, or stem: hold it in your hand, turn it around, and look at how all of the parts connect; look for overall shapes within the subject and try to make sense of the form by breaking it into manageable parts. Understanding the parts will make it easier to draw larger, more complex subjects. Try to draw the same subject in different positions rather than from one static position.

WORKING FROM LIFE

Working from live plants is actually much easier than working from photographs, but it takes a little more effort initially. It enables you to understand the three-dimensional nature of the subject and to get a real feel for it. The problem with photographs are many: first, the image is two-dimensional and you may misunderstand parts and make errors; then there is also the problem of lens distortion, which can cause nearer parts or those at the outermost edges of the frame to be much larger than they are in reality; later on, I will also discuss the problem with colour inaccuracy.

This doesn't mean that photographs should never be used. In fact, they are invaluable for reference if the plant changes or dies. They are also particularly useful for very small plant parts and for dissection drawings, which can be blown up on screen for ease of drawing.

Tools for observing and measuring subjects are invaluable when drawing, but only an H or HB pencil is required for simple sketching.

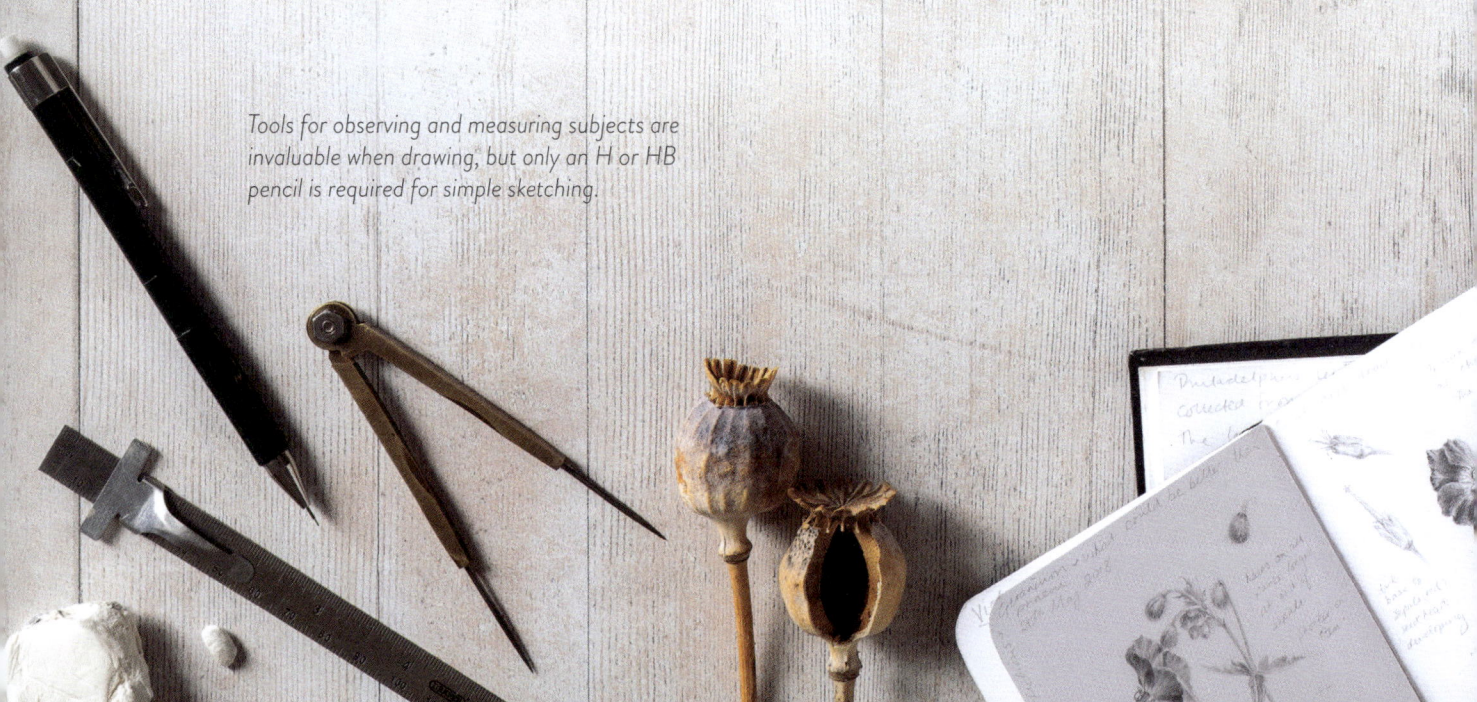

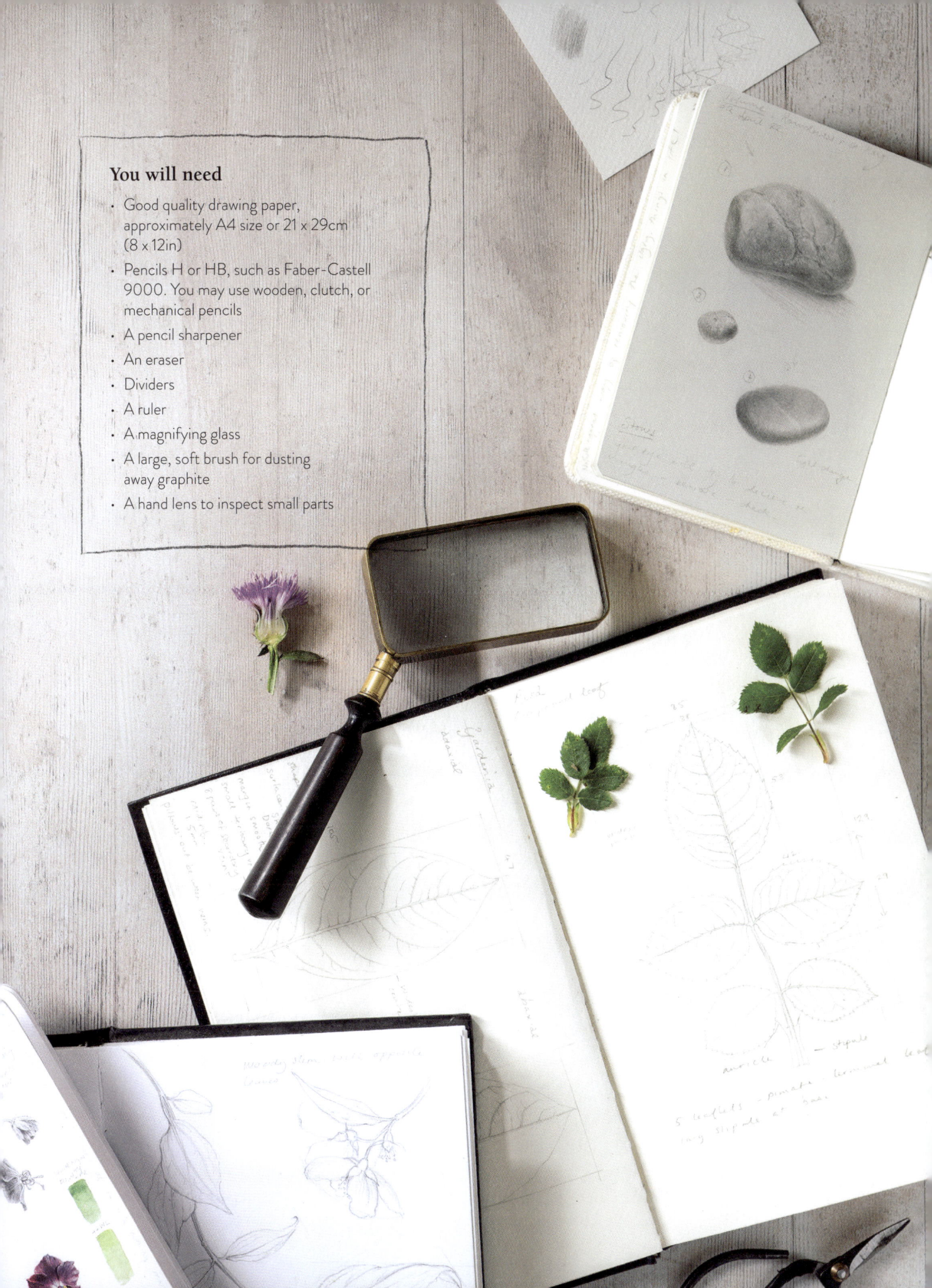

You will need

- Good quality drawing paper, approximately A4 size or 21 x 29cm (8 x 12in)
- Pencils H or HB, such as Faber-Castell 9000. You may use wooden, clutch, or mechanical pencils
- A pencil sharpener
- An eraser
- Dividers
- A ruler
- A magnifying glass
- A large, soft brush for dusting away graphite
- A hand lens to inspect small parts

CHOOSING PLANT MATERIAL

As you learned in Subject, Place, and Time, if you're a beginner, it's a good idea to start with simple subjects that can be easily sourced. Carry out drawing exercises at the comfort of your desk rather than outdoors, which is more challenging.

Avoid very small or large subjects as both can be difficult for beginners. Similarly, avoid overly complicated plants initially, which can be overwhelming. Good examples of subjects with simple shapes can be pot plants or florist flowers; even fruits and vegetables from the grocery store make good subjects. For leaves, select those that don't easily wilt. Flowers should not be overly complex with lots of petals.

Simple Subject Examples

Flowers: Tulips, Violas or Pansies, Cyclamen, daisy-type flowers, Calla Lily, and potted Orchids such as Phalaenopsis

Simple leaves: Ivy, Camellia, Lily, Daffodil, and Photinia

Fruit: apple, grapes, pear

Other subjects ideal for beginners include: bulbs, nuts, and fruit capsules

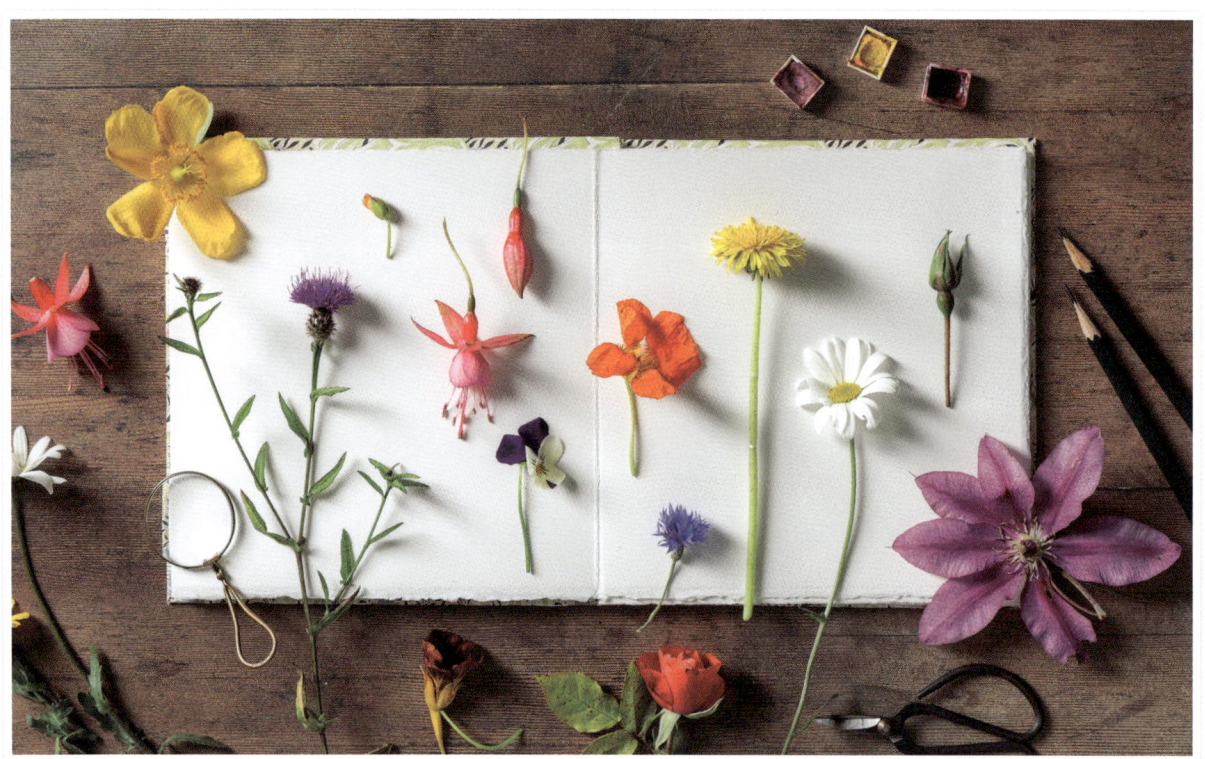

↑ *A selection of suitable flowers showing the diversity of shapes found in nature.*

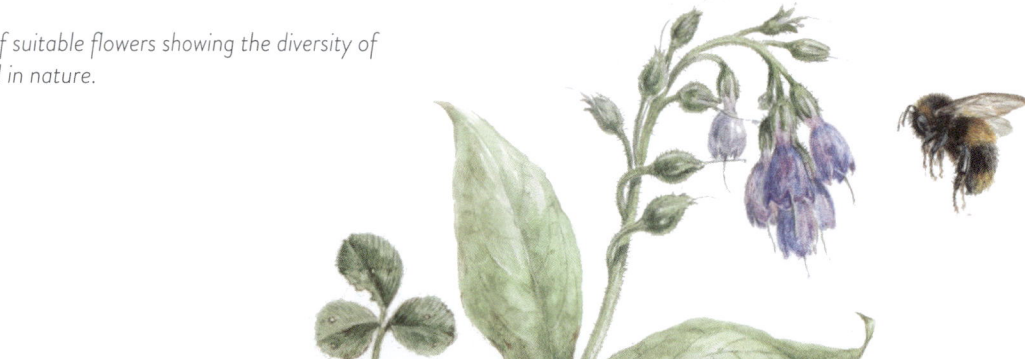

MARK MAKING

Drawing is the first mark to be made on the paper and there can be a barrier when it comes to making that mark for fear of ruining the paper. I suggest practising different pencil strokes beforehand as a warm-up exercise.

There are lots of different ways of mark making: long curved stokes come from using the upper arm, whereas shorter strokes require smaller motions and they come from the wrist; then, as strokes become shorter, they come from the movement in the hand and fingers.

Some lines can be bolder to give emphasis and others are light and delicate. Use very light pressure to create a light narrow line by holding the pencil in a more upright position. For a stronger line, apply a little more pressure; you can also drop the angle of the pencil to make a broader line. Thus there are many different types of strokes used when drawing.

One thing that should always be avoided though, even when drawing stronger lines, is heavy handedness, which will indent the paper. For this reason, always keep your drawing light in weight; it can help to hold the pencil slightly nearer to the middle rather than too tightly and very near to the tip.

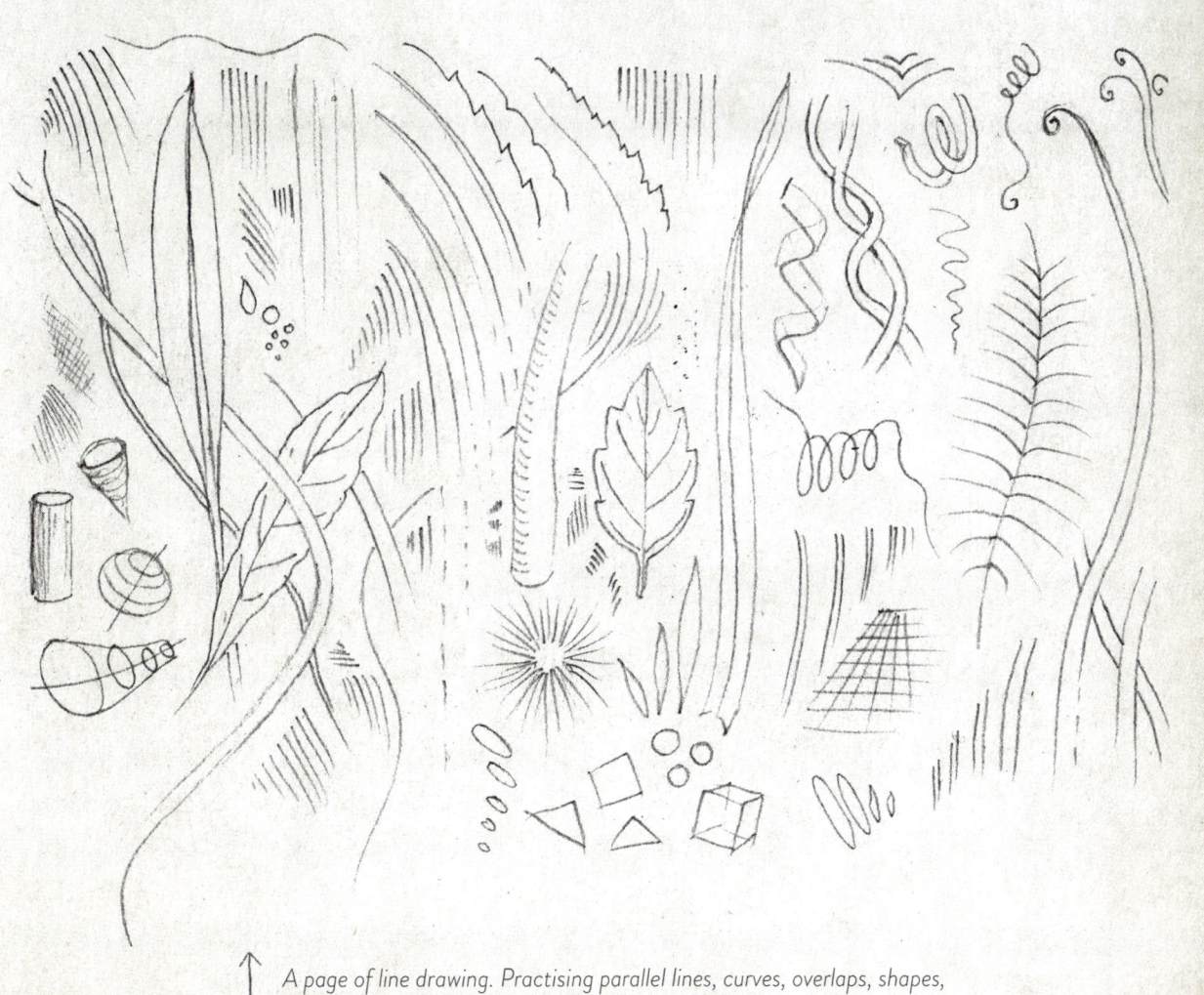

↑ *A page of line drawing. Practising parallel lines, curves, overlaps, shapes, folds, and bends makes a very good warm-up exercise.*

MEASURING

With any type of art, we should always aim for accuracy in the drawing. This means that the size and shape of the subject needs to be correct and some simple measuring is required to establish the basic dimensions of the subject first. Sometimes students get very confused by measuring, yet it's relatively simple to do.

The easiest way to get started is to use dividers. Position the dividers directly in front of the subject as though there were a glass pane in front of it. This keeps the measuring of all parts on the same plane, so that you are not moving the dividers nearer or further away. Closing one eye to view can help too. You can make a light mark on the paper for the overall height and width of the subject as your starting point.

Thereafter, you can measure other parts within the subject. The more you measure the easier it is not to make mistakes. Eventually your eye will be better tuned at observing, and drawing will become an easier task. Although measuring is important, also make regular checks to make sure everything looks as it should be, as it can be easy to make errors with measuring. In time, your eye will become trained and errors will be easily spotted.

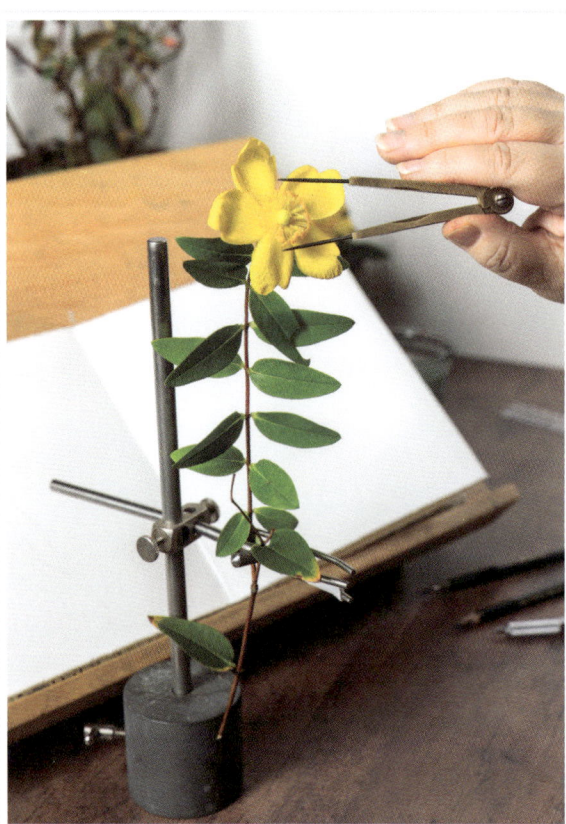 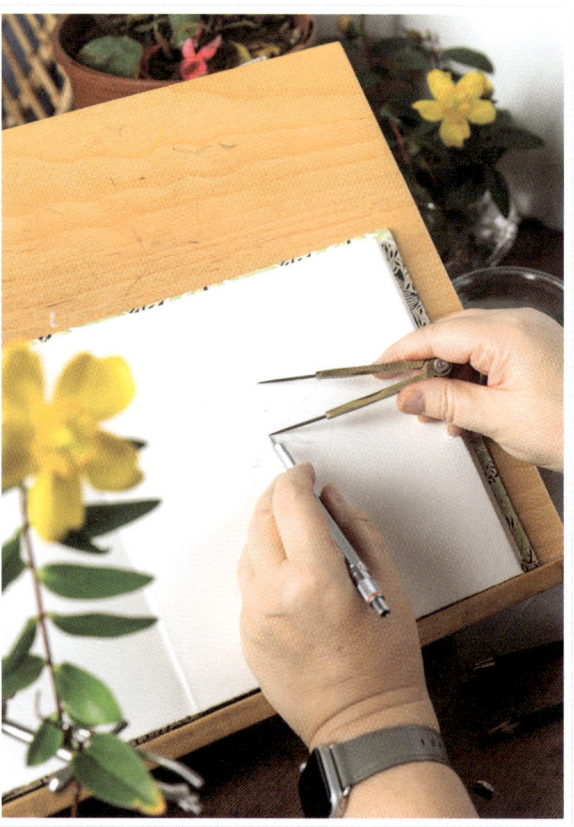

↑ *Using dividers is a simple way of measuring plant parts accurately. Here you can see how the dividers are held in front of the subject to measure a range of parts, from the overall height and width of the plant to the parts within the plant, such as petal length and width or distance between leaf veins.*

LOOKING FOR SHAPES

Look for basic shapes and angles within the subjects, because flowers come in all sorts of shapes; there are disc-, bell-, cup-, cone-, cylinder-, and star-shaped flowers. It is also useful to understand the overall symmetry of the shape. For example, daisies have radial symmetry, which means they can be divided up equally like a cake and all parts are the same. By contrast, flowers such as orchids have bilateral symmetry, which means that they only have two equal halves if divided down the centre.

Leaves also come in many different shapes, so looking for recognizable forms can really help you to understand a subject for drawing purposes. There are oval, palmate (palm-shaped, like an open hand with lobes radiating from it), rounded, sword-shaped, and even triangular leaves – look carefully for recognizable shapes.

Looking at the space around the subject is also helpful. This is called 'the negative space'. Looking at negative space can help you to check whether the distance between parts is correct.

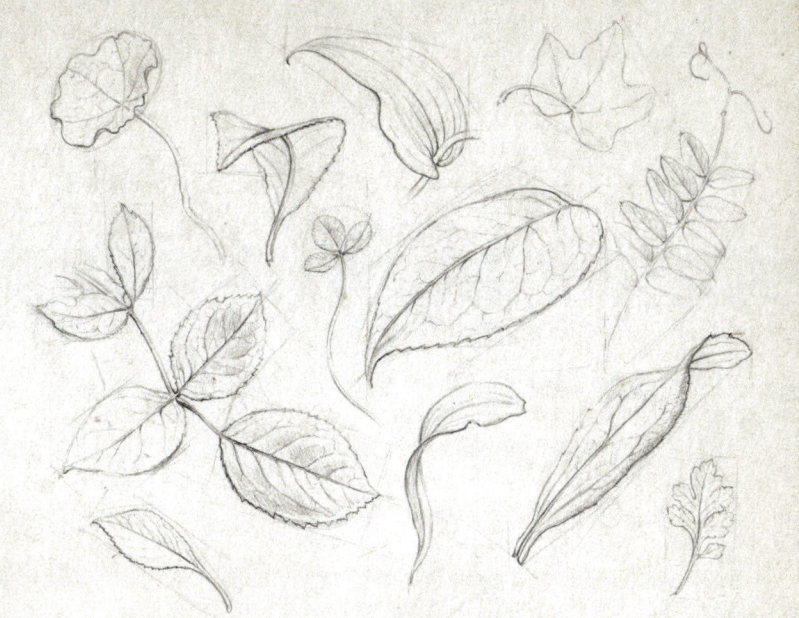

A selection of sketches of different leaf shapes, showing how the drawings are constructed with working lines.

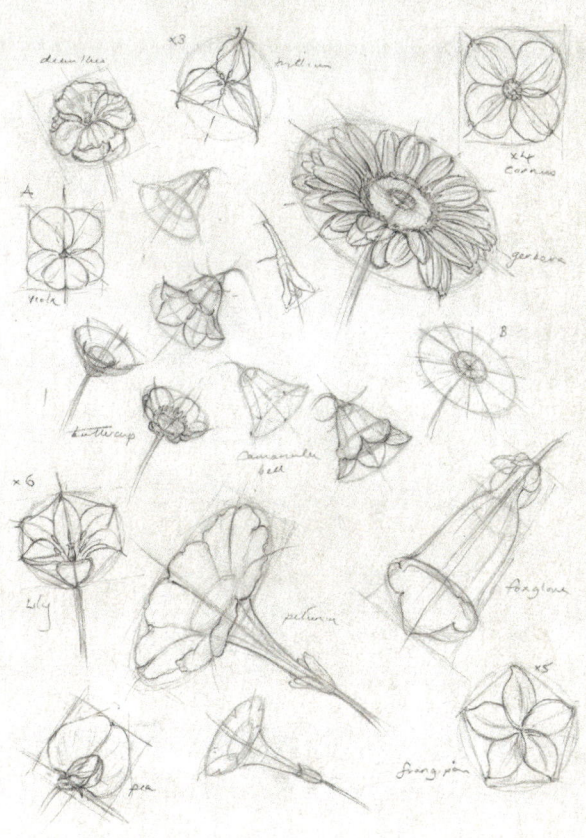

A selection of flowers showing the various geometric forms within flower shapes and also the negative space between parts.

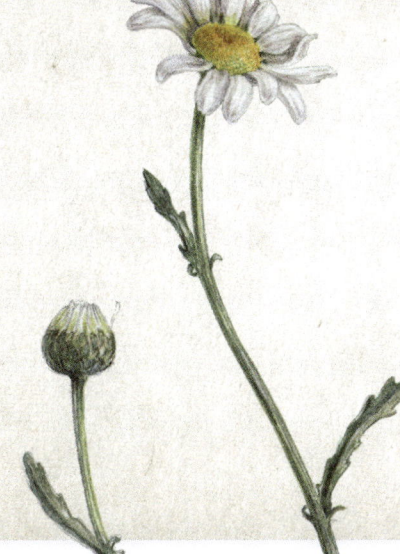

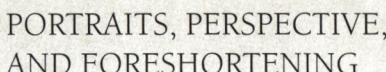

PORTRAITS, PERSPECTIVE, AND FORESHORTENING

I recommend beginning with portrait drawings and then moving on to drawing in perspective. A leaf or flower portrait is a face-on view of the subject. It is the most basic drawing of a subject and is useful in understanding the structure of the subject before attempting perspective drawing. The overall shape is easy to measure and plot. It will also allow you to observe details within each subject, such as the venation pattern (arrangement of veins) in leaves.

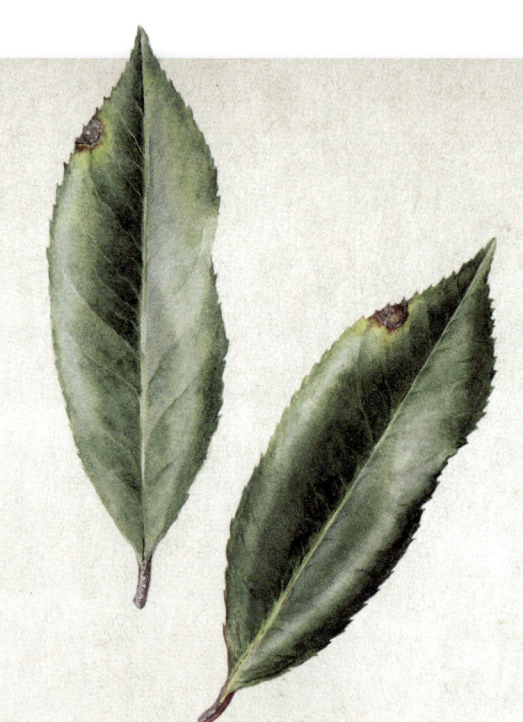

Gardenia

Adaxial

Abaxial

Shape: elliptic
Surface: leathery, shiny, dark
Margin smooth
Small tertiary veining
8 pairs of secondary veins
Midrib 1.5mm
Pillows out between veins

Widest at centre point

Veins on abaxial side much more pronounced

Indents between secondaries

Paler in colour

↑ *A leaf portrait showing adaxial (the front or upper side of the leaf) and abaxial (the back or underside of the leaf where veins are often in relief) views.*

Moving on to drawing in perspective, when you look at a plant, the leaves and flowers are at many different angles and positions – some come towards you and others tilt away. Foreshortening is a drawing technique used to create the illusion of this, to portray what we see in real life. This makes drawing more of a challenge; however, the same method of measuring described previously can be used to draw plants in any position. Make good use of your dividers and practise looking for the angles and negative space between parts. By doing so, you can begin to make sense of the plant and how it all fits together in three dimensions.

In a leaf and a flower, it is always best to put in a centre line first. In a leaf, this will be the midrib; in a flower, the stem through to the flower centre will help you to align the parts correctly. Again, in foreshortened drawings, look for basic shapes as this will help you.

Remember that drawing is a problem-solving exercise and it won't be perfect initially. It takes a little work and lots of corrections, so work lightly.

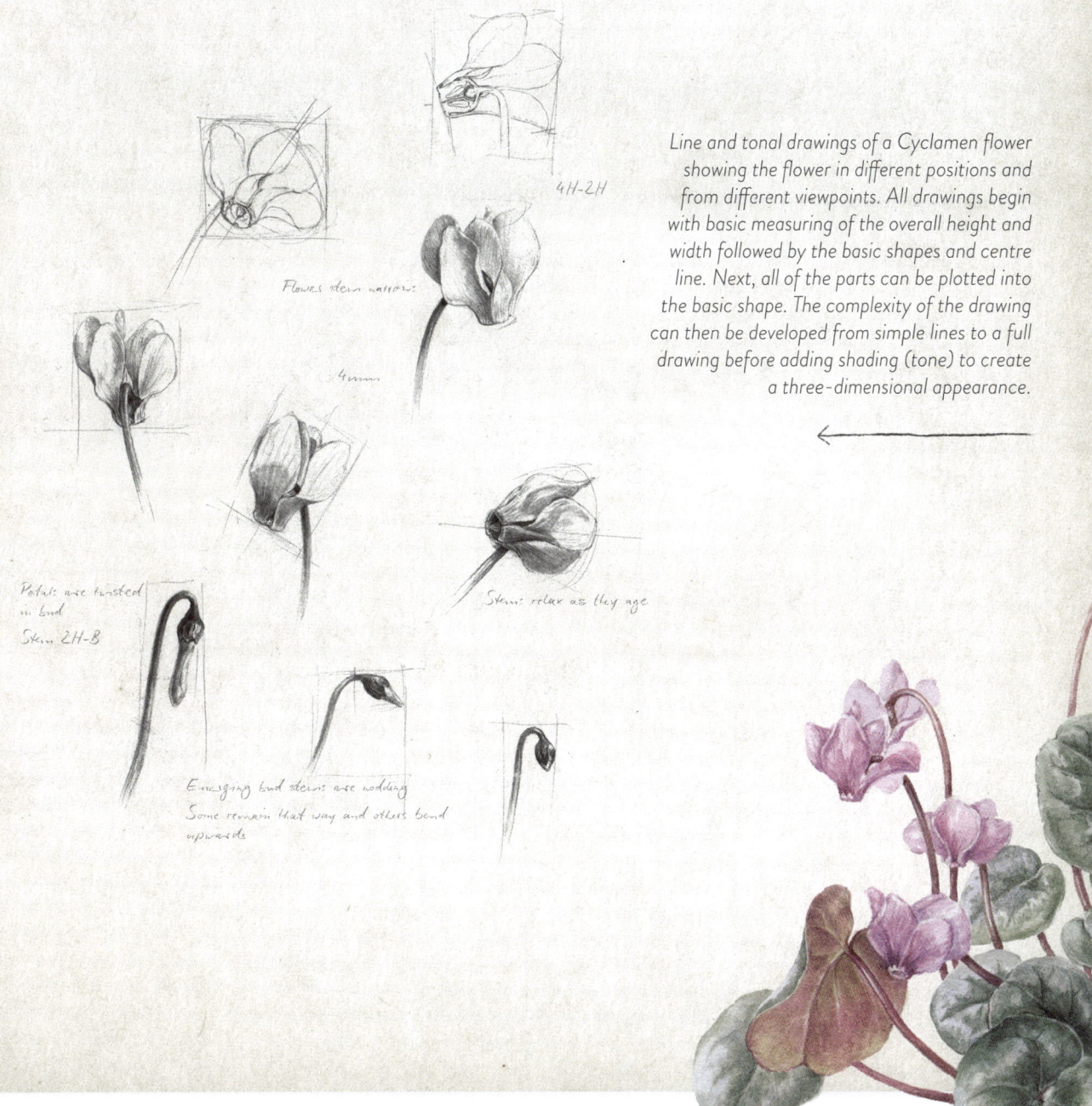

Line and tonal drawings of a Cyclamen flower showing the flower in different positions and from different viewpoints. All drawings begin with basic measuring of the overall height and width followed by the basic shapes and centre line. Next, all of the parts can be plotted into the basic shape. The complexity of the drawing can then be developed from simple lines to a full drawing before adding shading (tone) to create a three-dimensional appearance.

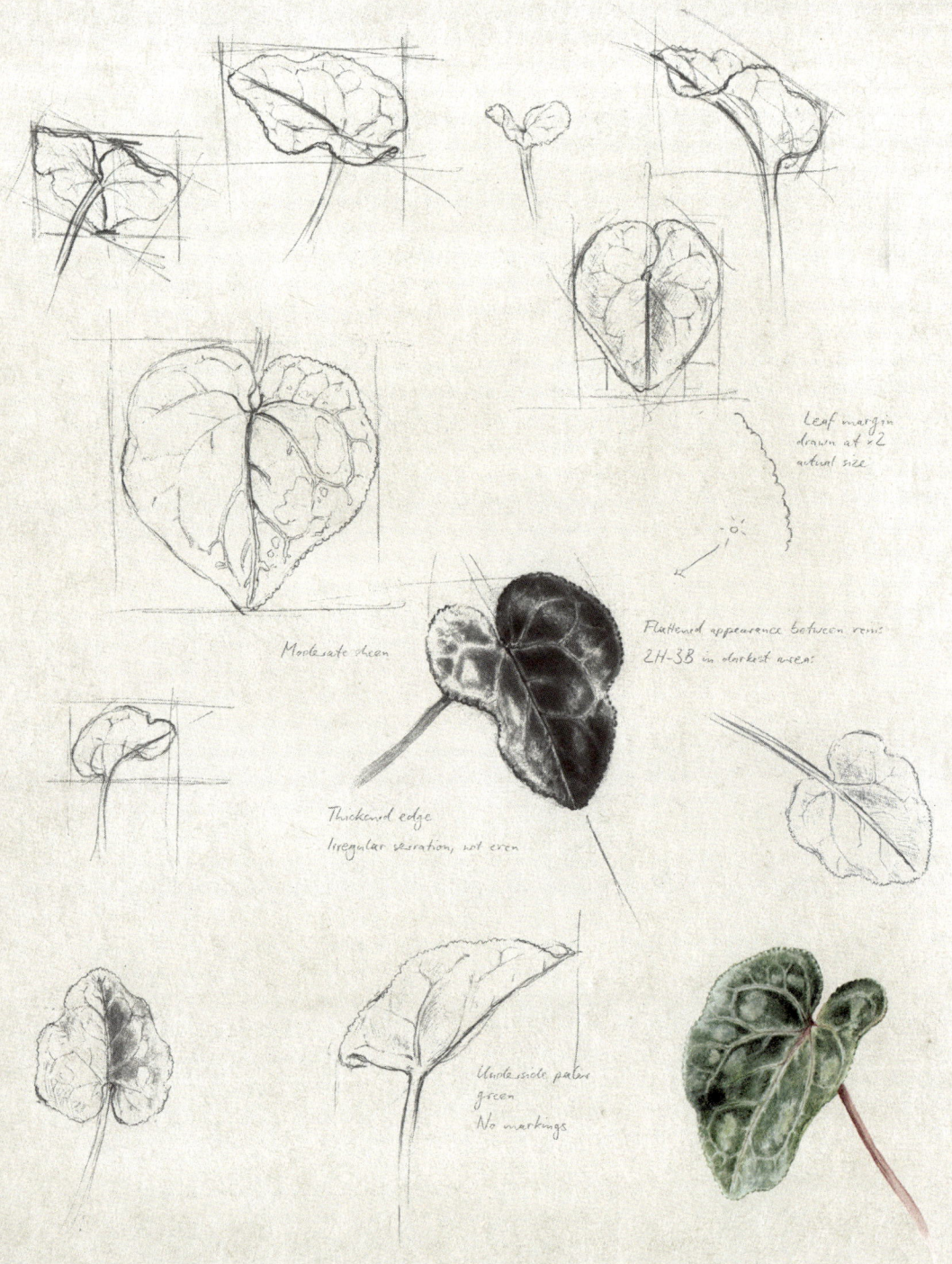

Cyclamen persicum leaves
Heart-shaped
Younger leaves paler, more green
Older leaves very dark
Silvery marking around veins
Size 80mm long × 50mm wide and smaller

Leaf margin
drawn at ×2
actual size

Flattened appearance between veins
2H–3B in darkest areas

Moderate sheen

Thickened edge
Irregular serration, not even

Underside paler
green
No markings

A page of Cyclamen leaves, different sizes and positions, as you would find on the plant. All are made using the same approach, measuring height and width and plotting the midrib first before adding all other parts.

LARGER SUBJECTS

Once some practice has been completed with individual plant parts, a larger section of plant can be attempted. This will no doubt include perspective and overlapping parts.

Drawing overlapping parts is best achieved if the parts are drawn as a 'skeleton' drawing, and as though all parts are transparent. This is a useful approach as it enables you to make sure lines are correctly aligned because you can see the full structure of connecting parts. Once the planning is complete, the working lines can be erased.

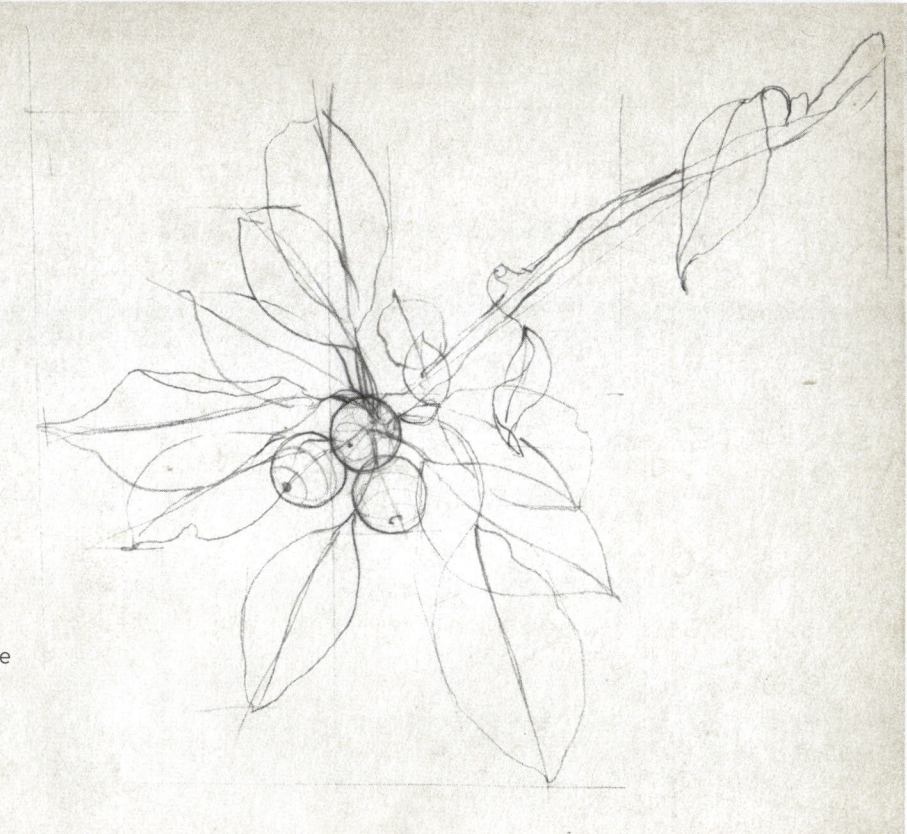

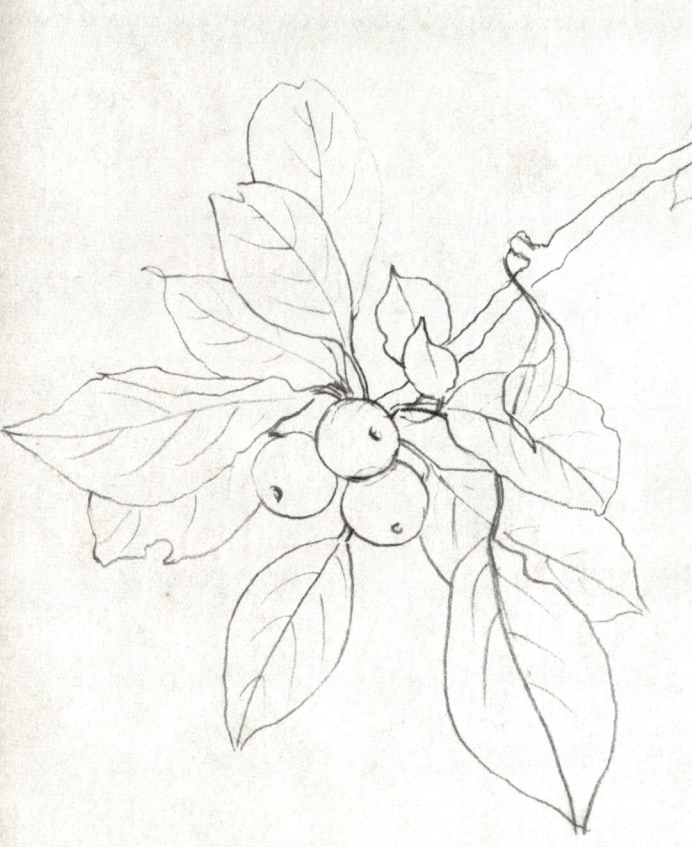

A skeleton drawing is a structural sketch that is first measured and then all of the parts are plotted in as though you can see through them. This means that you can see the overlapping parts and ensures that the alignment of lines is correct in all parts.

Thereafter, the working lines can be removed and the drawing completed.

Tonal Drawing and Painting

Tone refers to the relative lightness or darkness as influenced by the effect of light falling upon a subject. In tonal drawings or paintings, the artwork is created with varying shades of a single colour, using lighter and darker values to produce the illusion of volume or three-dimensional form. This technique, achieved through a range from light to dark greys, is often called a tonal or value study.

Some of my sketchbook pages have elements of monochrome work included, as I don't always want to paint everything in colour, and using different media can create a more interesting spread. For this approach, I use two broad methods to create light and dark tonal values within the work: the first is graphite shading and the second is tonal painting by using black or grey paint.

On occasion, I experiment with making all or most of the tonal work in black and white. However, I most commonly use tonal drawing and painting for additional parts on a spread; this keeps the focus on the main colour elements of the spread, while adding additional information about the plant in a subtle way; it also fills up the page.

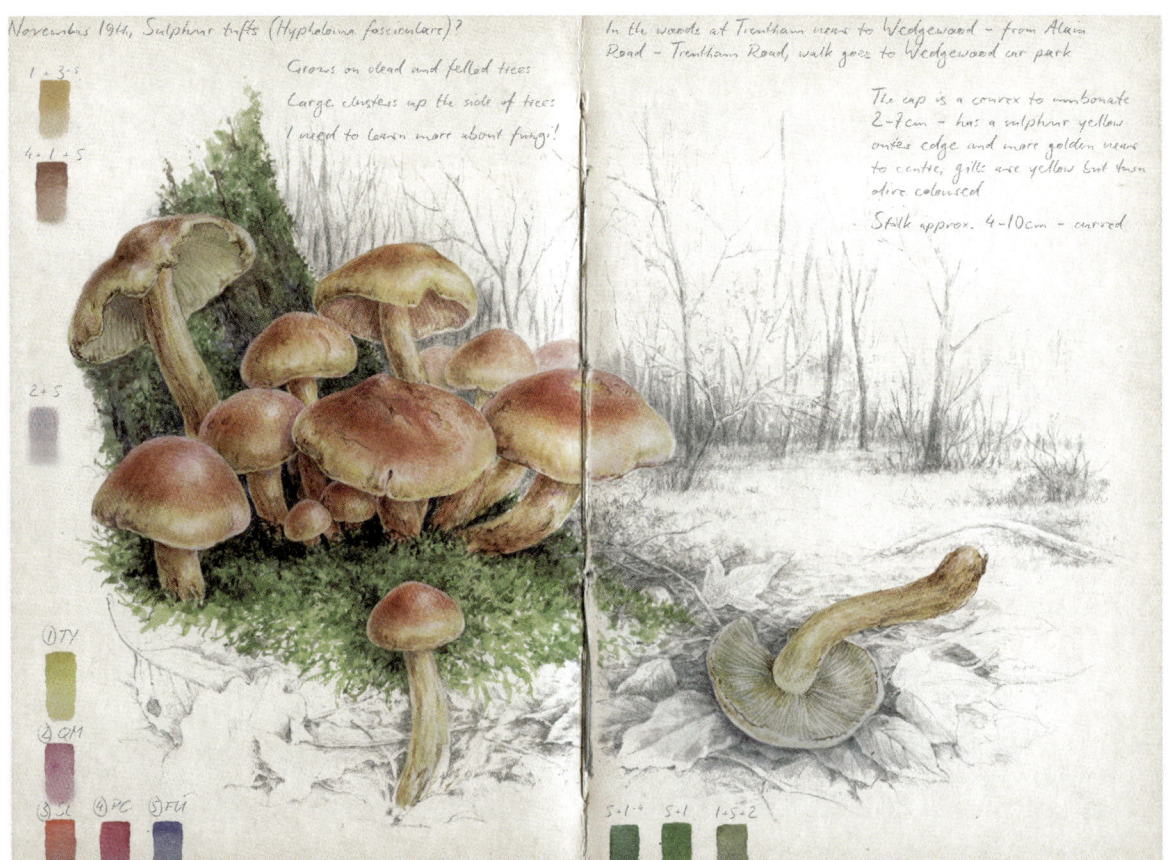

In this woodland fungi painting, the mushrooms were painted initially but I felt the page needed to include an indication of the habitat. The tonal drawing background of the forest floor and trees was added, which provided the perfect solution to the problem without detracting from the fungi as the main focus of the sketch page.

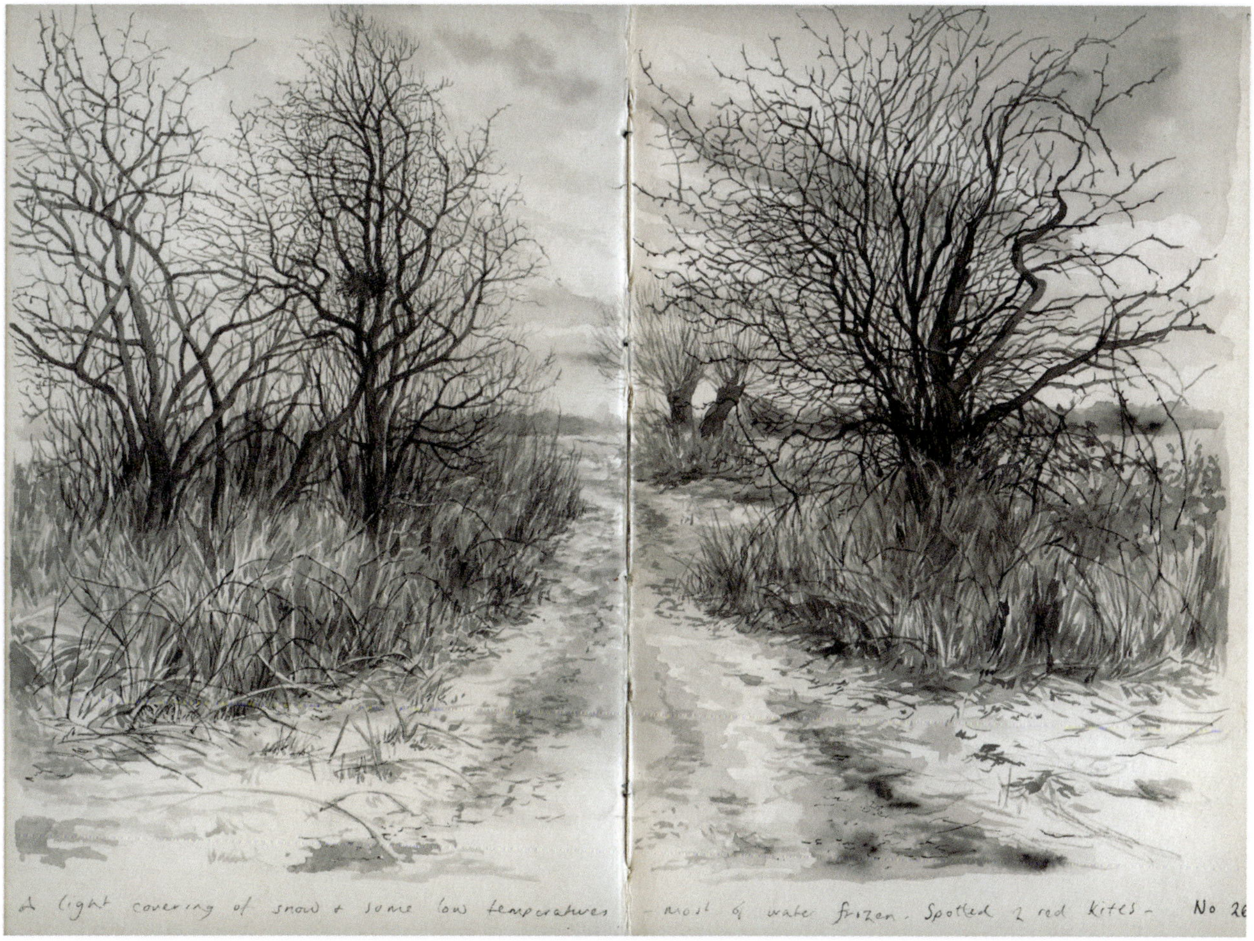

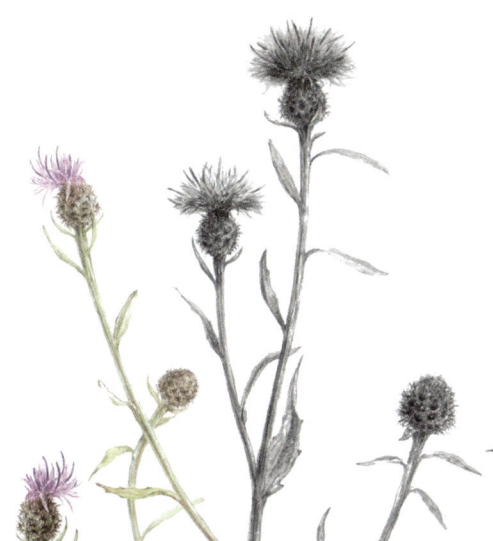

A light covering of snow + some low temperatures - most of water frozen. Spotted 2 red kites - No 26

↑ *This view was at the local marshes on a bleak winter day when there was little colour to be seen. I decided to paint the whole page as a value study, using only black paint. The distant parts being paler and the nearest trees as a black silhouette.*

Using monochrome elements within a page can provide more information about an environment while keeping the focus firmly on the main subjects. The tonal work can be carried out using a variety of media, such as graphite or grey or black paint. Don't be afraid to experiment with media – that's what a sketchbook is for.

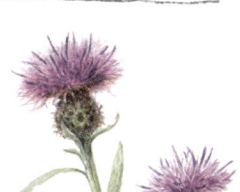

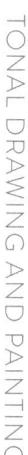

UNDERSTANDING LIGHT

The effect of light on the subject is extremely important because it creates a range of tonal values across the subject, with highlights, midtones, and shadows. You should always be clear about the direction that the light is coming from and this light direction should be equally clear in your illustration.

For example, on a rounded form where the light hits the surface from the upper front left-hand side, there will be a highlight, and this is the lightest area on the illustration. By contrast, on the other side there will be a darker shadow, where the surface curves away from the light. Then all other areas are composed of various midtones between the lightest and the darkest areas. In addition, on a rounded form the edges can be slightly lighter or softened beyond the form shadow, which creates the illusion of the edge receding away from view and this increases the illusion of roundness or volume in a drawing.

In this Mangosteen study the light hits the upper left of the fruit, and midtones are added around it, thus preserving the highlight. The shadow on the lower right is darker with a paler edge beneath it, creating the impression of a receding edge and enhancing the illusion of roundness. Below, the tonal values are translated into colour in the final painting.

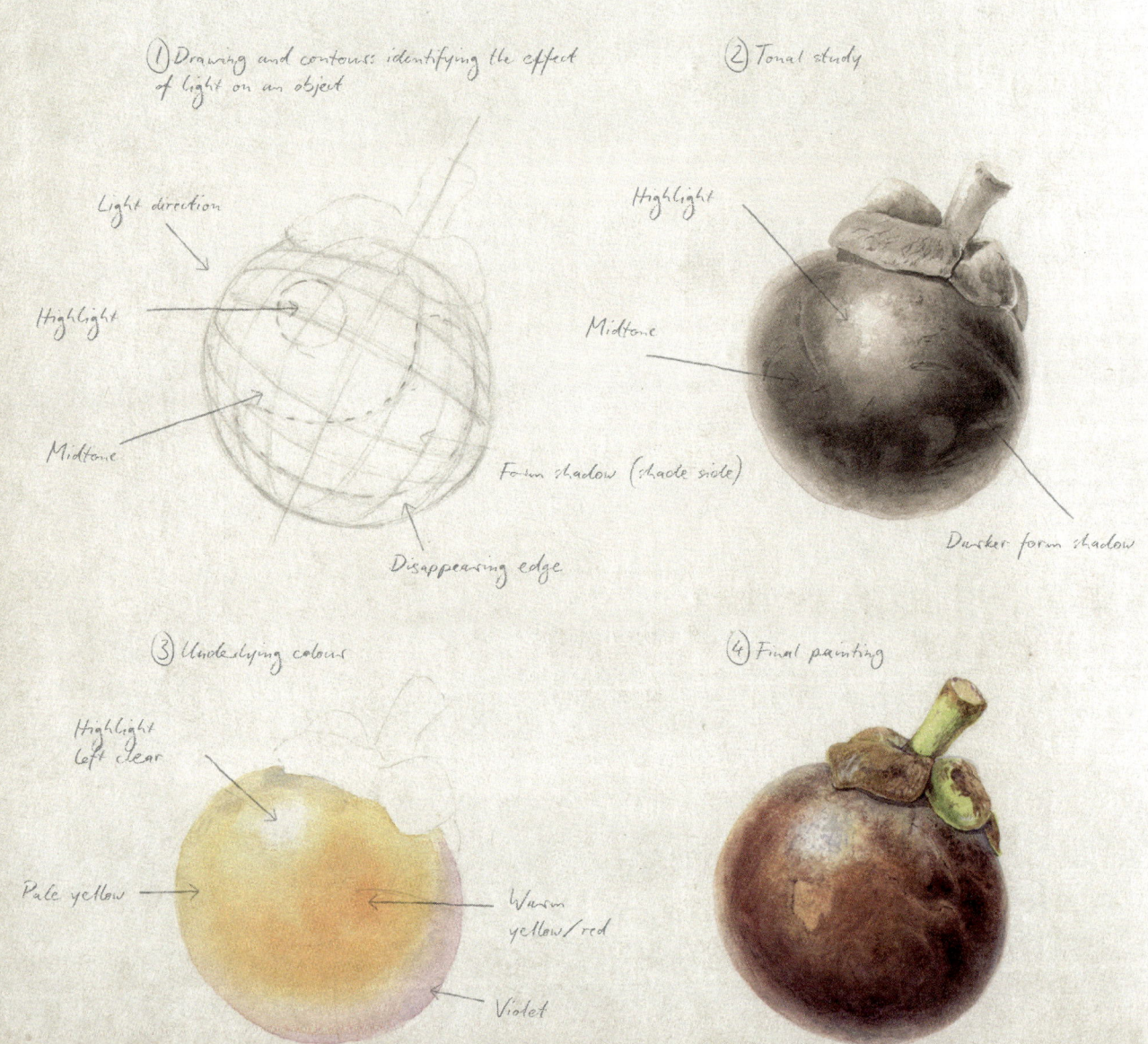

① Drawing and contours identifying the effect of light on an object

Light direction

Highlight

Midtone

Disappearing edge

② Tonal study

Highlight

Midtone

Form shadow (shade side)

Darker form shadow

③ Underlying colours

Highlight left clear

Pale yellow

Warm yellow/red

Violet

④ Final painting

TIPS FOR LIGHTING SET-UPS

While the theory of understanding light sounds simple enough, you will find that, in practice, working outdoors can be confusing, with the direction of light changing depending on time of day; it can also be highly variable, from bright sunlight to dull and cloudy, which changes both the colour and the light and shadows.

Light can also be confusing in the studio, especially if there are windows on different sides of the subject. To resolve this problem, position your desk next to a window; if you are right-handed, the window should be on the left-hand side, otherwise your hand will cast a shadow on your working areas (but be aware that the natural light will change depending on the time of day and the weather). You should close the blinds on any other windows.

Good natural light is the best option for colour matching. However, if this is not possible, an alternative approach is to use an angle-poise lamp positioned on one side of the subject (you can purchase lamps that omit light that is similar to daylight). The bulb should be white light and around 5500 Kelvin. If you are right-handed, the lamp should be positioned at the upper left side of the subject, which avoids the problem of creating a shadow underneath your hand. If you are left-handed then simply light from the upper right-hand side. This artificial light will create consistent lighting on the subject and a good range of highlight and shadows.

PRACTICE

Regular practice with each technique will improve your control and ability to manipulate graphite for desired effects. You will be able to create smooth transitions from light to dark using the different techniques.

As with all work, always keep in mind the direction of your light source as this will determine where your highlights and shadows fall.

Building up layers gradually will create a more controlled and refined shading. Start with light layers and gradually add darker layers for depth using softer grades pencils.

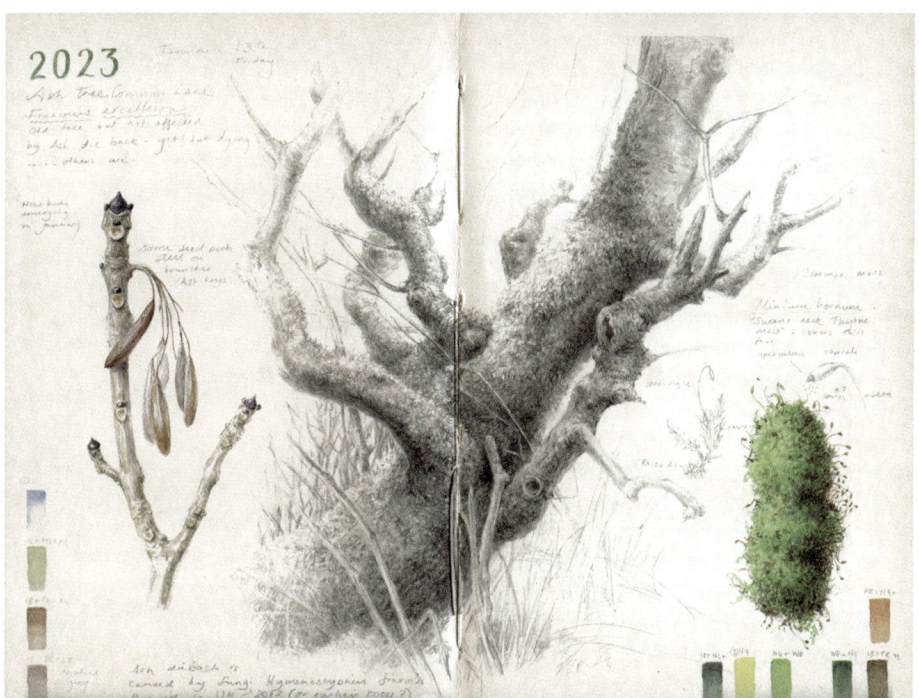

← Graphite seemed the best option for this old Ash tree, which is the focus of the spread, the surrounding additions being in colour, which is the opposite of my more regular approach. I used a variety of techniques with continuous tone and scumbling to create the mossy and gnarled effect.

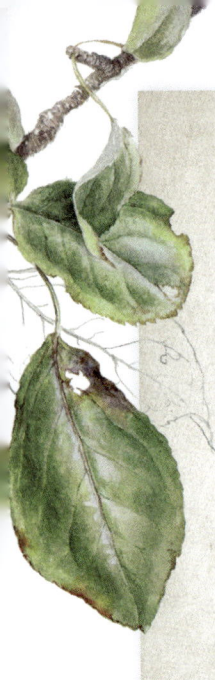

TONAL DRAWING

Tonal drawing is a relatively simple way of creating three-dimensional drawings using a grey scale. Understanding this scale is crucial for tonal painting, as it helps to identify and replicate the light and dark areas within the subject, and so is a very good method if you want to learn about light and shade.

Although it is possible to make a reasonable tonal drawing by using just an HB pencil, better results are achieved if several grades of pencil are used.

I generally use a range of pencils from 4H to 2B for most sketchbook work, with 4H being the hardest and lightest tone and 2B being the softest and darkest tone. I do sometimes use softer grades but this range is sufficient for most sketchbook work. You may also use a clutch, or lead-holder style of pencil, which, having a separate lead, is similar to a mechanical pencil but is thicker, usually with a 2mm thickness lead. It is called a 'clutch' because it has metal jaws that hold the lead in place.

Shading techniques are essential for adding depth, texture, and dimension to drawings. There are many graphite shading techniques but these are the ones that I find most useful and use in my sketchbooks.

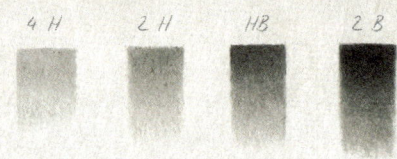

The grades I use in my sketchbook, from left to right, 4H, 2H, HB and 2B.

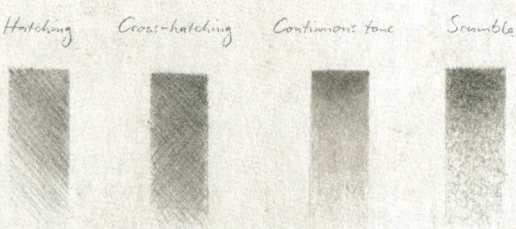

Four commonly used graphite techniques, from left to right: hatching, cross-hatching, continuous tone, and scumble.

Hatching

Hatching involves drawing closely spaced parallel lines. The spacing and direction of the lines can vary to create different tones and textures – diagonal, horizontal, or vertical. The closer the lines, the darker the shading will appear. The lines can follow the contour of the object being drawn; looser pencil strokes follow the object's contour across the curves, which enhances the volume. This can be a fairly quick method for adding a little form to a line drawing.

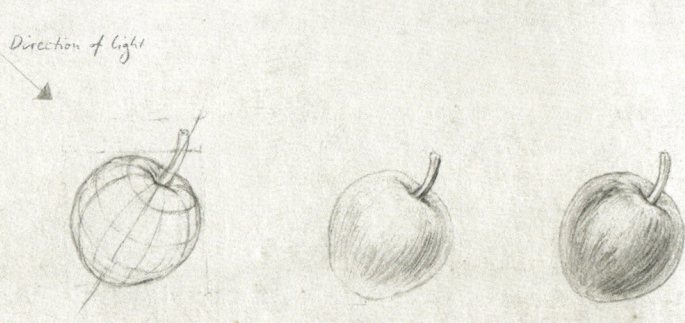

The hatching technique used on a small crab apple drawing.

Cross-hatching

Cross-hatching is a technique where sets of parallel lines are layered over each other in multiple directions. This method can achieve a wider range of tonal values than simple hatching; the lines can be loose or tightly positioned together so that they create denser shading the closer they are to each other. This is also a relatively quick method for adding form.

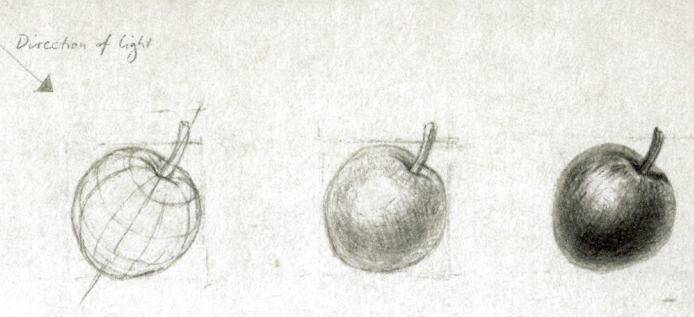

Direction of light

The cross-hatching technique used on a small crab apple drawing.

Continuous Tone

Continuous tone is a technique where small overlapping ellipses or a circling technique is used to create shading. This method can produce extremely smooth gradients and is particularly useful for subjects with smooth surfaces, making it ideal for many botanical subjects. It is a much slower process than other techniques. One of the key differences between this method and others is that it has no obvious outline – the initial outline drawing should merge into the tonal work, creating a more realistic three-dimensional appearance. Usually, several grades of pencil are used to create a range of values.

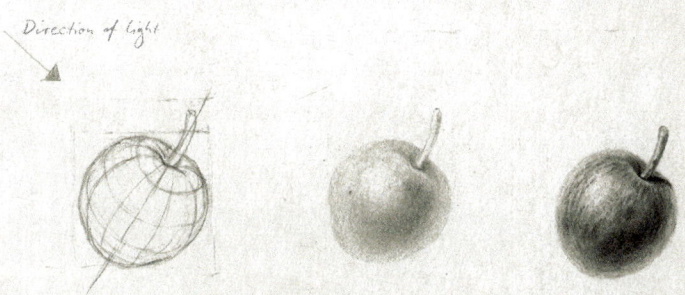

Direction of light

The continuous tone technique used on a small crab apple drawing

Scumbling

Scumbling involves using small scribble-type marks to build up shading. This technique creates a textured, grainy effect, which is useful for depicting rough surfaces like tree bark.

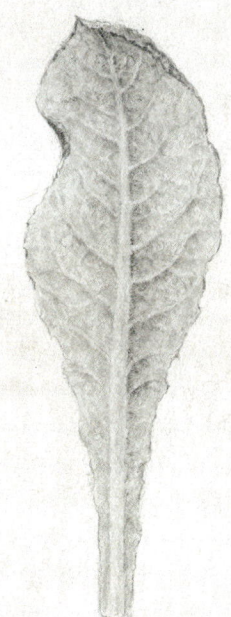

You could use the scumble technique to create the hairy surface of the underside of a Primula leaf, for example.

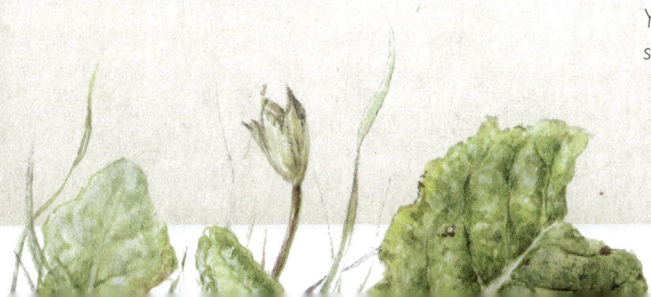

TONAL PAINTING

As with tonal drawing, tonal painting focuses on using different shades of grey to depict the varying light and shadow in a subject by emphasizing the lightness and darkness. This approach uses the same value scale from white to black with multiple shades of grey in between.

Tonal painting tends to be faster than tonal drawing and it is possible to create more dramatic effects with greater contrast because a wider range of values can be used if black paint is used.

However, tonal painting can also be used in a more subtle way to create a softer appearance. I often paint details and backgrounds with paler grey mixes for this purpose. Soft greys can be mixed from three primary colours.

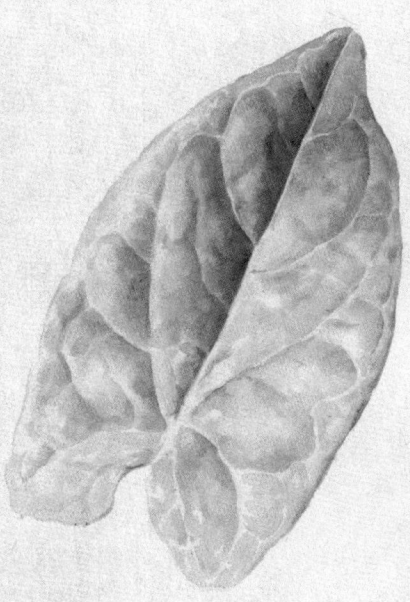 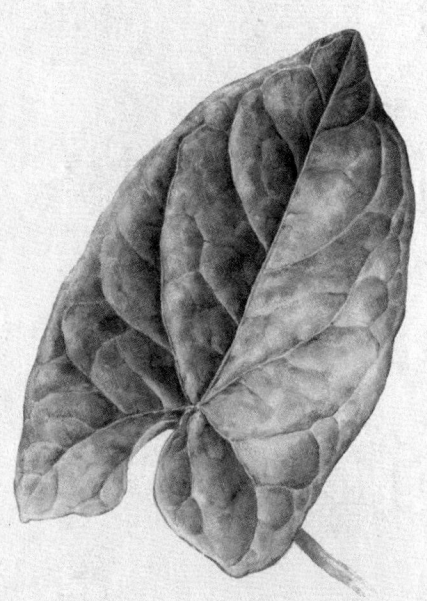

The stages of a tonal painting of a Bindweed leaf painted with black watercolour: the first layer is pale but retains the light; the second image has darker tonal values added with more layering of the dark greys but it also retains the light.

Technique

The technique is much the same as for any painting, which will be described in the Watercolour Painting section of the book, but of course using just one colour. That colour doesn't have to be black, however; it can be sepia, or any dark colour.

The most important aspect of tonal painting is that it focuses your attention on the light and shade from the outset, instead of focusing on the colour. This crucial aspect is often overlooked, resulting in flat-looking paintings. If you learn about value painting first, it will greatly help you with colour work too and will help you make a more dynamic painting. Another bonus is that it's much quicker to create a tonal painting than it is a tonal drawing.

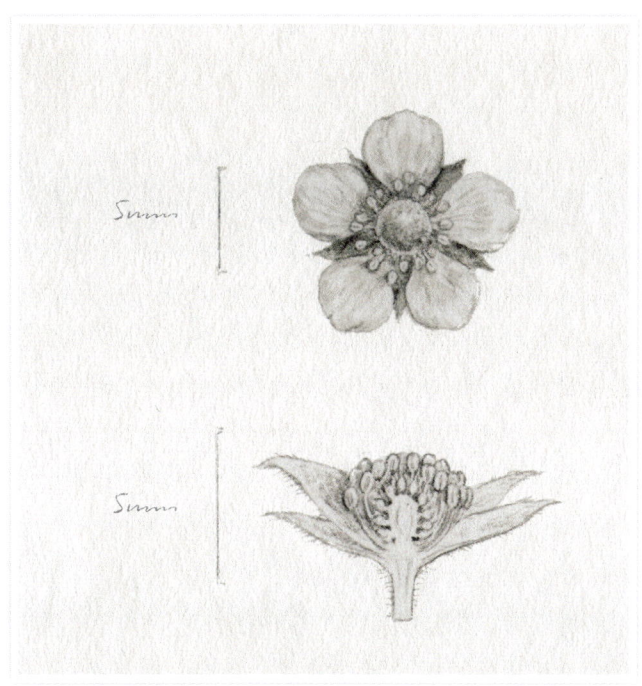

Details, such as this flower portrait and dissection (flower cut in half) are added for the wild strawberry illustration. Such details can be painted in grey paint, as an alternative to using graphite. The advantage with this method is the paint does not smudge and crisp details can be achieved.

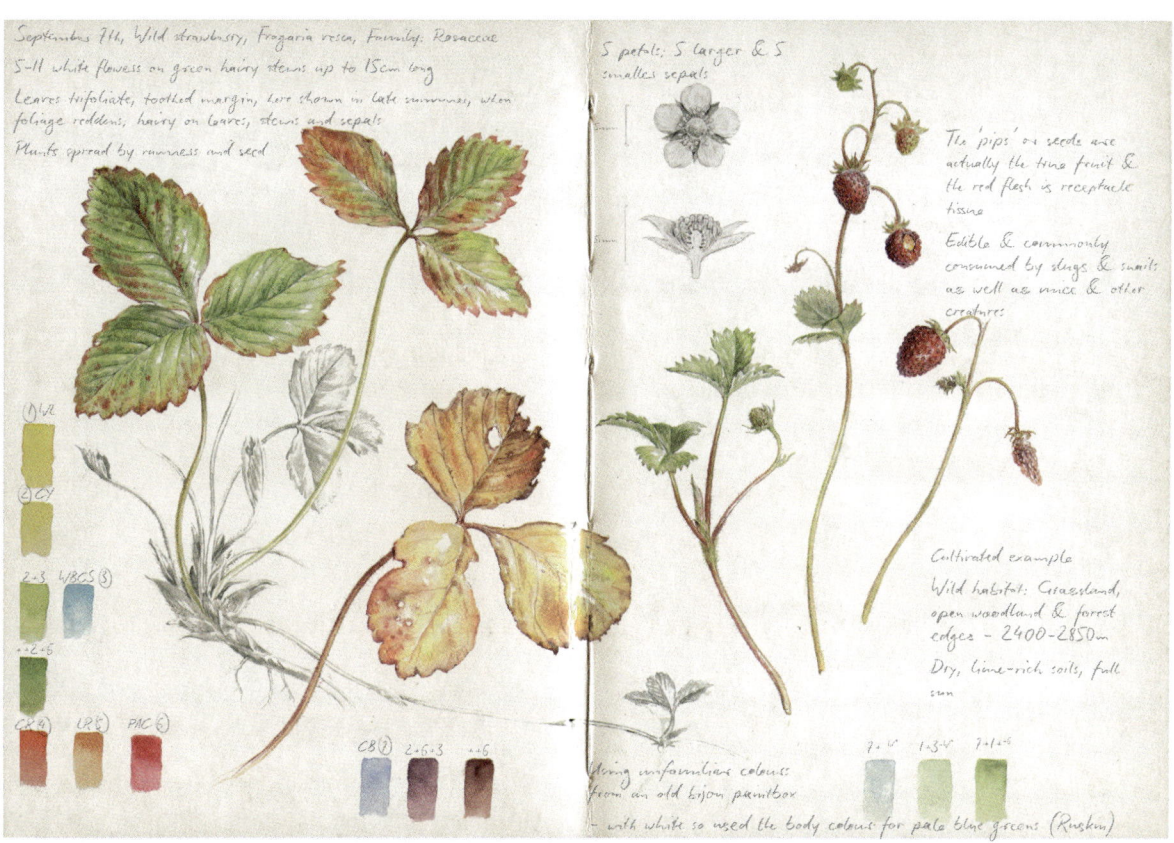

The full illustration of the wild strawberry. This page was painted using a vintage paintbox that I bought at a sale so there are a few additional colours here to the ones I usually use, and they are Cadmium Yellow (CY), Cadmium Red (CR), Light Red (LR) and Permanent Alizarin Crimson (PAC).

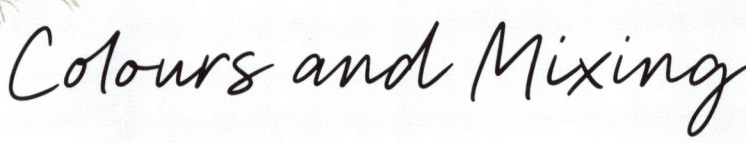

Colours and Mixing

Colour mixing is probably one of the most daunting areas of painting for a beginner; it's easy to get caught up with painting endless colour charts and, in reality, this can just add to the confusion. Here are a few simple points that may help.

USING A PRIMARY PALETTE

As you may already know from the Tools and Materials section, the colours in my sketchbook are all mixed from a range of primary colours: four yellows, five reds, and five blues. You might have heard of some painters using just three primaries (one red, one yellow, and one blue) to mix all other colours. However, when painting from nature, especially when aiming for vibrant hues, a limited palette can fall short. For instance, trying to mix a light, bright purple from Permanent Carmine and Indanthrene Blue may not yield the desired result, even when diluted. Similarly, achieving a deep purple with only light-toned primaries can be impossible.

This is why I have chosen a palette that includes cooler and warmer versions of each primary hue, featuring some of the brightest colours available. I use this palette for all my paintings and find it sufficient for my needs. A controlled number of colours simplifies the mixing process.

To get started, paint a colour chart of your chosen colours, like the one shown here. Keep this chart in the back of your sketchbook for easy reference.

PAINT PROPERTIES

Additionally, make a note of the properties of each colour by visiting the paint manufacturers' websites. Paints can be transparent, opaque, semi-transparent, or semi-opaque, which affects how they should be used. Some paints are more lightfast than others, which is important for the longevity of your work, and others can be granulating (granulating paints are those that have some separation of particles, which creates texture). Understanding your paints will help you make better use of your colours.

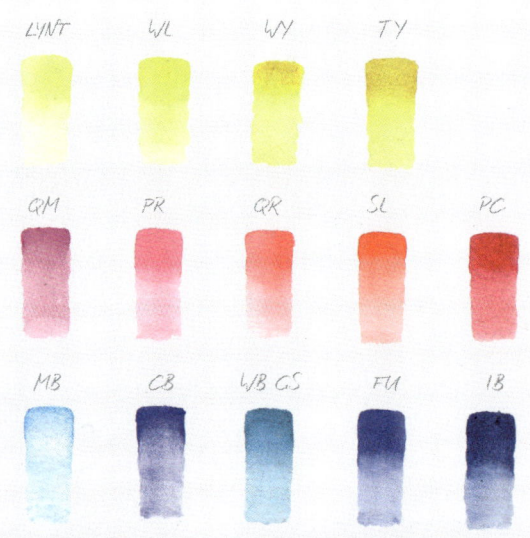

A painted colour chart of the primary colours in my palette with a range of yellows, reds, and blues. Each colour should be initialled in order to identify it. On the top row, you can see the yellows: Lemon Yellow Nickel Titanate, Winsor Lemon, Winsor Yellow, and Transparent Yellow; on the middle row, the reds: Quinacridone Magenta, Permanent Rose, Quinacridone Red, Scarlet Lake, and Permanent Carmine; on the bottom row, the blues: Manganese Blue (or Cerulean Blue), Cobalt Blue, Winsor Blue Green Shade, French Ultramarine, and Indanthrene Blue.

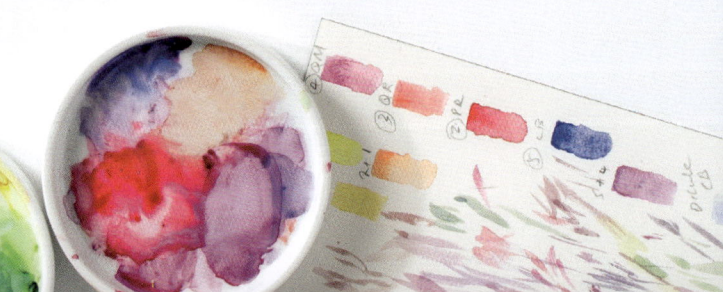

COLOUR TEMPERATURE

Colour temperature is how warm or cold a colour appears. Looking at the three primary colours, it is clear that red is the warmest colour and blue the coolest, with yellow in the middle. Also, within the range of each hue, there are warmer and cooler colours. For example, Quinacridone Red is warmer than Quinacridone Magenta.

While we don't need to be overly concerned with colour temperature, we do need to think about the effect of light falling on a subject and how it affects the colour.

For example, when the light hits a red subject:

• The highlight can be bleached to almost white.

• The brightest, most saturated red can often be found in the nearest parts in the middle.

• Either side of the saturated red, the colour is less saturated, being darker and maybe warmer in the shadows and lighter and cooler on the side nearest to the light.

This means that if a single red is used, it probably won't look very realistic, instead it is better to use two or more reds – including one cool and one warm red.

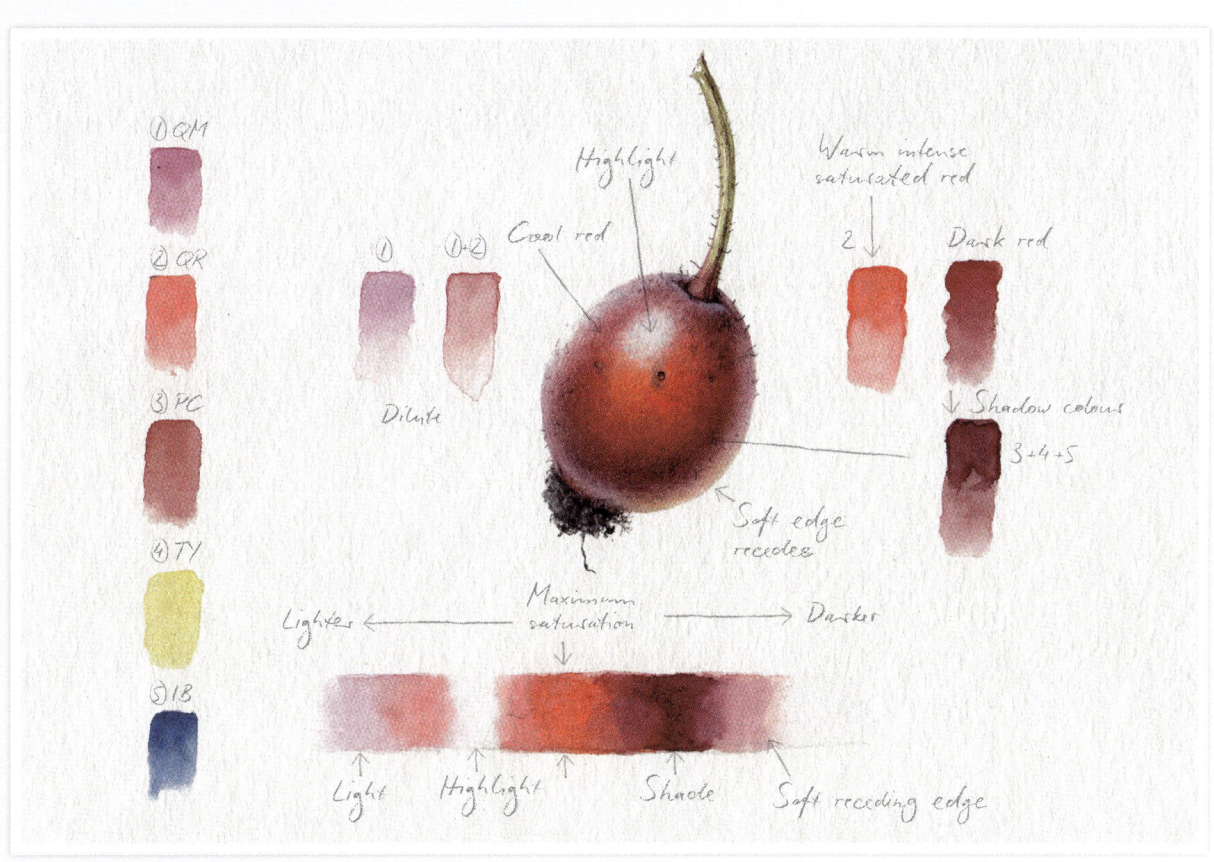

In this rose hip study, three different colours from the reds palette create cooler and warmer colours in relation to the light. The most saturated red is nearest to the middle of the hip; a darker red shadow is mixed using a touch of blue and yellow for the deepest shadows; at the outer edges is a paler, cooler colour, giving the impression of the edge receding away.

COLOUR SATURATION AND VALUES

It's easy to find colour wheels in art books and online, but I never found them particularly useful beyond the basics, such as understanding that secondary colours are mixed from primaries (red + yellow = orange, blue + yellow = green, and blue + red = purple) and, similarly, tertiary colours are mixed from secondary colours.

More interesting is the ratio of colours in a mix, which can bias a colour towards one of the neighbouring hues on the wheel. For example, an orange mix with more red will lean towards the red spectrum, while one with more yellow will lean towards the yellow spectrum. This also relates to how colours shift in relation to light, making them appear warmer or cooler.

Even more fascinating is breaking down colours into their light values. In the three colour charts shown here, I divided nine colours from the palette into light, mid-, and dark tones, yielding very different outcomes. This exercise

provides a wide range of colours to play with. Additionally, in these wheels, the colours are painted from saturated at the outer edge to diluted in the centre, showing how they appear with varying amounts of water. If you look at my sketchbooks, you'll see that the colour swatches are always painted from saturated to diluted.

It soon becomes obvious that if you want to make a light green, there is little point in trying to do so with a dark blue because even though it may look okay diluted, it will most likely end up too dark, and therefore a light green needs a light-to-mid-blue in the mix. This sounds obvious but it's surprising how many students go for a colour that has the wrong light value when mixing and it ends up too dark. Understanding the importance of the colour saturation (and dilution) and the tonal value of the colour will therefore be of great benefit to you.

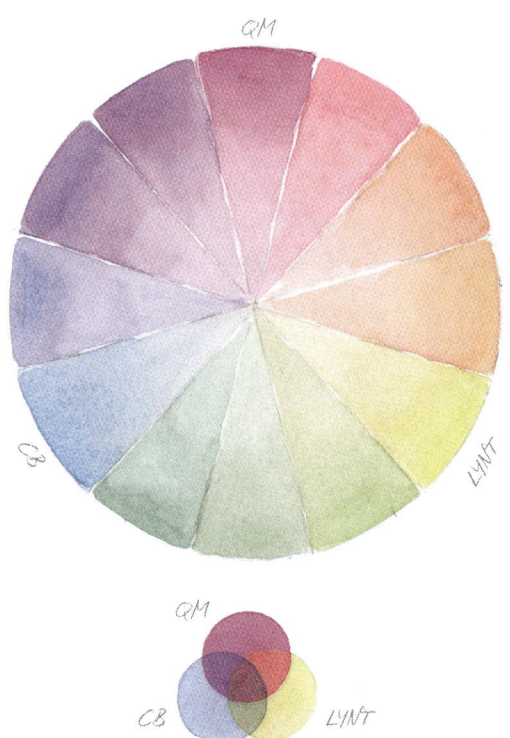

The highlight value colour wheel is created using three of the lighter primary colours: Quinacridone Magenta, Lemon Yellow Nickel Titanate, and Cerulean Blue. These are mixed in varying ratios to create all of the secondary colours shown in the wheel.

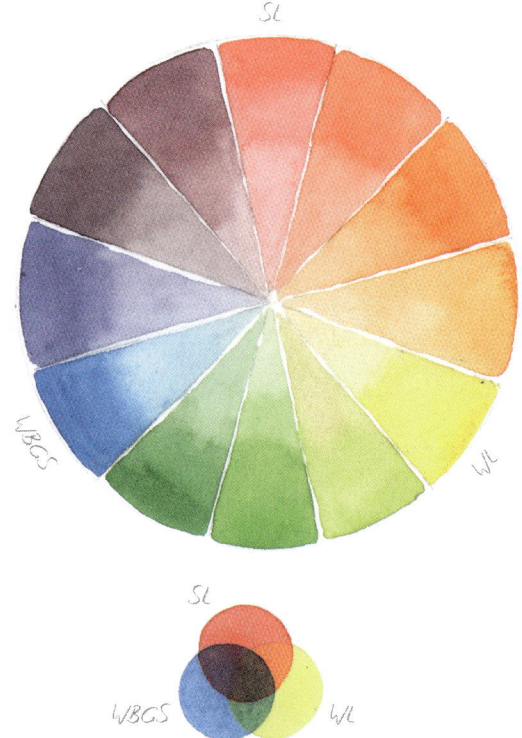

The bright mid-value colour wheel is created using some of the most vivid primary colours in the palette – Winsor Lemon, Winsor Blue Green Shade, and Scarlet Lake – to create a range good range of bright colours.

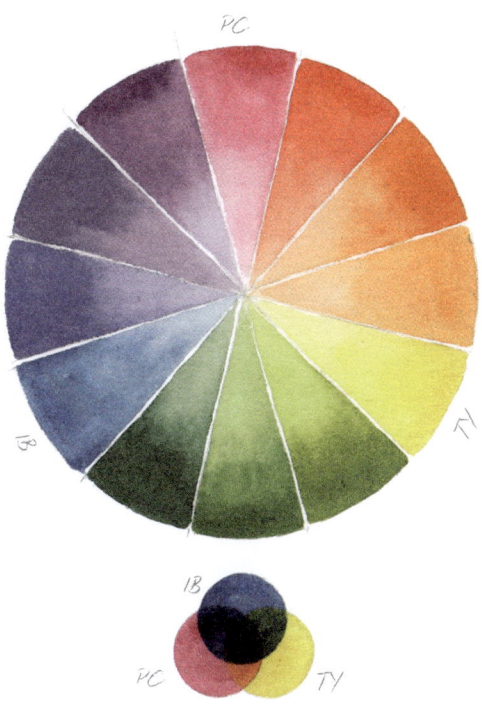

The rich, dark value wheel is created by mixing three of the darkest primary colours from the palette: Transparent Yellow, Indanthrene Blue, and Permanent Carmine. This creates a lovely range of rich colours.

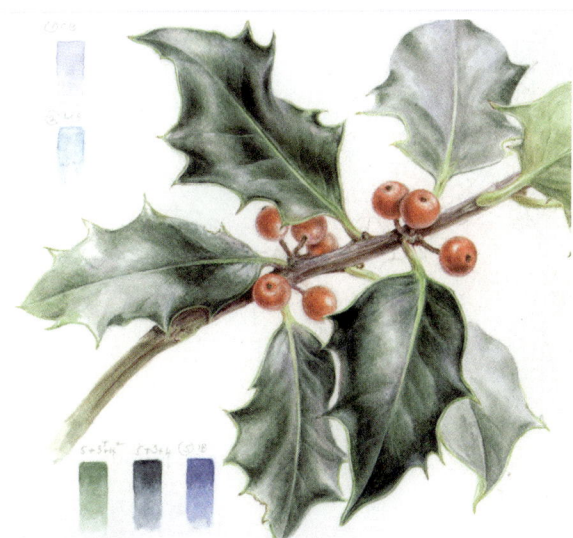

↑ A pale blue underlying wash, such as Cobalt Blue, can provide a useful base when painting a shiny green leaf. For example, in this Holly leaf it effectively represents the highlight reflecting the blue of the sky.

MY TIPS FOR COLOUR MIXING

There is much to learn about colour so here are some useful additional points to consider.

How Many Colours in a Mix?

When mixing, it is best to keep it to no more than three colours; the more colours that are added, the greater the likelihood of things turning muddy.

Optical Mixing

You can achieve different results by overlaying colours rather than mixing them on the palette. For example, you may achieve a brighter scarlet red colour if you paint the red over a dry layer of yellow. Try experimenting and comparing mixes with overlaid colours.

Underlying Colours

Many subjects need underlying colours, such as yellow under red, blue under green, and violet under browns. Underlying colours need to be painted in the first layer. Although it can be difficult to identify such colours when you first start painting, it soon becomes apparent that the use of certain colours creates visual illusions by interacting with another colour applied later.

Shadow Colours

There are many different options with shadow colours; however, don't be tempted to use dirty grey or brown mixes for shadow. Look instead for darker versions of the same colour, or other examples include violets for pinks, pale blue violets for white, dark warm reds for light red flowers, deep blues in some dark greens, and warm yellow for vivid yellow flowers.

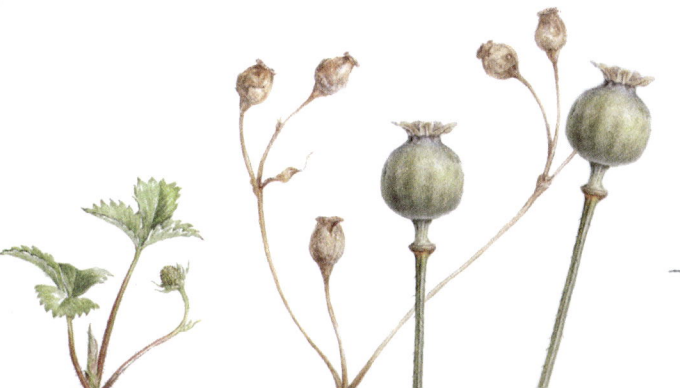

Watercolour Painting

Watercolour is a very versatile medium that can produce a range of effects and textures that are perfect for painting plants and natural objects. It's important to have a good range of techniques in your skill set in order to make the most of the medium.

There are lots of resources available on how to paint in watercolours but often they are not all that suited to smaller botanical subjects, so don't get too stuck on technique as though it were a linear process. Instead, the best approach is to use the techniques as an introduction or guideline and then experiment yourself to find what works best for you. There is no one right or wrong way.

CONTROLLING THE WATER

One of the main challenges when painting with watercolours is the ability to manage the amount of water on your brush and on the paper. Watercolour can take a little time to master but regular practice with different techniques will allow you to discover the range of possibilities in your sketchbook and will help you to control the paint more effectively.

As you learned in the Colours and Mixing section, understanding the properties of each colour in your palette is also important as not all colours behave in the same way. For example, colours can have varying degrees of transparency, being opaque, semi-opaque, semi-transparent, or transparent. Of course, when sufficiently diluted, they are all transparent but it is important to know how each of your paints behaves. Thus, working with a fairly limited palette will allow you to learn the properties of each of your colours and know how best to use them.

The layering of paint using different techniques is used in most subjects, often allowing it to dry before applying the next layer in order to avoid muddy colours. As you will see, watercolour techniques are usually split into wet or dry categories. However, paint can also be added into dampened surfaces rather than wet. I use this approach with a lot of my sketchbook work because it's so versatile and easier to control.

One of the most common problems with painting watercolours in botanical painting is the use of too much water, which is hard to control. In smaller subjects, very wet techniques can be difficult to manage; such techniques are more commonly used in landscapes and larger subjects but they can still be useful in botanical painting if used correctly.

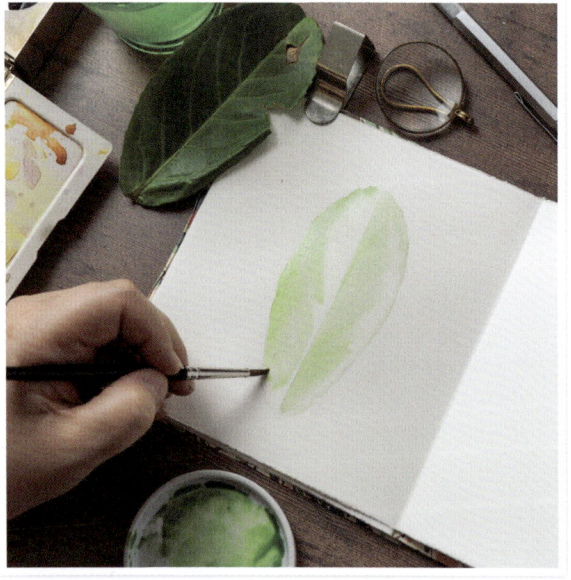

Painting a leaf wash in the initial stages. A painting can be started in several different ways and a combination of techniques can be used.

THE WET TECHNIQUES

The wet techniques are mostly used in the initial stages of the painting before other techniques are used but there can be some alternation of these techniques in reality. I have limited the techniques discussed to those that are most useful. Usually they are painted with larger brushes, sizes 4–6, depending on the size of the subject.

Graded Washes

This is a wash that has a smooth transition of colour into the white of paper, so it's a light-to-dark gradient or vice versa. This an important skill to have and can be used very effectively for highlights, such as on stems, leaves, flowers, and fruit. It creates form very early on in the painting but in a controlled way.

Description: grades colour into highlights and lighter parts of a subject.

Method: dampen the area to be painted first, then load the brush with colour (not too much); when you want to transition into white, dip the brush into clean water and continue. The amount of water in the dampening and brush is key to success.

In the initial layers of this Clematis petal, colour is gently graded into the white of the paper, creating a sense of volume and depth.

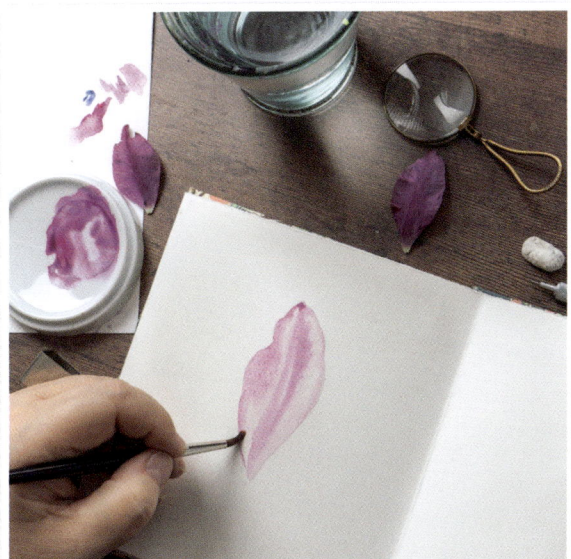

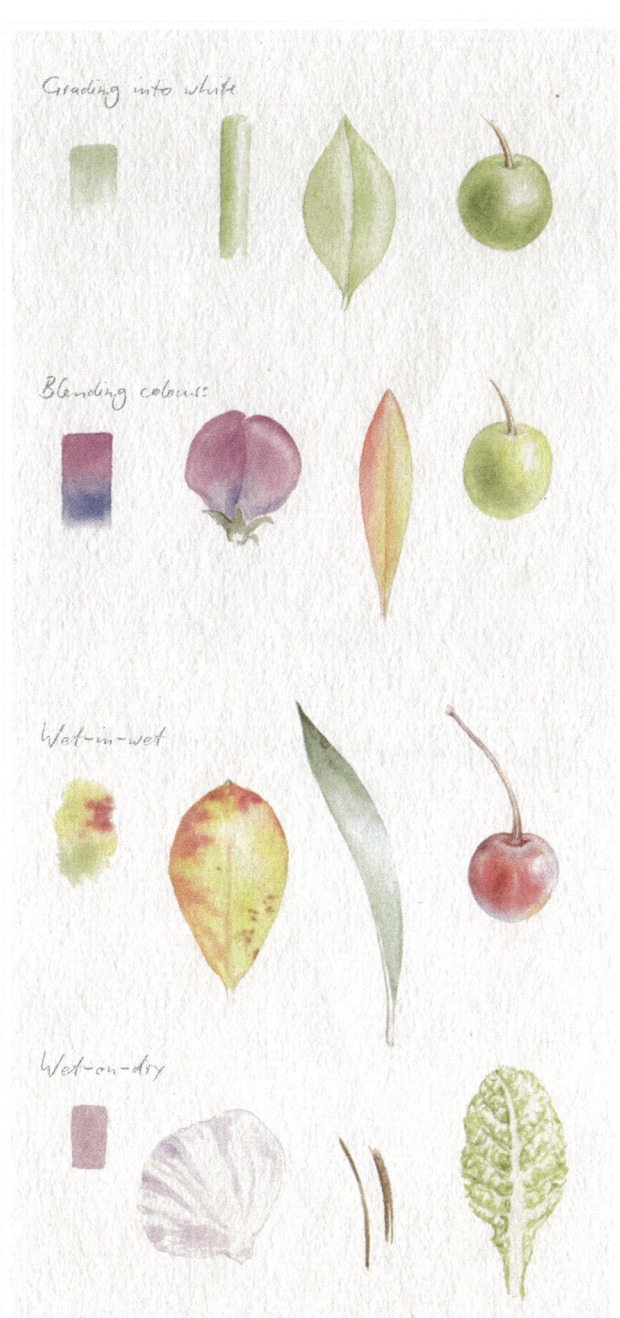

Four different approaches for beginning a painting. Sometimes the techniques are used together; for example, the blending technique example shown here also uses graded washes to lead into highlights. The wet-on-dry technique is an approach that I use a lot when I want to establish structure before adding washes. It is ideal for pale-coloured flowers or complex leaf structures.

Blended Washes

This is a useful technique used in many subjects and allows one colour to lead into a second colour, achieving a smooth transition in a controlled way by dampening the paper first. It is ideal for subjects such as a ripening fruit, or a petal with two colours.

Description: creates a smooth transition from one colour to another.

Method: dampen or wet the paper, then apply one colour at the point where the colour change is needed; clean the brush and continue with a second colour, allowing the two colours to meet and blend in the middle with a smooth transition.

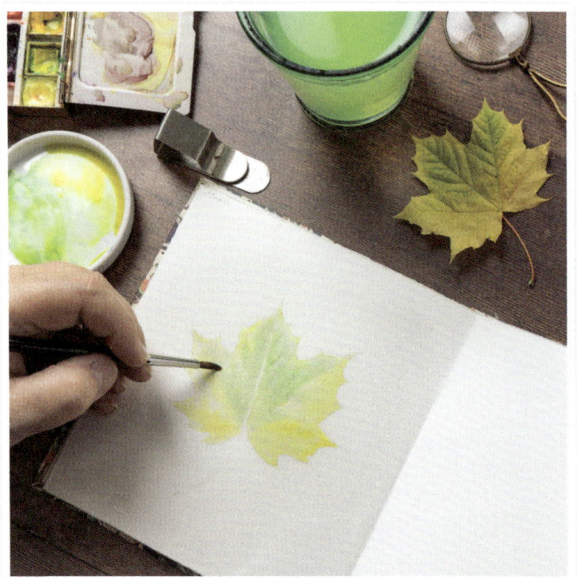

A blended wash allows two colours to merge seamlessly, an excellent foundation for this Maple leaf painting.

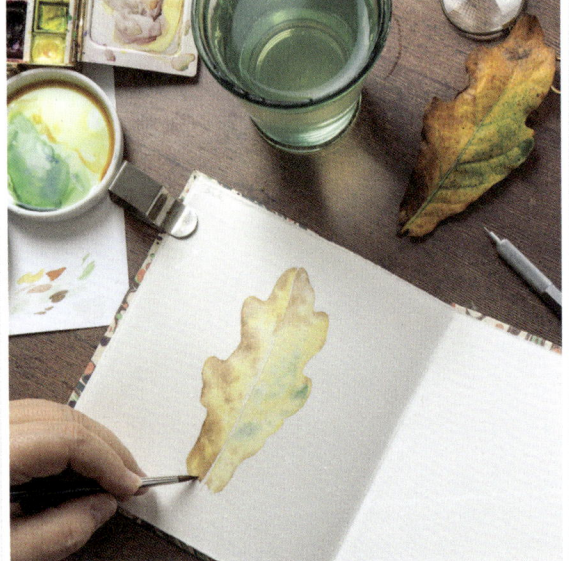

Painting wet into wet allows colours to flow and merge beautifully, perfect for capturing the vibrant hues of this multicoloured Oak leaf.

Wet-in-Wet

This technique involves applying wet paint onto a wet surface. It can be used to add multiple colours, and the flow of colour is used to create smooth transitions. The flow varies depending on how much water and paint is used and the surface can be worked into until it starts to dry, which allows more focused colour to be applied. It is ideal for larger subjects or smaller ones, whereas the blending and grading techniques described earlier are more controlled approaches and particularly well suited when working in smaller areas.

Description: allows colours to blend and flow into one another in a controlled way.

Method: wet the paper with clean water by filling the belly of the brush. While the paper is still wet, apply watercolour paint and colours will spread and merge. More paint or additional colours can be added as the paint gradually dries. If too much water and paint is added, hard edges will form and colour may separate from the water, so water management is key.

Wet-on-Dry

This is a more controlled technique that allows sharper edges and shapes to be painted, either onto the white of the paper or in layers onto previously dried layers of paint. It can be useful in smaller areas and is ideal for painting veins and lines. Importantly, it is useful for establishing form and definition in the early stages, creating small patches of colour, but can also be used in the mid- and later stages for detail and crisp shadows. You will see that I use this technique a lot.

Description: applying wet paint onto a dry surface to create well-defined edges and shapes.

Method: apply watercolour paint directly onto dry paper by loading the paint onto the brush to give you more control over the shapes and lines.

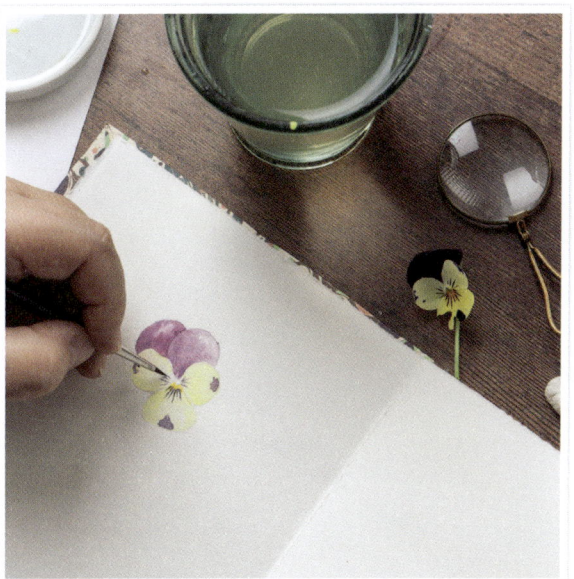

Painting wet onto dry layers allows for the precise markings on this Viola to be sucessfully applied.

Painting into Damp

If you want to intensify colour in specific areas or add spot colour, you can paint into a dampened surface as a controlled way of adding more colour by only dampening the areas where colour is needed. This approach can be used at various stages of a painting to build and intensify colour while ensuring that other areas stay clear of colour. The colour added will also have soft edges that naturally blend into the layers beneath, with no hard edge.

Description: intensifying colour by painting into dampened areas with soft natural colour transitions.

Method: dampen the area where the colour needs to be added with clean water and add the colour into the dampened area so that it spreads within that area. In some circumstances, colour can also be added to a previous layer of colour while it is still damp, such as when darker, soft veins or markings are needed.

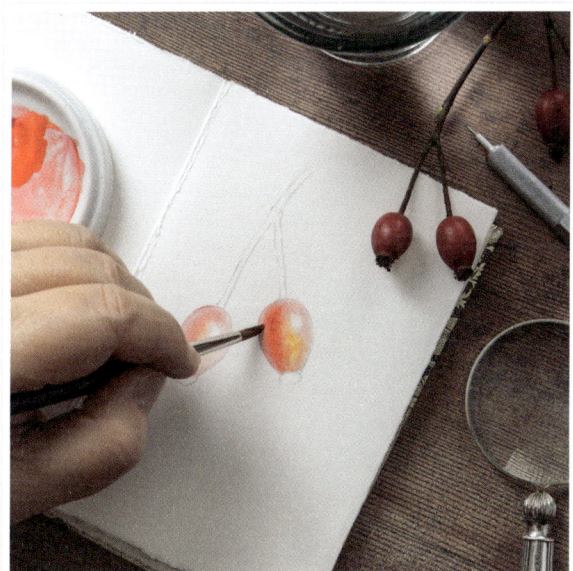

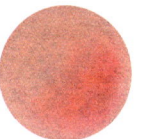

Pre-dampening with clean water allows for greater colour saturation in specific areas, as in the red of this rose hip.

Glazing

Glazes of diluted colour can be added over dry layers of paint, either all over an area or in smaller selected areas, to build depth of colour or to unify areas; and by adding one colour over another in a glaze, a third colour is created, in a process known as optical colour mixing. Glazes are usually added in the mid-to-late stages of a painting. They are useful in many parts of a painting if used selectively.

Description: layering transparent washes of colour over a dry layer of paint to create depth and richness; allows for subtle colour changes.

Method: apply to previous dry layers of colour as a transparent layer.

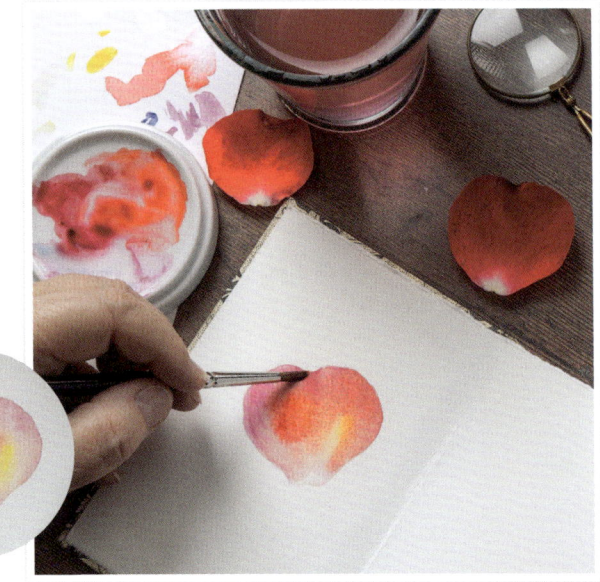

↑ *Glazing over colour can intensify or change the colour in a subject, as seen in this Rose petal detail.*

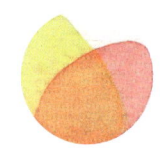

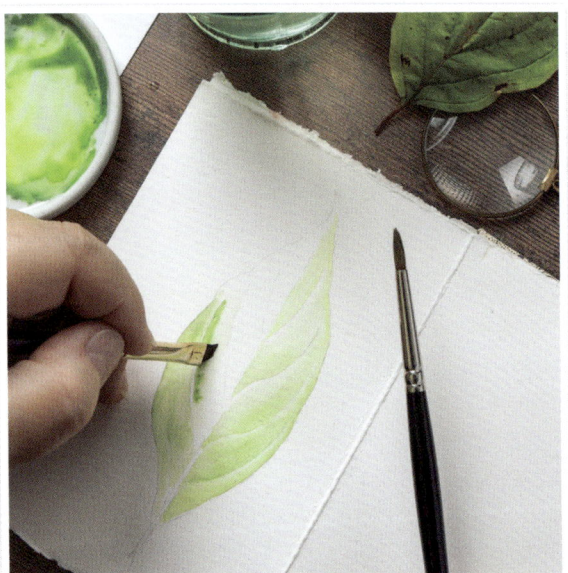

↑ *Lifting or moving paint can be used as a technique or to repair areas. Paint is best lifted or moved while still wet, as seen here on this leaf.*

Lifting, Moving, or Softening

Occasionally, it is necessary to move a little paint or to soften an area, usually in circumstances where too much paint has been applied or a hard edge has formed. Some artists use lifting with a pointed or flat brush in the wet stage to create highlights, but I prefer to use the grading techniques instead for highlights. Try out different approaches.

Description: removing paint from the paper to create highlights or correct mistakes where too much paint has been applied. Use this technique sparingly and never scrub with a brush to lift paint.

Method: use a damp brush, sponge, or tissue to lift the paint from the paper. For best results, lift the paint while it's still wet.

THE DRY TECHNIQUES

The term 'dry' brush is a little misleading and would probably be better if it was termed 'damp' brush because the brush isn't actually dry. A lot of dry brush work is more like using a pencil, using small strokes that scumble the paint onto the surface. Because it's 'dry', it sits on the surface rather than sinking in, therefore less paint and water is required.

There are various dry brush techniques, but all involve using a dampened brush with minimal water and paint that can be painted onto dry or damp surfaces to create different effects. These techniques are usually painted with smaller brushes, such as sizes 1–3, and are mostly used on top of previous layers to create smooth colour or texture. They can be transitioned from dark to light and vice versa. Several different dry techniques are shown here.

All of these subjects were painted using a number of dry brush techniques. Dry techniques are used over the initial wet techniques, demonstrating the results achieved.

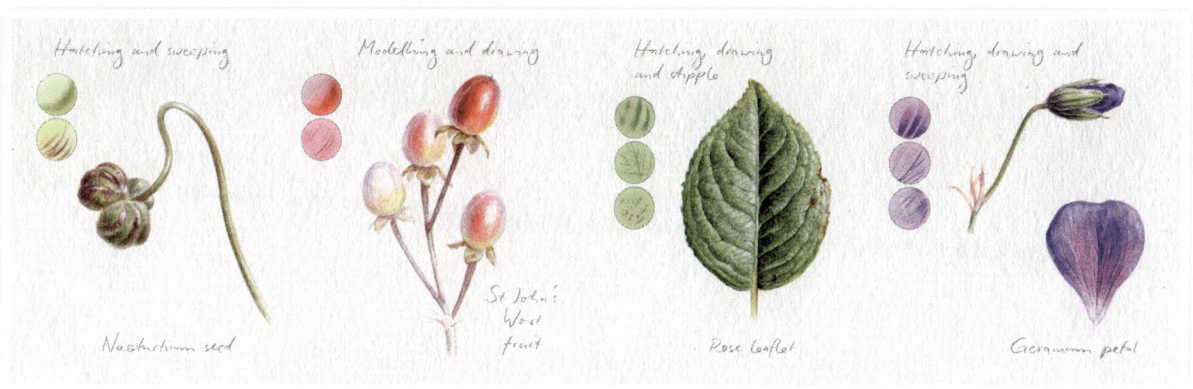

Nasturtium seed — Hatching and sweeping

St John's Wort fruit — Modelling and drawing

Rose leaflet — Hatching, drawing and stipple

Geranium petal — Hatching, drawing and sweeping

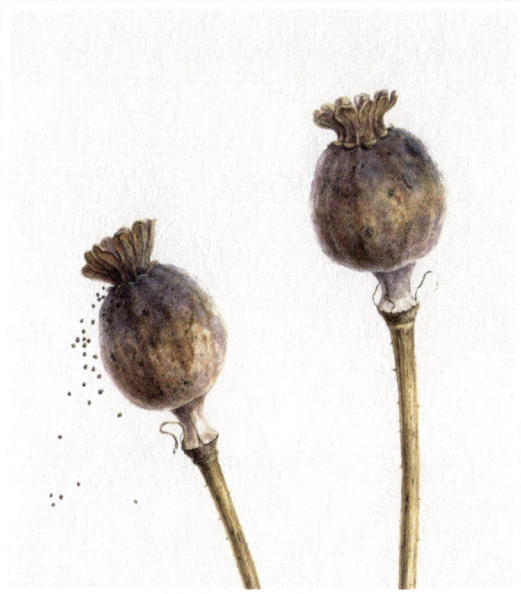

Dry brush modelling is used to apply rich colour with precision, enhancing both detail and form, as demonstrated in these Poppy seed heads.

Modelling

In this technique, small motions of the brush are used to model a three-dimensional-looking form. It is usually applied over the initial washes, either onto a dry surface to create a more textured finish or onto a dampened surface for a very soft, smooth effect. The aim is to add a layer of dry colour, and is akin to polishing the paint on, using a continuous motion.

Description: intensifying colour, and building form and texture with paint applied onto dry or damp surfaces.

Method: load the paint onto a lightly dampened small brush and remove the excess onto a cloth; never use kitchen paper because it contains chemicals. Next, test on spare paper to check that the paint is not too wet. Moving on to the actual painting, apply the brush lightly to the paper and slightly flatten the tip, and use the small motions of the brush to apply the paint. The effect can be further softened with a clean, damp brush for smooth transitions. Paint must be applied in very light layers. This technique is perfect for areas between veins on leaves and intense colour on rounded fruits.

Hatching

A method for rendering a surface is to use tiny hatching lines using the tip of the brush. These lines are so small and closely positioned that a smooth surface is created. The direction of the strokes tends to follow the contour of the surface. The paint is slightly wetter than the modelling technique. This method of building colour can be added to dry or slightly dampened surfaces with different outcomes. The small lines can also be cross-hatched in multiple directions. It can be used in the same way as the modelling dry brush technique to create colour and form.

Description: intensifying colour, building form and texture with paint applied to the surface of previous layers, either onto dry or damp surfaces.

Method: load the paint onto a lightly dampened small brush and remove the excess onto a cloth or on a spare piece of paper to check that the paint is not too wet. Apply using the absolute tip of the brush with very light strokes. When using this technique, paint must be applied in very light layers and the strokes can also be cross-hatched.

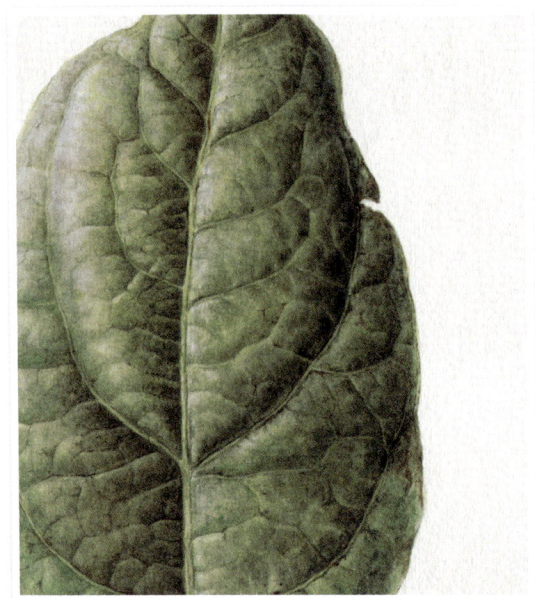

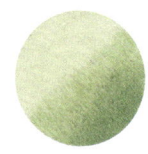

Hatching lines are so small that they look smooth, and they have been used to build rich colour in the areas between veins in this Calycanthus leaf.

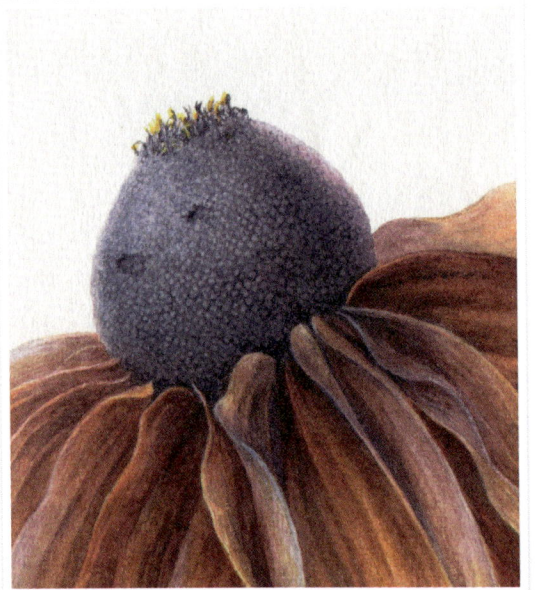

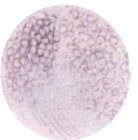

Drawing dry brush was used in the centre of this Rudbeckia to create the texture of the tiny flowers in the centre. It was painted onto a slightly dampened surface.

Drawing

It is possible to create a range of textural effects and lines by using the tip of the brush to draw using a creamy mix of paint. This is useful in areas such as in shadows under veins, where a deep, fine line is needed, or to create a textured surface. It is also useful for fine hairs.

Description: painting fine lines and texture with drawing motions.

Method: load a damp brush with paint and draw to create lines or texture, just as you would with a pencil. This can be used on dry surfaces for sharper lines, or on damp surfaces for a slightly softer effect.

Stipple

Some surfaces are pitted or have pores, they may have fine markings or blemishes, as in this pear, or textured surfaces, such as the surface of an anther releasing pollen or an aged leaf. For such surfaces, stipple is a useful technique.

Description: creating texture, pitting, and small markings.

Method: use the tip of the brush to apply small dots of colour to create the desired effect. Stipple can be applied onto dry surfaces for harder dots or lightly dampened surfaces for softer markings. Dots can be grouped together for larger areas and markings, or can be far apart, in the case of pores.

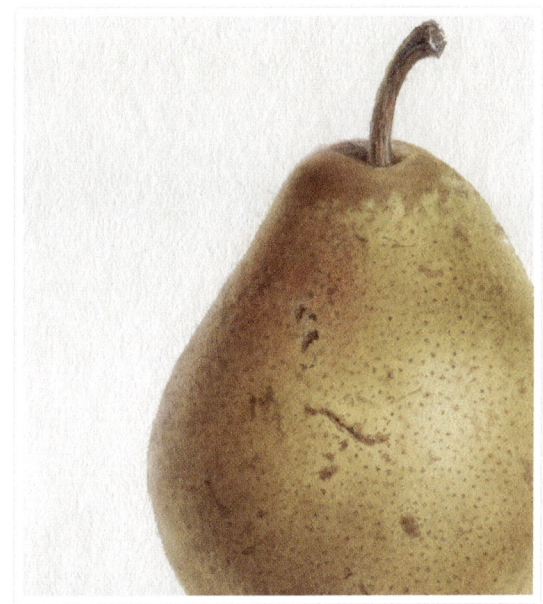

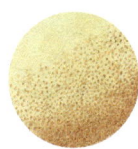

↑ *The stipple technique has been used to create the spotted surface and blemishes on the skin of this pear.*

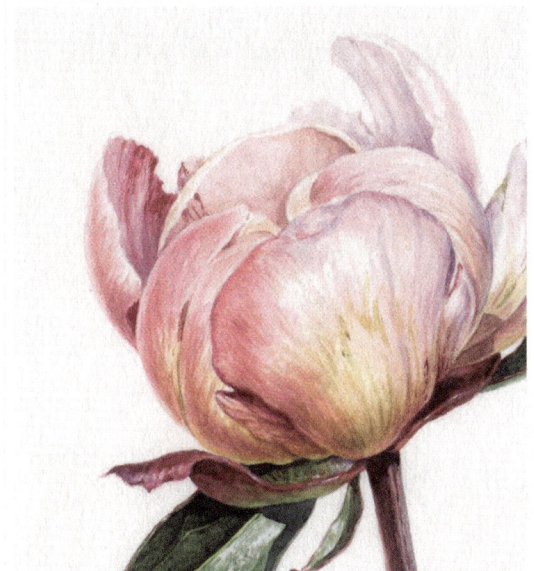

↑ *The sweeping dry brush technique was used to create the markings and texture on this Peony bud.*

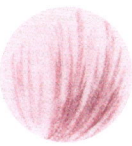

Sweeping

This method uses a slightly splayed brush tip to create texture or the indication of veins. As the name suggests, the brush sweeps across the surface, creating textured or pencil-like markings. This can be applied to dry or damp surfaces.

Description: texture that creates long broken lines following the contours of the surface.

Method: load the brush with paint and splay the tip on spare paper to remove excess paint. Then sweep colour over the surface contours in the direction of any veins or markings to create the desired effect. It can be applied on a dry or lightly dampened surface.

Composition

Arranging a plant illustration is probably one of the most challenging aspects of a sketchbook page. In this section, a range of compositional ideas and approaches are presented in order to provide guidance and inspiration. As you will see, there are many different strategies that can be used to accommodate a broad spectrum of plants, and which create an interesting and engaging spread within a relatively compact space.

A sketchbook doesn't need a 'strict' arrangement but we do need to incorporate all of the necessary elements on the page to represent the plant as accurately as possible, in a well-balanced way. This can mean that it is balanced in both the arrangement of the content and with the colour on a page.

However, it's also worth remembering that sketchbook entries are not finished botanical illustrations and there should be flexibility in the approach; after all, this is your sketchbook and it's your decision on how a plant is represented. At times, you may want to focus on one small aspect of a plant, such as the flower and its component parts, and at other times you may want to document as much information as possible about a whole plant, depending on the purpose of your page, of course.

Overall, your sketchbook should be an enjoyable experience. Not everything needs to be finished or scientific – it can be an eclectic mix of subjects. Therefore don't restrict yourself with too many rules about what a sketchbook should be, otherwise the book can become a chore.

WHAT TO INCLUDE

A sketchbook page should aim to tell the story of a plant by incorporating all of the relevant parts. This can be complex or simple depending on what the purpose of the page is. For example, a sketch page that is made as preparation for a final painting will need to document as much information as possible about the plant. Alternatively, a page can be created for practice with no end purpose other than the desire to document the plant for enjoyment.

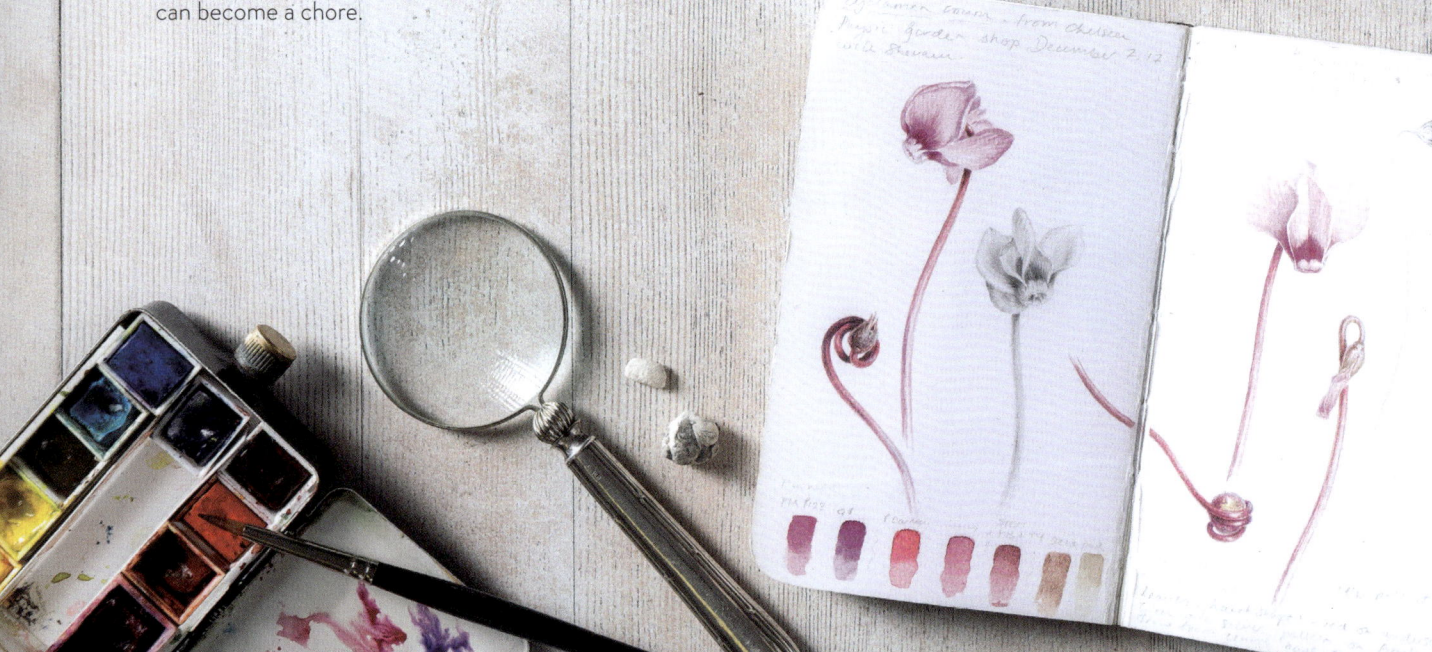

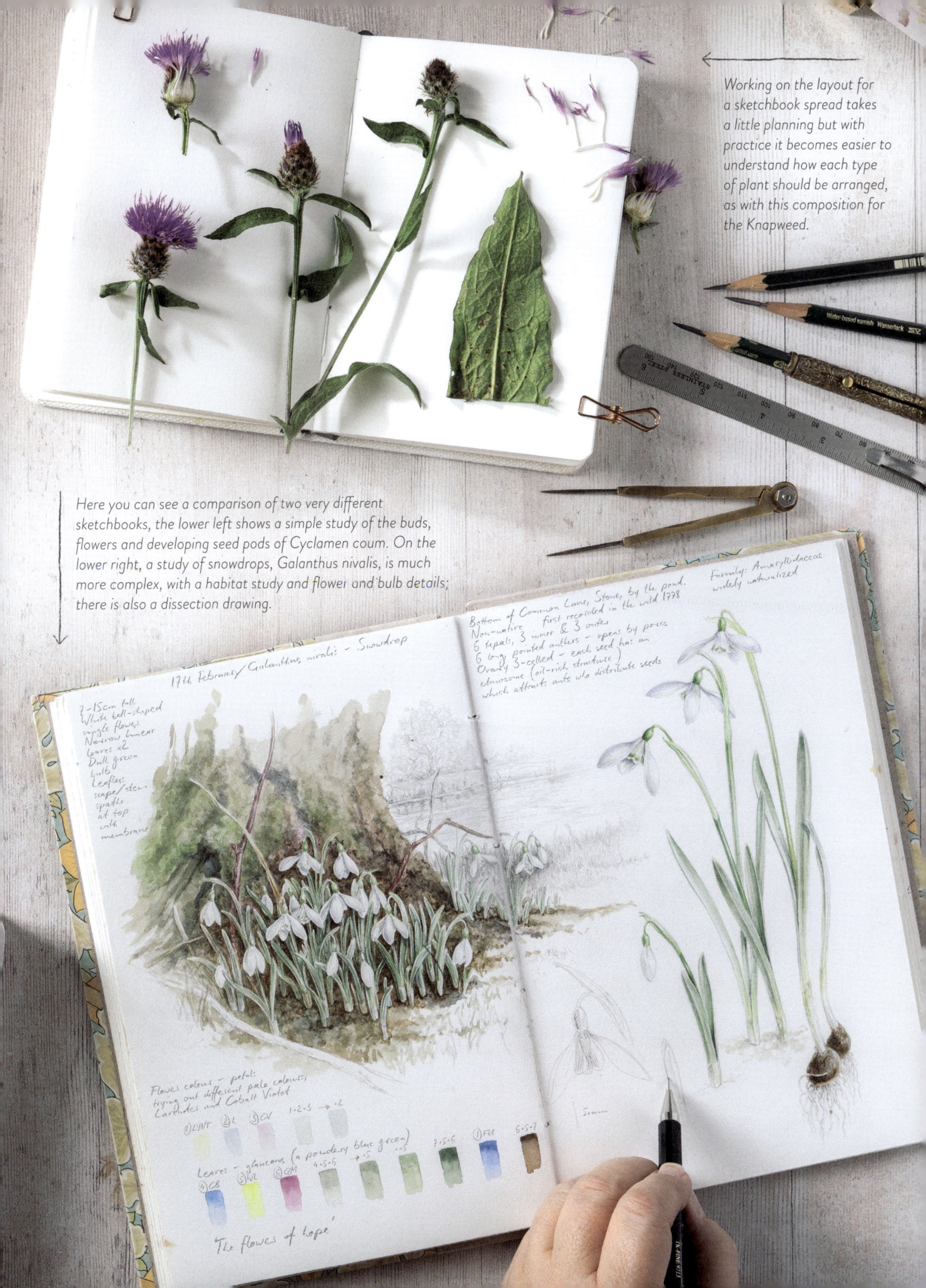

Working on the layout for a sketchbook spread takes a little planning but with practice it becomes easier to understand how each type of plant should be arranged, as with this composition for the Knapweed.

Here you can see a comparison of two very different sketchbooks, the lower left shows a simple study of the buds, flowers and developing seed pods of Cyclamen coum. On the lower right, a study of snowdrops, Galanthus nivalis, is much more complex, with a habitat study and flower and bulb details; there is also a dissection drawing.

17th February / Galanthus nivalis – Snowdrop

Bottom of Common Lane, Stone, by the pond.
Non-native   first recorded in the wild 1778
6 tepals, 3 inner & 3 outer
6 long, pointed anthers – opens by pores
Ovary 3-celled – each seed has an
elaiosome (oil-rich structure)
which attracts ants who distribute seeds

Family: Amaryllidaceae
widely naturalized

7–15cm tall
White bell-shaped
single flower
Narrow linear
leaves x2
Dull green
bulb
Leaflet:
scape/stem
spathe
at top
with
membrane

Flower colour – petal:
trying out different pale colours:
Cerulean and Cobalt Violet

① LNT ② L ③ CV 1·2·3 → ·2

Leaves – glaucous (a powdery blue green)
④ CB ⑤ VL ⑥ CGH

The flower of hope

UTILIZING THE SPACE

Documenting the important parts of the plant within a limited space can be challenging and space needs to be used efficiently. After many years working as an artist, I have developed a fairly broad approach to my sketch pages but certain features, such as the inclusion of colour swatches and annotations, are constants. In other aspects I keep it flexible, leaving parts unfinished if I'm short of both time and space.

Learning to use different approaches can help to avoid issues such as tonal clashes or 'touching' parts. Tonal clashes occur where parts merge together because the tonal values of separate parts are too similar. Touching parts occur where two parts accidentally meet or overlap without separation, and such areas can appear strange or misleading. The white space around and between the plant parts therefore needs to be carefully considered when creating a sketch page.

From my initial observations of the plant, I usually have a good understanding of what I want to show and how to present it. This is based on the features of the particular plant but I also need to consider other aspects. For example, I may have to wait for other parts, such as fruits, to develop. In this case, I will need to leave space for these too by leaving areas of the page free to add such parts at a later date.

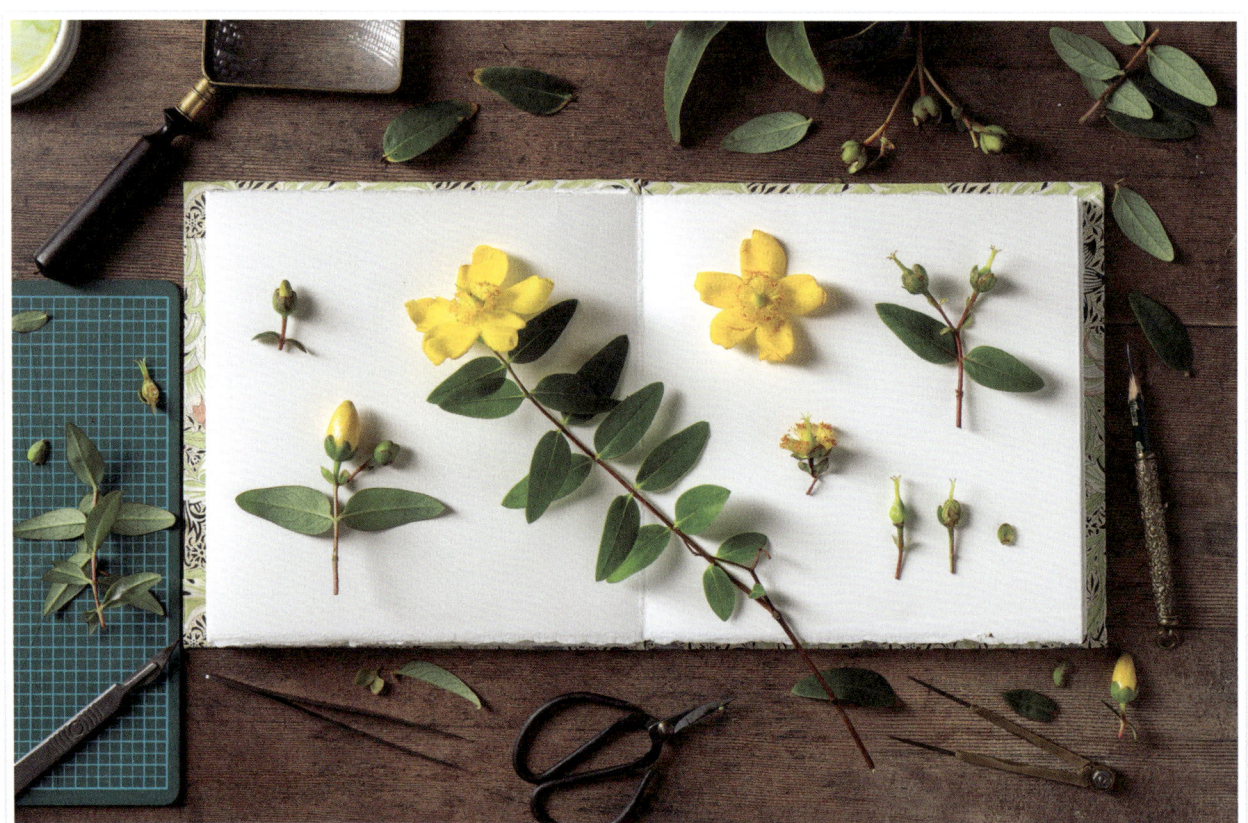

Laying out the plant parts on the spread can help to visualize the composition before drawing starts. It can be useful to take photographs of different arrangements to see what works best and how the space on the spread can be filled.

USING THE GROWTH HABIT

Plants grow in different ways: some are upright and tall; others form short, low rosettes; there are scramblers or climbers; and some have parts that hang down. However, the same format of book has to accommodate all of these different growth habits.

I almost always use a double-page spread because it will be the case that there is more than enough content to fill two pages, and working across the gutter of the page creates a much larger space to work within. If possible, I begin by laying parts of the subject on the paper first to see how they might fit. If the plant grows upright, it must be presented in this way; a low or rosette-shaped growth could be illustrated from above; if the plant is a climber or scrambler, it should show this habit; and if parts are hanging down or curving, they should be shown in the correct orientation.

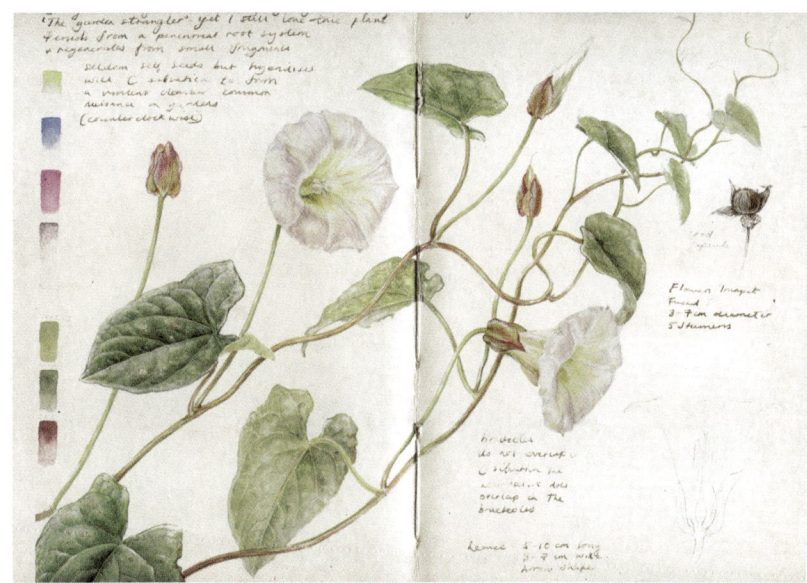

In this composition, the upward climbing habit of a Bindweed plant, Calystegia sepium, is captured and sprawls upwards and across the two-page spread as it vigorously clambers over other plants towards the light.

OBSERVING THE NATURAL ORDER

If possible, I try to order parts in the natural stages of development. For example, if there is a flower, I will position the fruit next to it, simply because the fruit develops from the pollinated flower as part of the natural order. However, I also have to consider what space is available on the sketchbook spread and this may not always be possible if it compromises the overall balance of the spread. Similarly, I position higher-up parts nearer to the top of the spread and lower parts at the bottom because it makes no sense to put flowers at the bottom of the spread when they are at the top of the plant or roots at the top of the spread when they are at the bottom of the plant.

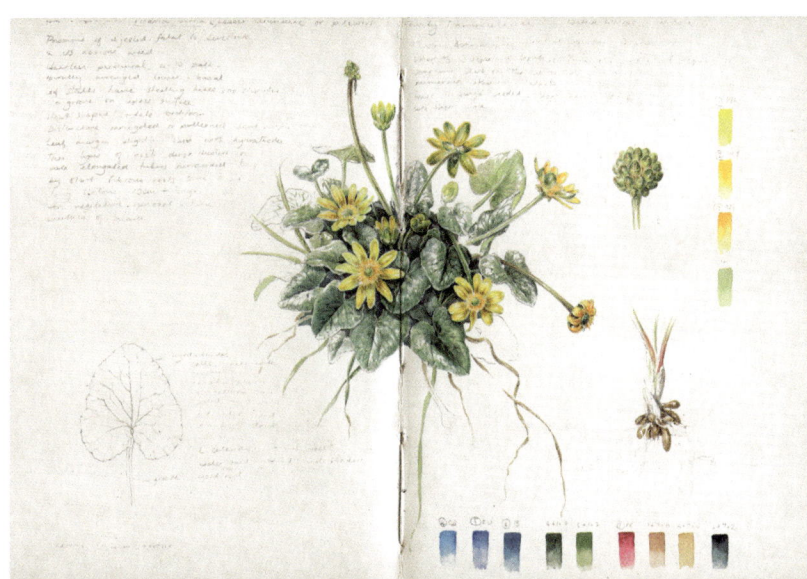

The natural order of parts is demonstrated in this spread illustrating the Lesser Celandine, Ficaria verna; the enlarged fruit is positioned and scaled up by x2, on the upper right-hand side, next to the flower, and the root detail is positioned at the bottom right of the spread, lower than the main plant illustration.

COMPOSITION STRATEGIES

With larger or complex plants, it may be too difficult to fit everything on the spread separately, and in this case it may be possible to overlap parts. Care must be taken, however, to retain clarity between the overlaying parts. There are a few different approaches that can be used, and different media can also be used. It is also possible to visually cut a stem or even a leaf, and overlay stems, to reduce the overall height of the plant.

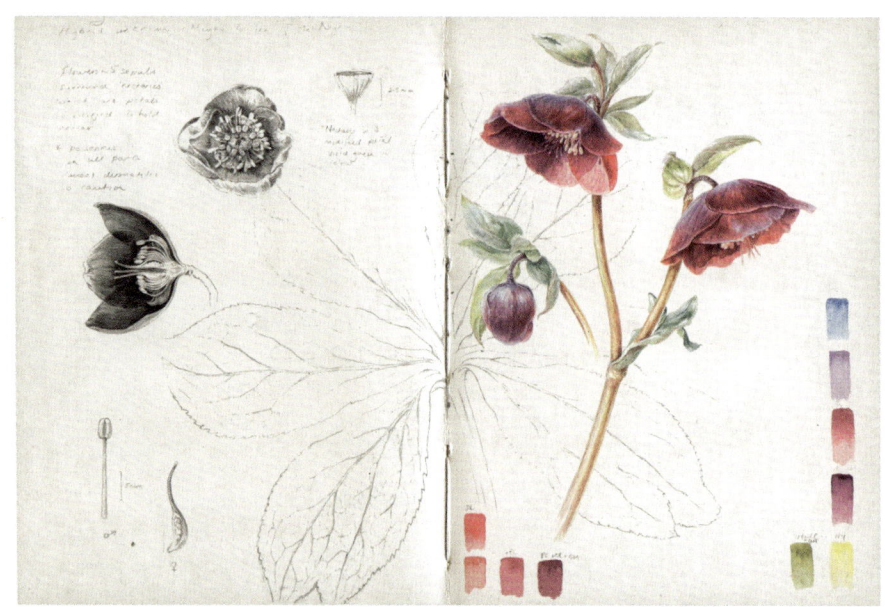

Due to the large leaves of the Hellebore plant, I chose to depict the leaf behind the flower in graphite, saving time and space. The additional flower details in graphite help balance the composition, as they were already painted in colour on the main stem.

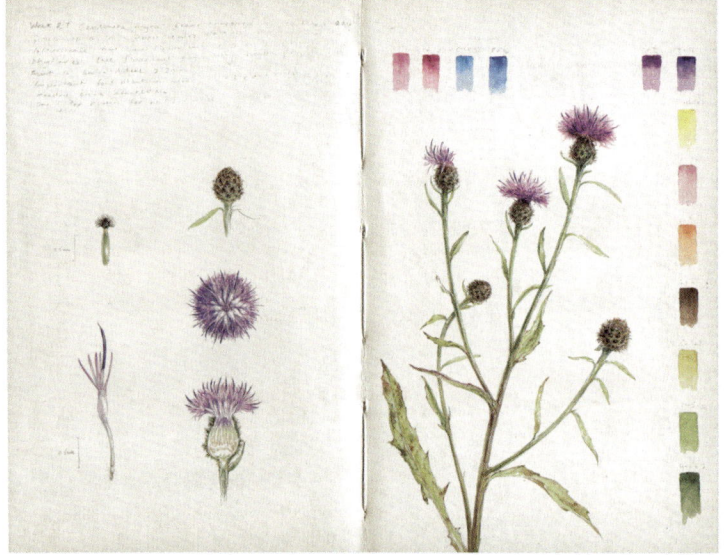

A detailed illustration of a Knapweed flower (Centaurea nigra) shows its composite inflorescence, with many small flowers. The enlarged individual flower at bottom left reveals intricate structures that are hard to see at life-size, with a scale bar indicating actual size.

SCALING UP OR DOWN

If parts are very small, they can be difficult to draw. In this scenario, it is possible to enlarge part of an illustration. This is typically done with close-ups of flower dissections and the dissected parts from the internal parts of a flower. For example, a small flower could be doubled in size by multiplying the height and width by two or however many times is necessary to make it clear to see. Similarly, if very large parts are reduced, such as in the case of a tree, the scale must also be written.

TABLE-TOP STUDIES AND COLLECTIONS

A good approach for beginners is a table-top study or collection of separate plant parts. This is a spread that has a number of small subjects that collectively fill a whole spread. 'Table-top' simply means that they are painted as arranged on a surface or they can just be floating individual studies. The approach can be useful with small subjects, such as flowers, seed capsules, fruits, fungi, or even leaves.

It can be useful to use different media to avoid the page being too busy or unevenly weighted. For example, dissection or detail drawing can be made in graphite as this approach avoids the page losing its focus. As long as colour is used in one part of the page, it may not be necessary to use it in another.

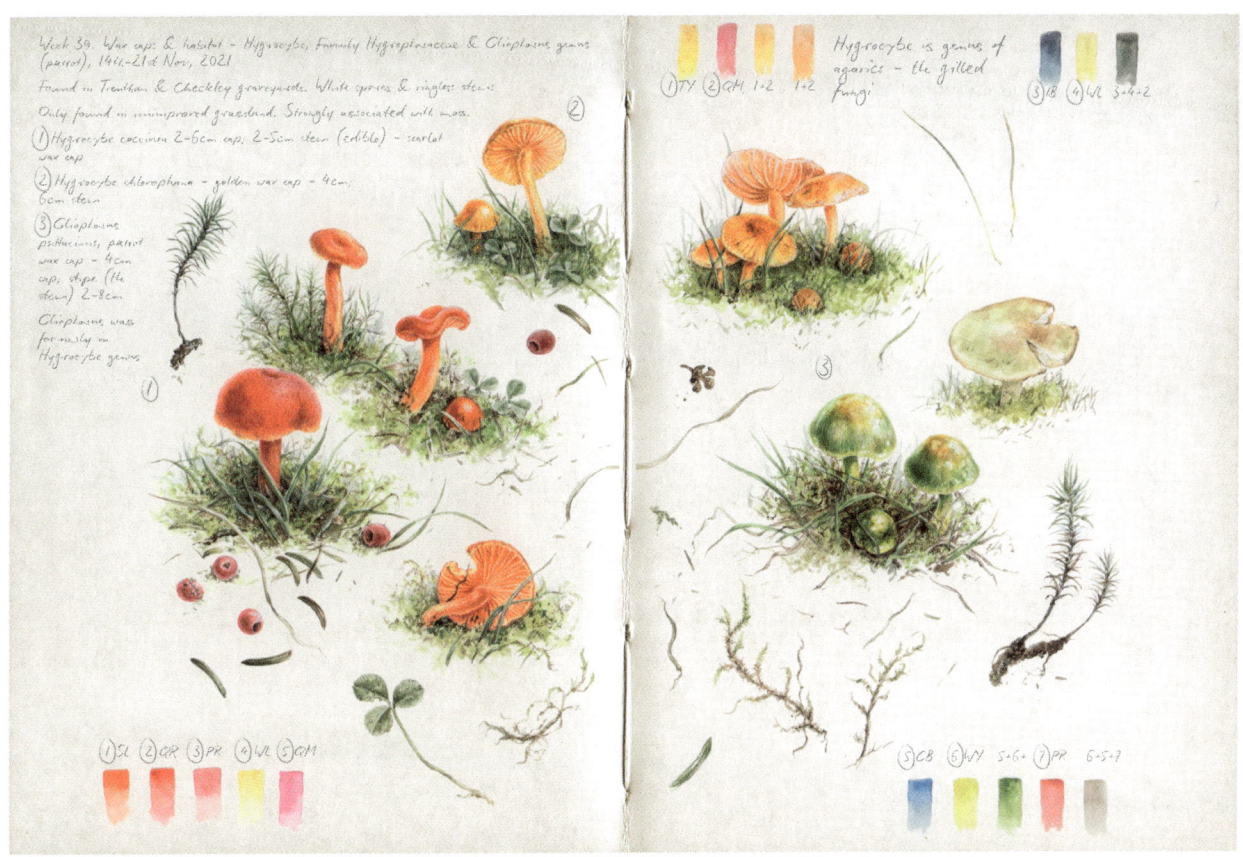

A whimsical collection of wax cap mushrooms fills the spread, accompanied by floating yew fruits, leaves and mosses, reflecting the short grassy habitat where these fungi were found. I included various fungi, autumnal debris, growth stages and colours to capture the scene.

MIXED COMPOSITIONS

You may want to include plants from a particular habitat or community and in this case several plants will be included on one spread. Special attention will need to be given to any overlapping areas to avoid confusion between parts of the different plants. Staggering the stems will no doubt be required but be sure to keep the relative heights of the plants accurate.

A collection of Scottish wildflowers painted during my first journey away from home following the coronavirus pandemic. This is a slightly more complex method of recording. The overlapping of stems was used to carefully position the taller and shorter stems and to balance the colour across the spread. I used Lavender (L), Violet Dioxazine (VD) and Cadmium Yellow (CY) here but the recommended palette can just as easily be used and there are many ways to achieve much the same outcome.

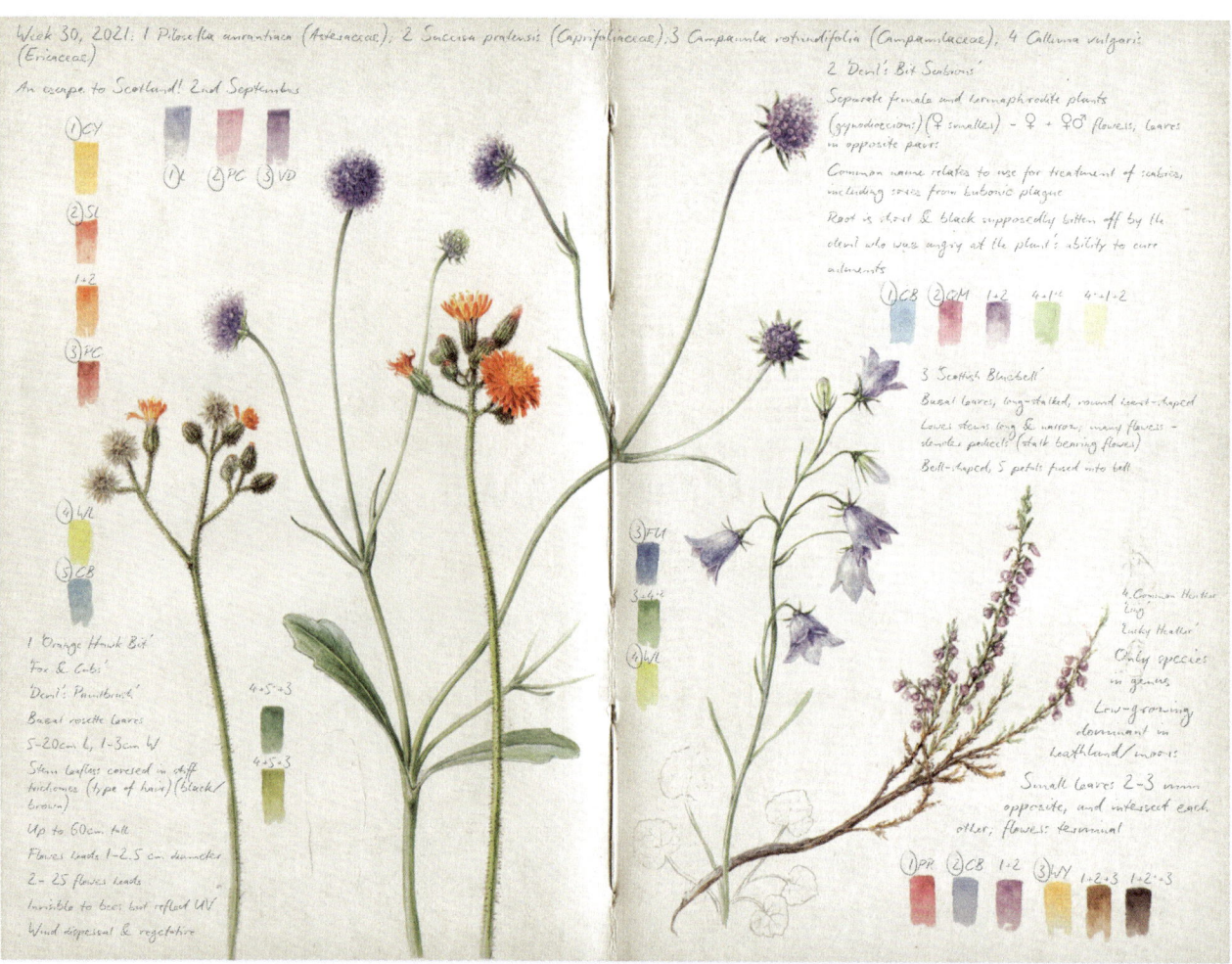

EXTRAS AND CREATIVITY

Keep the sketchbook dynamic and avoid homogenizing the pages by trying to stick to an overly rigid format. Instead, I recommend keeping a fairly relaxed approach to your compositions, which should be led by the plant. You may add extras, such as habitat drawings and pollinators and other associated insects, which can all add to the plant story.

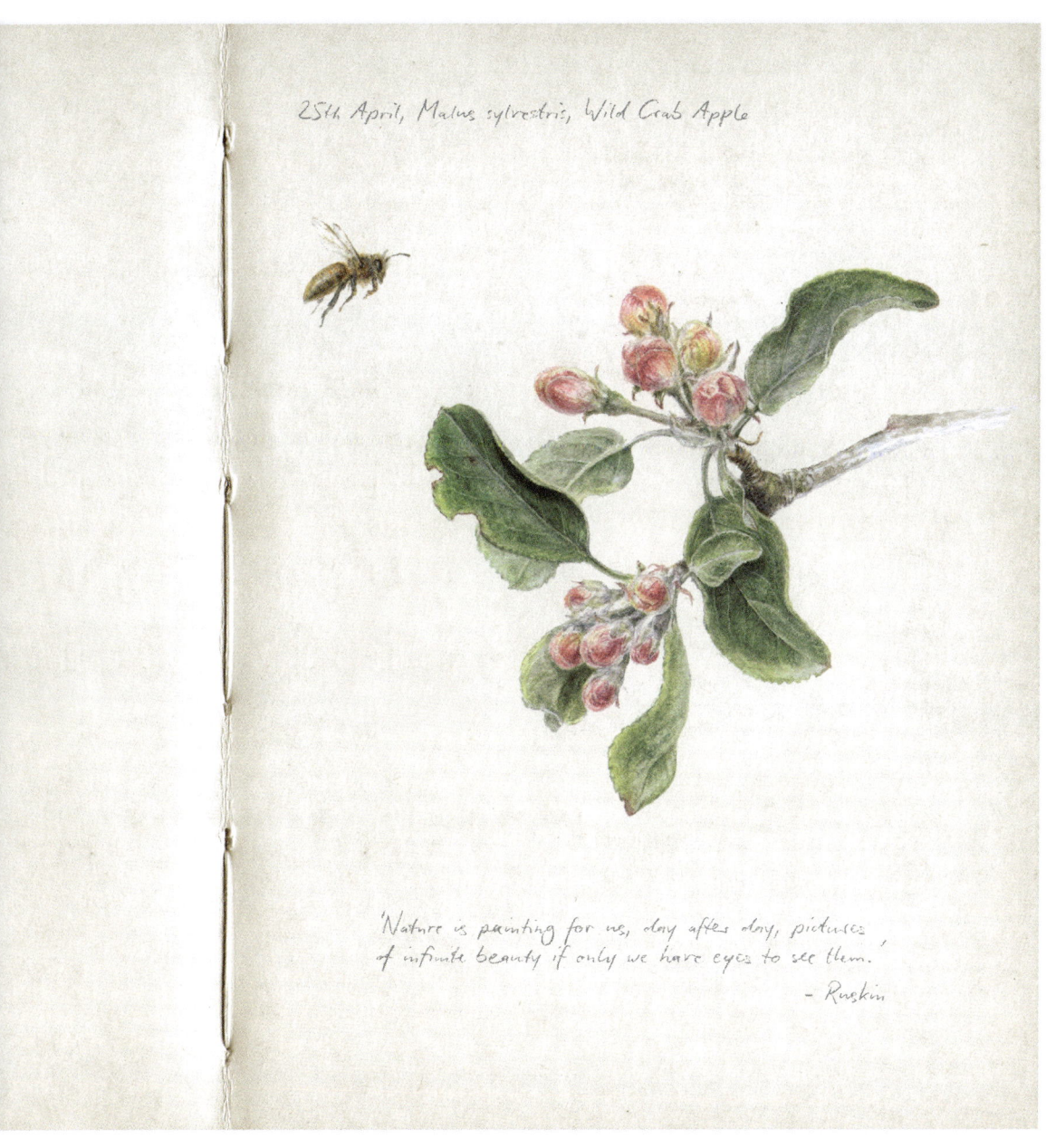

25th April, Malus sylvestris, Wild Crab Apple

'Nature is painting for us, day after day, pictures of infinite beauty if only we have eyes to see them.'
– Ruskin

Sketching nature helps me to see those small things that might otherwise be overlooked, and as I sat and watched the bees approaching the flowers of this apple blossom, I was reminded of Ruskin's famous quote, which often comes to mind when I'm working in my sketchbook.

Adding Extra Details

On every sketchbook page it's a good idea to add information to document the time, place, and contents of the page. This type of information will give the book a chronological order and will also make excellent reference if you want to return to the subject to illustrate it at a later date.

Imagine someone is picking the sketchbook up in the future and what they might like to know about the pages. Here is a guide to the type of information that can be added to pages.

ESSENTIALS

Starting at the top of the page: the date, the plant name – in Latin (if you know it) and any common names – the plant family name, and the location. If in the wild, you could add a map reference or just an area or address, something as simple as 'home'.

Colour notes: if the page is in watercolour, I always include the colour swatches with notations indicating which colours were used. This starts by numbering the primary colours used, which I label with both the initials of the colour and a number. Then the mixes are annotated with the number combinations for each mix. For example, if I used the primaries Cobalt Blue, Winsor Lemon, and Permanent Rose, I would label the colours as follows: 1. CB, 2. WL, and 3. PR. If, for example, a green mix of the three colours is mixed, I simply write 1 + 2 + 3 above or below the green swatch. Furthermore, if more or less of a colour is used, I add a small + or − next to the colour number, so for example, if a small amount of colour number 3 (Permanent Rose) is used, I write 1 + 2 + 3⁻. This is a very useful way of learning about colour but, more importantly, if you return to this plant in the future, you will know exactly what colours were used.

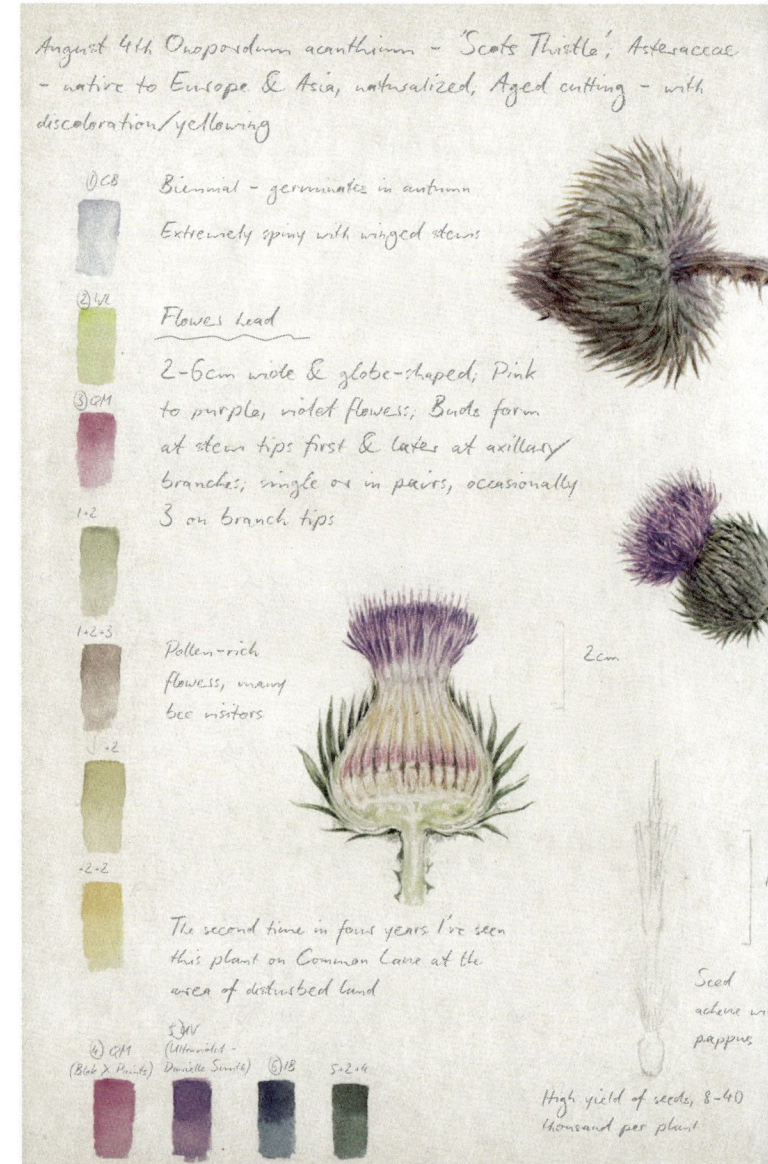

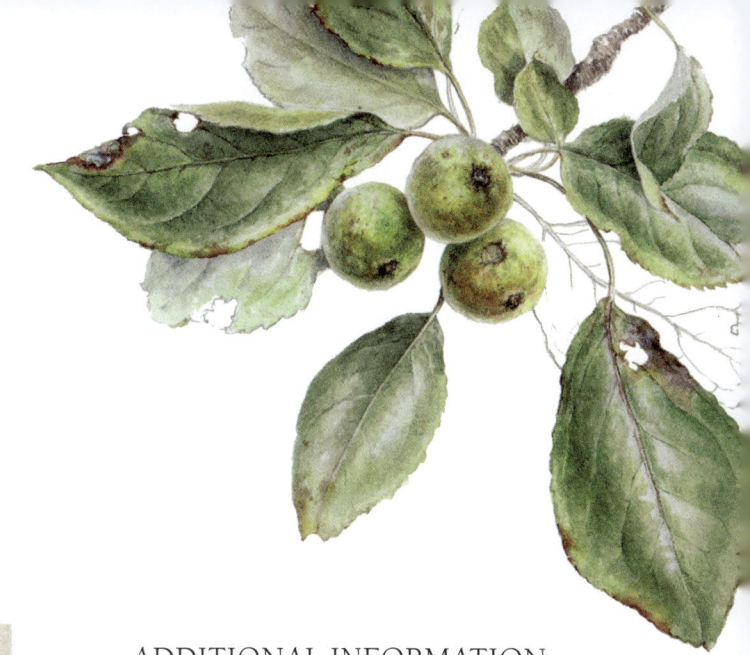

large plant, which was blown down by high winds - 2.5m tall!

Medicinal

Has been used in cancer treatment & demonstrated some effect on glioblastoma. Vegetal parts & juice can act as a diuretic & stimulate central nervous system

Plant has large tap root - up to 30cm

Leaves

10-50cm wide, alternate, spiny, covered with hairs that give silvery appearance

Stems

Up to 10cm wide broadly spiny/winged

Did you know?

All plant species have a two-part Latin name. Known as botanical nomenclature, this is an international system used by botanists, to avoid any confusion caused by the many common names given to plants. In this example the plants bi-nomial name is Onopordum acanthium: the first part is the genus, and the second part is the species or specific epithet.

ADDITIONAL INFORMATION

Plant description: I add details about the plant from my observations and research. Although this can vary from page to page, there is always some descriptive information, such as the height of the plant, whether it is annual or perennial, the type of leaf arrangement, and reproductive arrangements.

Anecdotal information: you could also add details such as other plants observed nearby, whether the plant is earlier or later than last year, or information about the weather. In addition, you can include any personal recollections, for example, associations or memories with a particular plant – maybe it grew in your grandmother's garden? Many of us have childhood memories of certain plants.

Other information: this could include medicinal information, folklore, or anything you feel is relevant or important. Some people add poems or snippets of texts. It's always interesting to discover something new about a plant and to read the artist's thoughts at the time. It's also good to look back over your own book and remember the page and the time you made it.

Scale: if you enlarged or reduced any parts, be sure to write this down. You can use a discreet scale bar or simply write 'x' next to the part that has been enlarged.

ADDING EXTRA DETAILS

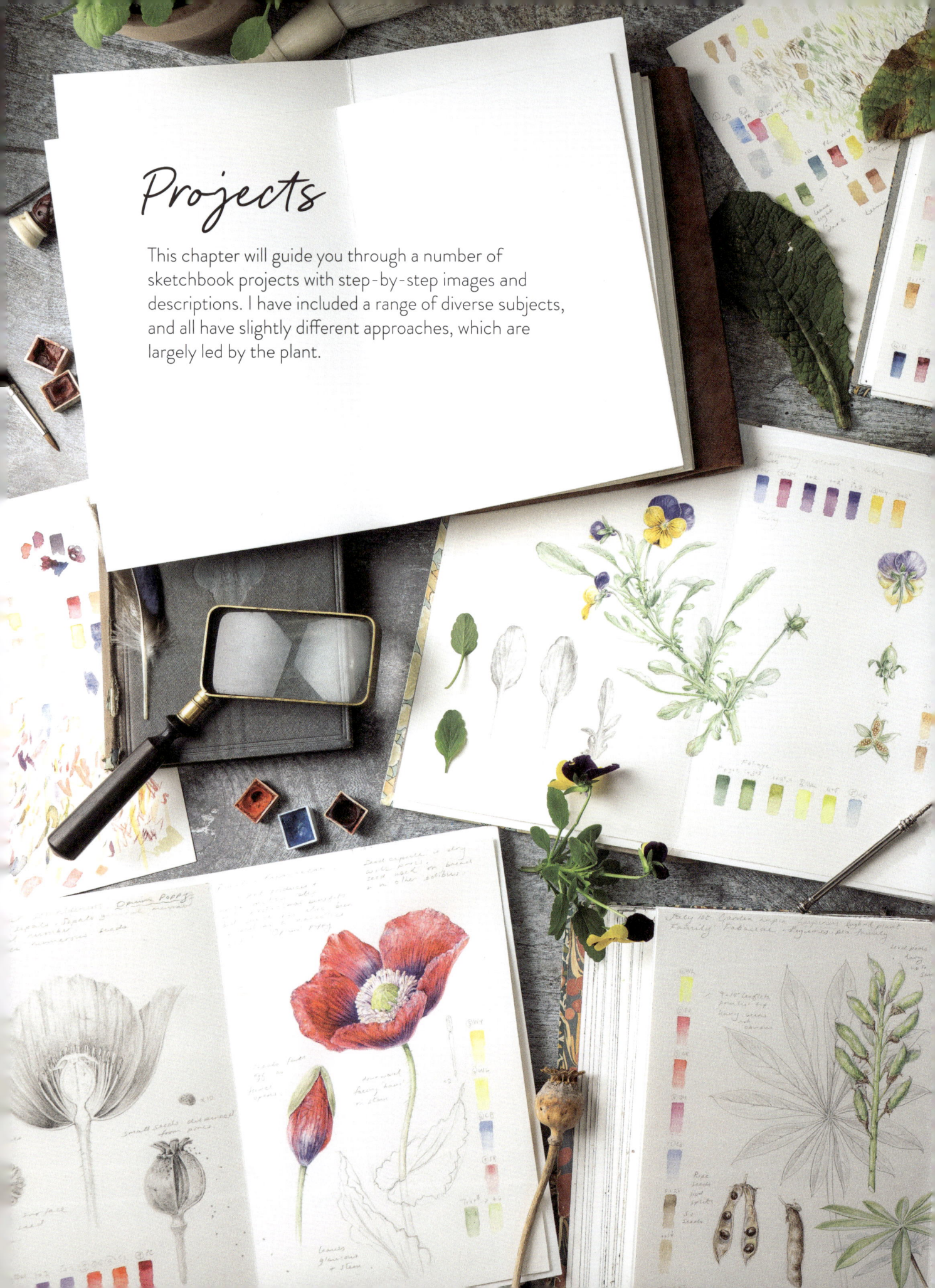

Projects

This chapter will guide you through a number of sketchbook projects with step-by-step images and descriptions. I have included a range of diverse subjects, and all have slightly different approaches, which are largely led by the plant.

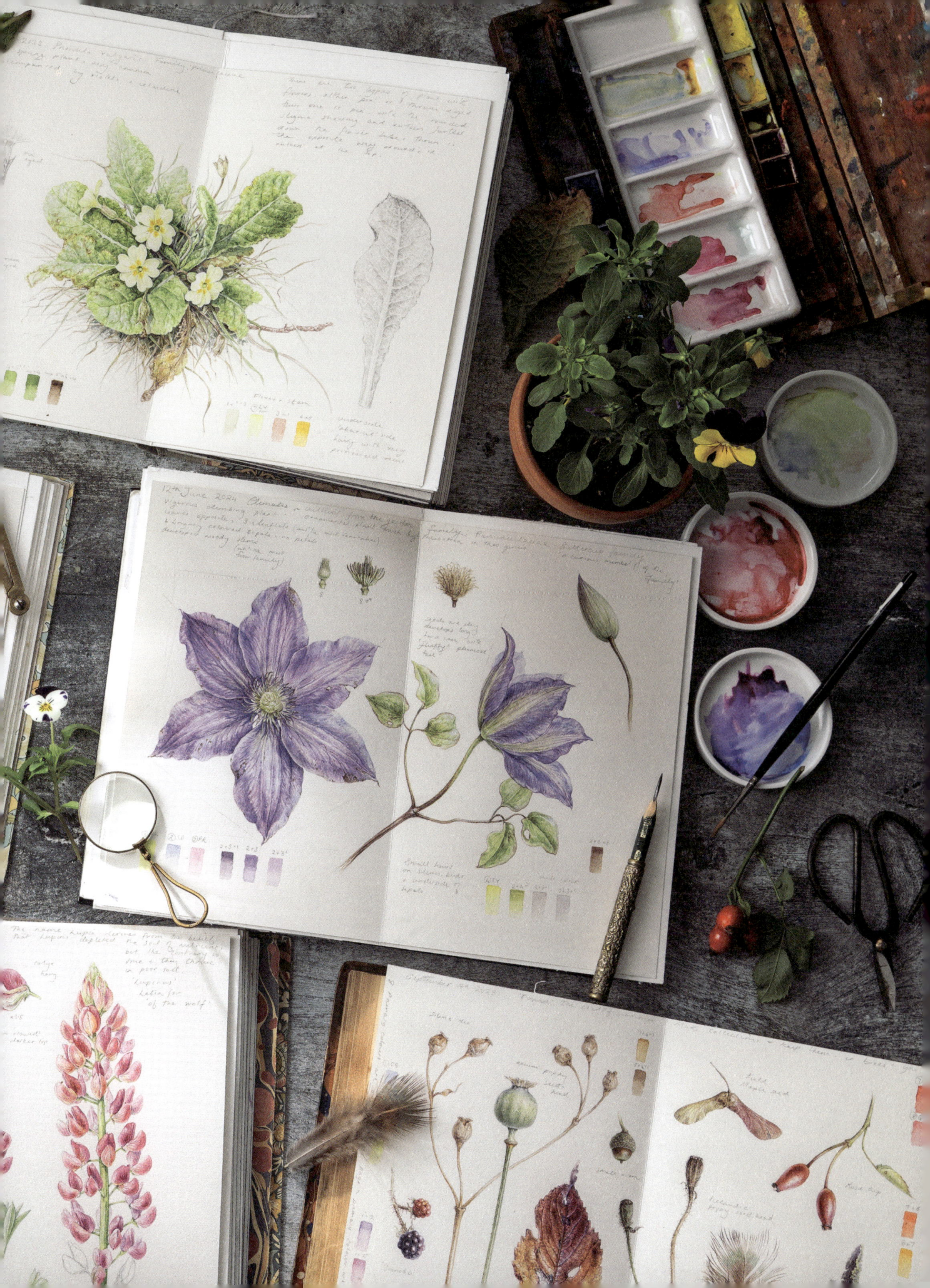

A Summary of the Process

My simple aim with each sketchbook page is to tell the story of each plant as best as possible within the relatively small space available. I do not wish to be overly prescriptive about using my approach and you should aim to develop your own way but there are some constants within my process that you may find helpful to begin with.

RESEARCH AND OBSERVATION

Learning about the plant you are about to record means using research and observation to help you understand your subject. A little detective work goes a long way and it is worth taking time to first observe the plant from life, viewing it from different angles and understanding the parts and how they fit together. Begin by making notes on the main features and also look in books and search online to find out more about your subject.

Identifying the plant name and which family it belongs to is the obvious place to begin but it's not always that easy. It's important to remind yourself that you do not need to be a botanist to document plants in your sketchbook, so please don't feel overwhelmed – the main thing is to make a start.

Fortunately, today we have much technology at hand and there are many plant identification apps available that you can use on your phone or tablet. Although they're not always accurate, they can give us a starting point. There are also online plant identification groups and don't forget to use plant identification books for reference too.

The description of the plant is a very good place to begin as it helps with understanding the parts of the plant before beginning a study. I also find it useful to take the plant apart, deconstructing it into its parts in order to identify them.

For each page, I aim to discover some key features of each and every subject, such as the arrangement of leaves, the number of petals, the type of reproductive parts and fruit, and maybe even what's underground. Then I look closer for more details, such as whether the plant has hairs or not. These are just a few things to look for and there are many more features to observe that may not be obvious until you look closely. You can also choose to focus on a small part of a plant, such as the flower structure, and this is a good way to begin, too.

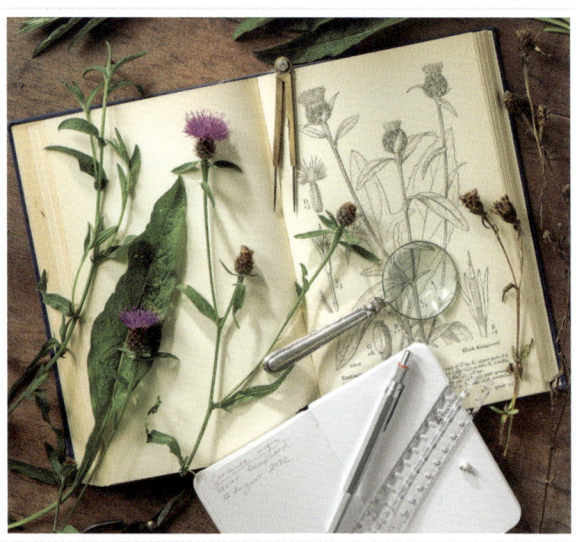

Undertake research first: observe the plant carefully and learn about it.

COMPOSITION

My overall approach is to let the subject lead the way based on my observations. Before undertaking sketchbook pages, I like to think about composing the pages and what elements to include, otherwise I might run out of space. For this reason, I sometimes make rough sketches of what to include first using basic shapes and simplified sketches that can be adapted as the page develops. There are many compositional arrangements and options, and these are covered in more depth in Techniques: Composition. The composition should be determined by the plant and its growth habit; for example, a tall plant could be cut into sections and overlapped, climbers or scramblers can span across the gutter of the spread, and clump-forming plants can be illustrated from above.

If possible, I lay the plant or parts of it onto paper to view the position and placement. However, do not do this on your sketchbook without placing protective paper underneath. Graph paper can also be useful for judging the size and relationship of parts.

To ensure that the drawing is not overly complicated, you may wish to remove sections of the plant, being careful not to deter from accuracy. Similarly, a page should not contain too much repetition of parts as this can become cluttered and confusing.

SKETCHING

I begin by making measured sketches of the plant, and tend to begin with the main focus for the page, such as a flowering stem. Next, I plot the positions of all other details to be added, leaving a space for the seed details to be added later, such as in the case of developing seed capsules.

The drawing should not be heavy; using an H or HB pencil for sketching, the sketch should be light enough to be erased and clear enough to understand all parts.

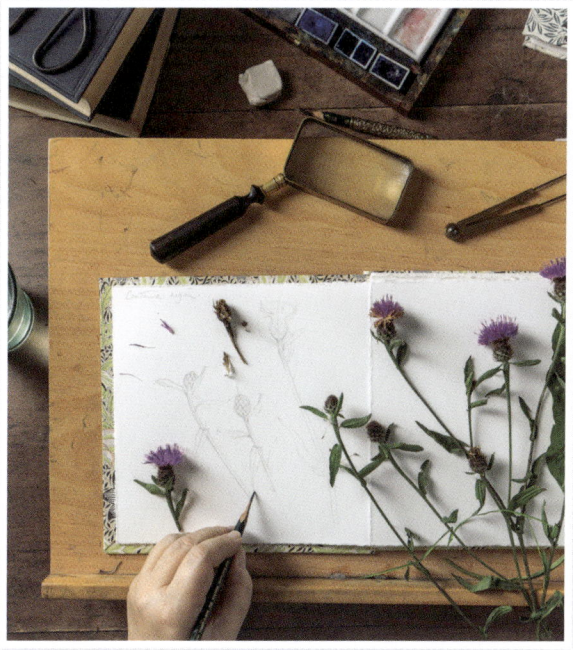

↑ *Make loose sketches plotting them directly from the plant using simple shapes and lines to gain an understanding of its growth habit. This doesn't have to be the final composition.*

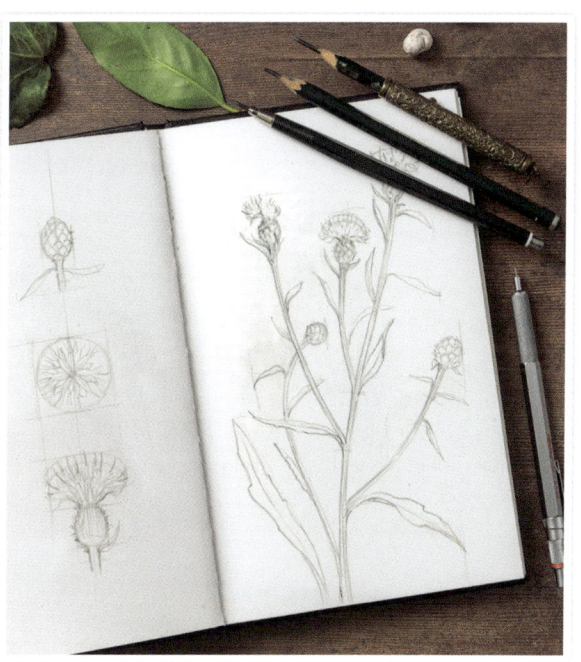

↑ *Make a more detailed sketch of the plant directly into your sketchbook in preparation for the painting.*

COLOUR STUDIES

It is important to work out the colours in advance of painting each part, and I make some rough colour notes on spare paper and keep these in a separate notebook. Otherwise, my whole sketch page might be filled with too many paint swatches, which makes it hard to make sense of them and uses up valuable room.

Working with a primary palette means that most colours have to be mixed or overlaid. I write down all of the primary colours and the mixes.

Once colours are roughly decided upon, I paint swatches in my actual sketchbook, although I may make some small changes if needed. Remember that nothing has to be final in the sketchbook and alterations and additions can be made.

PAINTING PROCESS

There are many approaches to the painting process and there are no set rules, so do what works best for you. When working on larger sections of a plant, I find that it is preferable to work up a whole painting in sections by working gradually rather than completing any one part of a plant. This allows more control over tonal values, lighting, and colour consistency, and creates a more harmonious finished page. I often begin with the underlying colours of the main flowering stem, then move to another section, such as the leaf and other stems, before returning to the flowers later. However, if a part of a plant is likely to wilt and die, I prioritize it and deal with everything else later.

The next part of this book will demonstrate some of the points already discussed by leading you through a range of different botanical sketchbook projects. These detail the stages of developing an illustrated sketchbook page from start to finish.

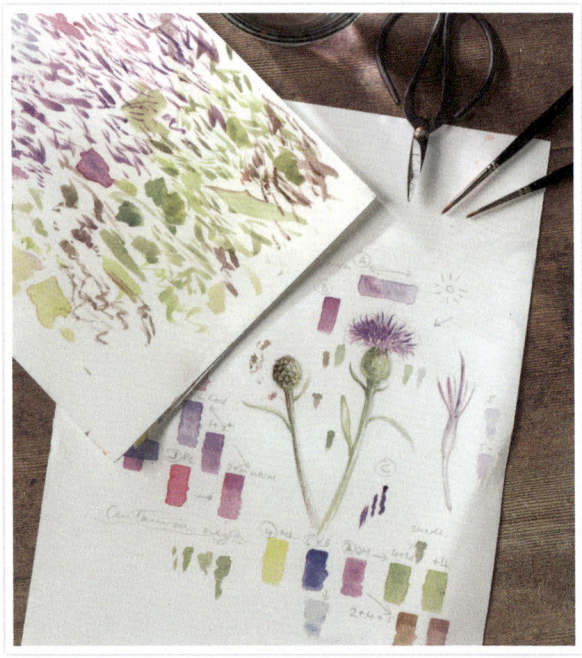

↑ *Always work out the colours in advance of painting each part.*

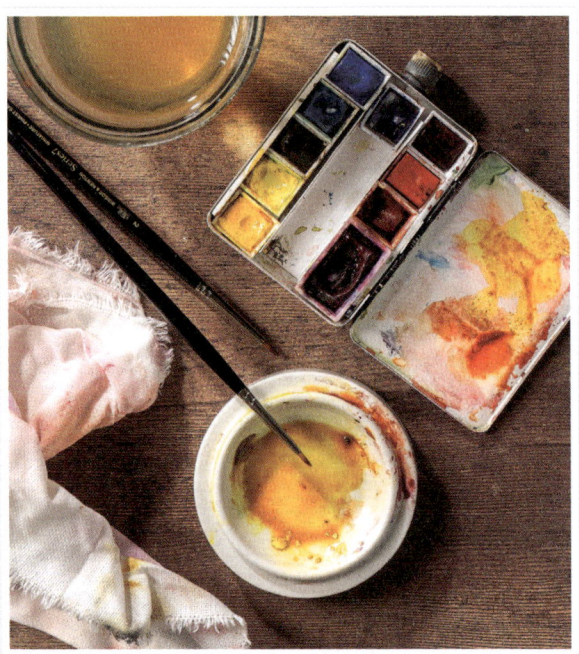

↑ *The painting process varies from plant to plant as you will discover in the projects, in the following pages of the book.*

A FEW BOTANICAL TERMS

Here are some of the botanical terms used in this book. If you want to learn more, consider investing in a botanical terminology book.

Anther: the part of the stamen that produces pollen, which are the male reproductive cells.

Calyx: collective name for the sepals, which are the outer parts of the perianth or flower.

Carpel: a female reproductive organ, comprising stigma, style, and ovary.

Corolla: the collective name for all of the petals in a flower.

Corolla tube: when petals are fused together and form a tube, such as in a Primula.

Filament: the structure that attaches the anther to the flower.

Leaflets: part of a compound leaf, where the leaf has a number of leaflets.

Midrib: the main vein in a leaf that runs from the base to the tip of the leaf.

Nectary: a glandular organ, secretes nectar.

Ovary: the female organ of a flower which contains the ovules.

Ovule: the organs housed within the ovary which, after fertilization, develop into seed.

Pedicel: an individual flower stalk.

Petiole: a leaf stalk, attaching leaf to stem.

Pistil: the female ovule-producing part of a flower; can be a single carpel or several carpels fused together.

Sepal: a single part of the calyx.

Stamen: the collective name for the filament and the anther.

Stipule: a leafy outgrowth found at the base of the leaf stalk where it joins the stem.

Stigma: where the germination process begins, found at the top of the style.

Style: the part of the carpel between the stigma and the ovary.

Tepal: petals and sepals that look similar, as in Tulips and Lilies.

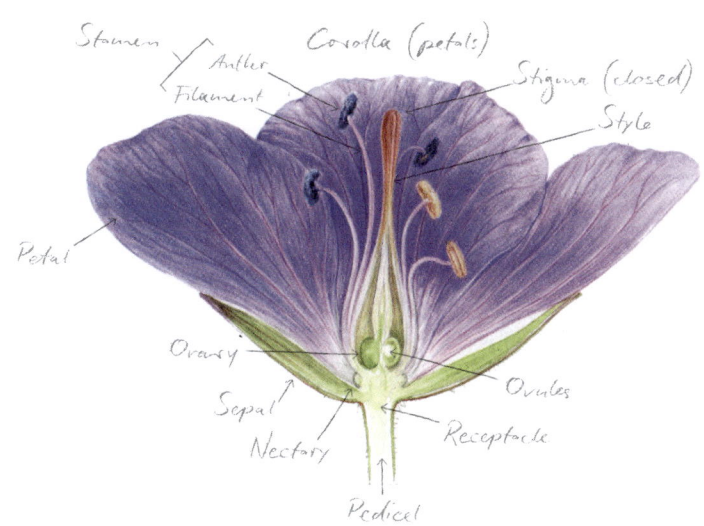

Labelled parts of Geranium flower, Geranium pratense.

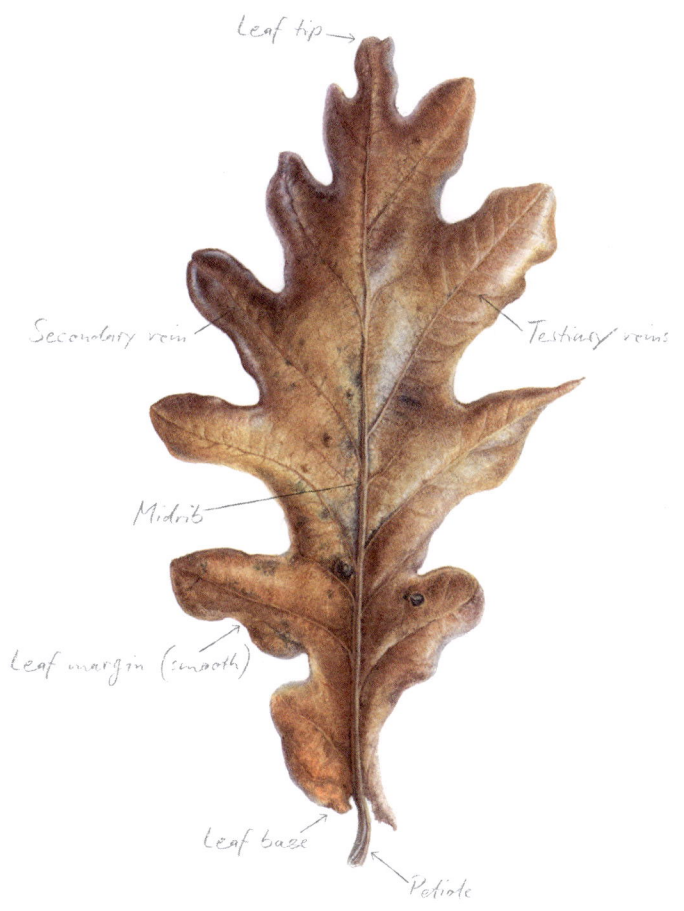

Labelled parts of an Oak leaf.

Clematis

A deconstructed flower

A common garden flower that makes a great beginner's subject is a Clematis. The flowers are quite flat and are not too small, so they will easily fill a double-page spread with just a couple different views.

For this first project, I have chosen to focus on a violet-coloured flower because it's a good colour to start with for beginners. They come in a wide range of colours but I suggest avoiding white or very pale flowers because replicating white subjects on white paper can be difficult, even for the more experienced painter. Similarly, it can take a long time to build up the desired colours for rich or dark coloured flowers, and so violet is a good option to try, as is pink.

The finished double-page spread of a Clematis study, alongside a range of materials and equipment and alternative plant material used in the project.

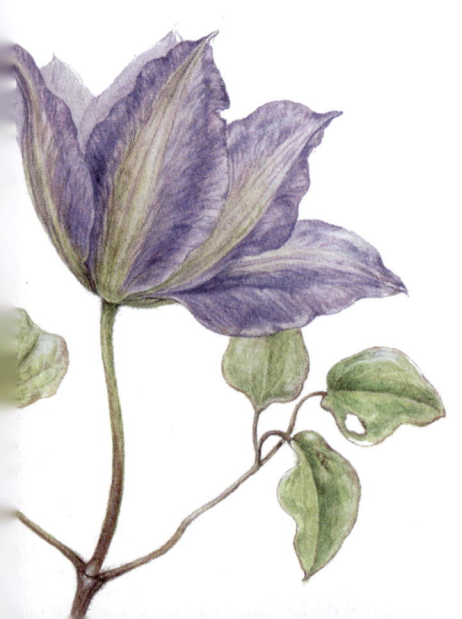

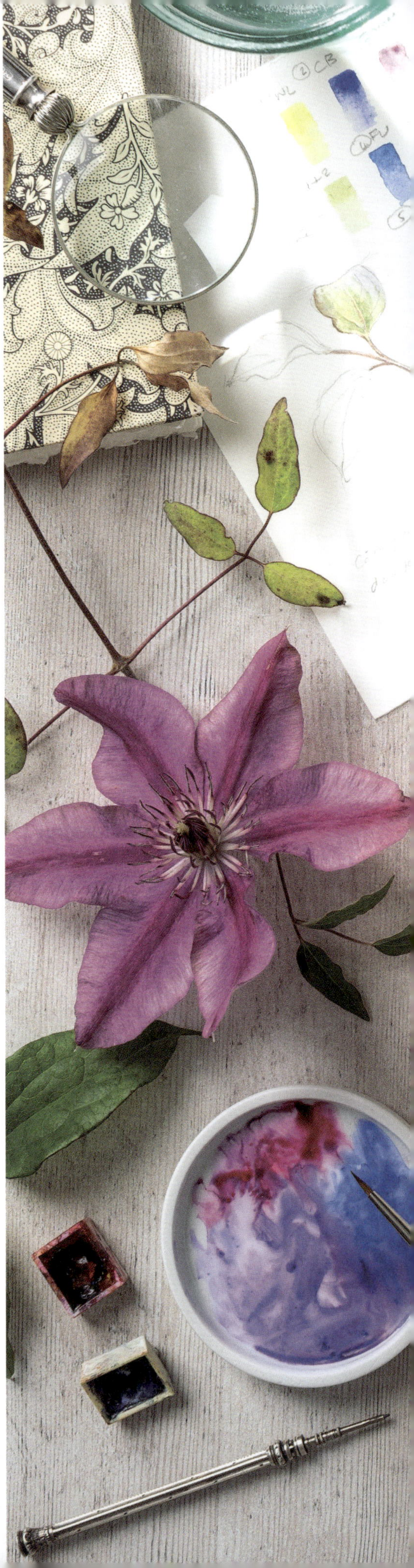

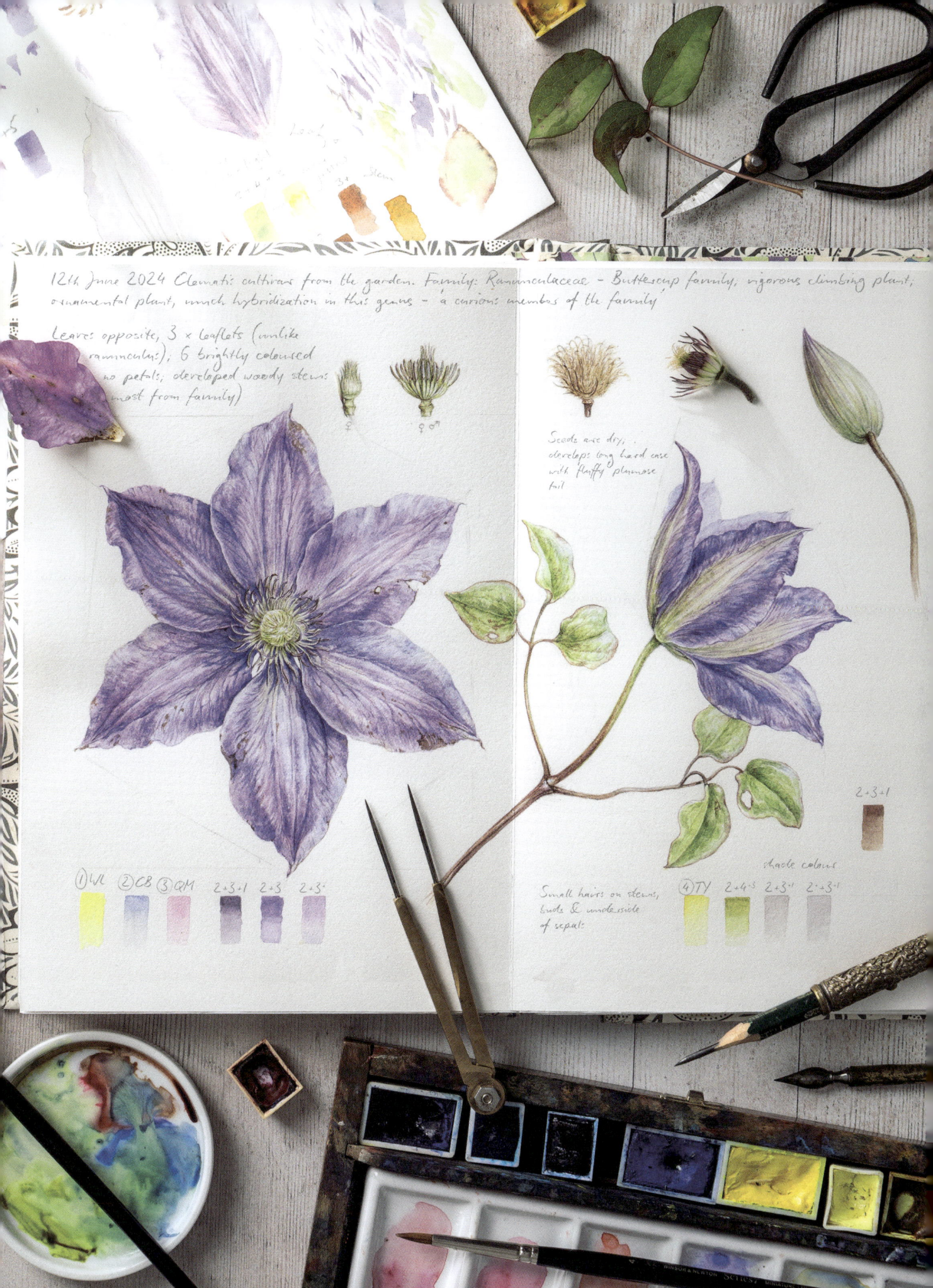

12th June 2024 Clematis cultivars from the garden. Family: Ranunculaceae - Buttercup family, vigorous climbing plant; ornamental plant, much hybridization in this genus - 'a curious member of the family'

Leaves opposite, 3 × leaflets (unlike ranunculus); 6 brightly coloured no petals; developed woody stems (most from family)

Seeds are dry; develops long hard case with fluffy plumose tail

Small hairs on stems, buds & underside of sepals:

shade colours

2+3+1

① WL ② CB ③ QM 2+3+1 2+3 2+3¹

④ TY 2+4·5 2+3¹¹ 2+3·1

RESEARCH AND OBSERVATION

Clematis belong to the Ranunculaceae family, which is known as the Buttercup family. This might seem surprising, as plants in this family are quite diverse, with members including Buttercups, Wood Anemone, Delphinium, and Aquilegia, which all look very different. However, there are common features in this family: for example, flowers are radially symmetrical, usually with five petals and sepals, which can look very similar. By contrast, in Clematis, there are no petals and the petal-like structures are actually sepals, which simply look like petals. In the chosen flower, there are six sepals, but other Clematis differ in number.

More typically, all flowers in this family have many stamens and often many superior carpels, which produce dry fruits. In Clematis, the fruit are quite feathery and easily carried by the wind. These are a few of the things I learned about the plant and its family, which greatly added to my understanding.

COMPOSITION

Clematis is a vigorous climber with many flowers, leaves, and stems, but in this study, I decided to keep things simple by focusing mostly on the flower.

The approach for the spread is a simple deconstructed flower: it includes a front and side view of the flower, as well as a bud. I decided to include just two leaves to show their opposite arrangement on the stem, as I felt it was important to do so.

In most of my pages, I try to tell the story of the plant by showing some of the main features during its life cycle. For this project, I chose to include the reproductive parts and the developing feathery carpels, because they are a key feature in the plant family. If you choose a similar approach, you will need to wait a while for the seeds to develop, as is often the case when sketching plants. In the meantime, you can carry on with other areas of the double-page spread.

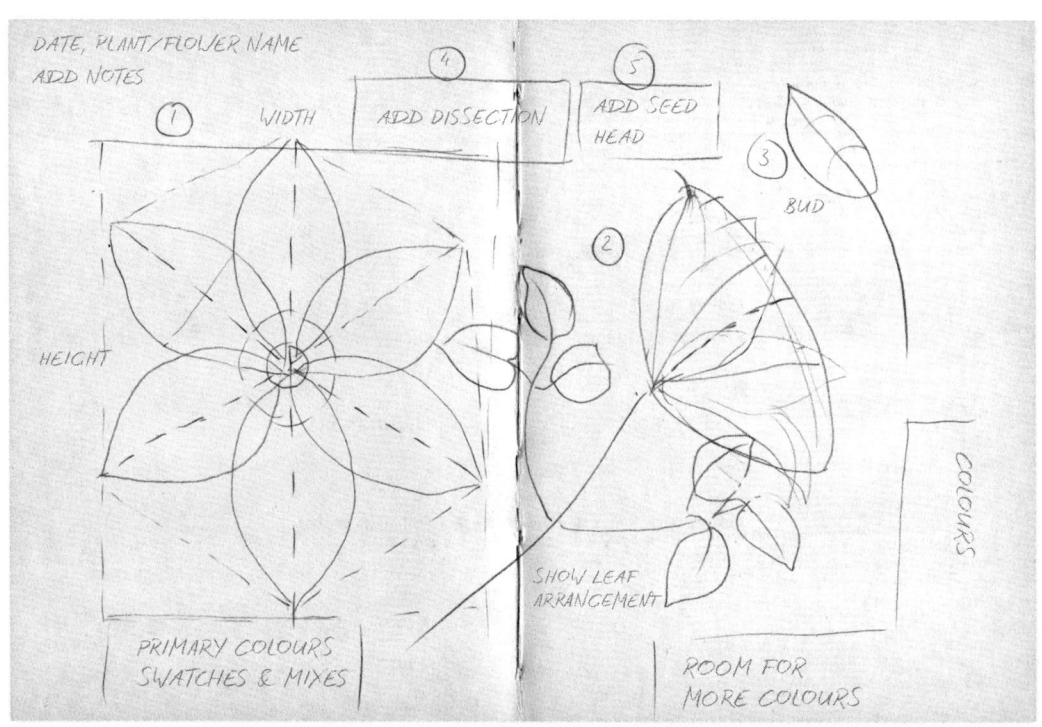

If unsure about where to place elements on the page, start with a rough sketch on A4 paper. Use measurements and basic shapes from the plant parts intended for the double-page spread. This simple deconstruction can include various views, stages of the flower and separate plant parts.

SKETCHING

After taking measurements of all the plant parts, lightly draw the structure of the front-facing flower by using the overall height and width and then marking in the six sepals; you can do this by measuring the angles and distance of sepals in relation to each other. This overall shape looks like a hexagon, and understanding the shape makes it easier to draw. Measure the width of each sepal to ensure they are correct. You can also include a side view of the flower, the bud, and add the reproductive parts above the flowers.

Make a rough layout and then refine the drawing until it is ready for painting.

COLOUR STUDIES

In all pages, I suggest working out the basic colours in advance using the primary palette; additions can be made as the work progresses. In this subject, the pale underlying colours should be quite dilute in the early stages of the painting of the flower, with more saturated mixes made from the same colours as the work develops.

Add swatches of the primary colours and each mix to the spread as the painting develops, making any adjustments where needed. Adjusting the colour mix ratios can create a wide range of colours to be mixed and more colours can be added if needed; generally it is better to use fewer colours but in different mixes, as using a limited range of colours creates more continuity in the painting.

Colours used: Winsor Lemon, Cobalt Blue, Quinacridone Magenta, and Transparent Yellow.

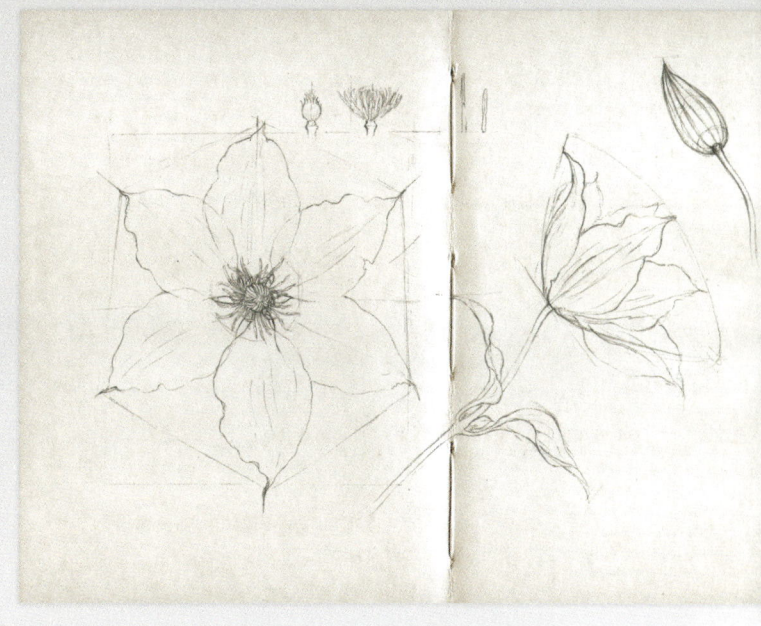

Make the rough layout and line drawing using an HB pencil. The outline drawing should be as light as possible, so just enough to be able to see the lines. Once the first layers of paint are added, remove the outline with a putty eraser.

The colour palette and swatches show the dilute mixes that will be used in the first stage of the painting. These mixes are made using primary colours Winsor Lemon, Cobalt Blue, and Quinacridone Magenta, which will be used in the initial painting of underlying colours in the main flower and then in the side view. Two mixes are made with the same three colours.

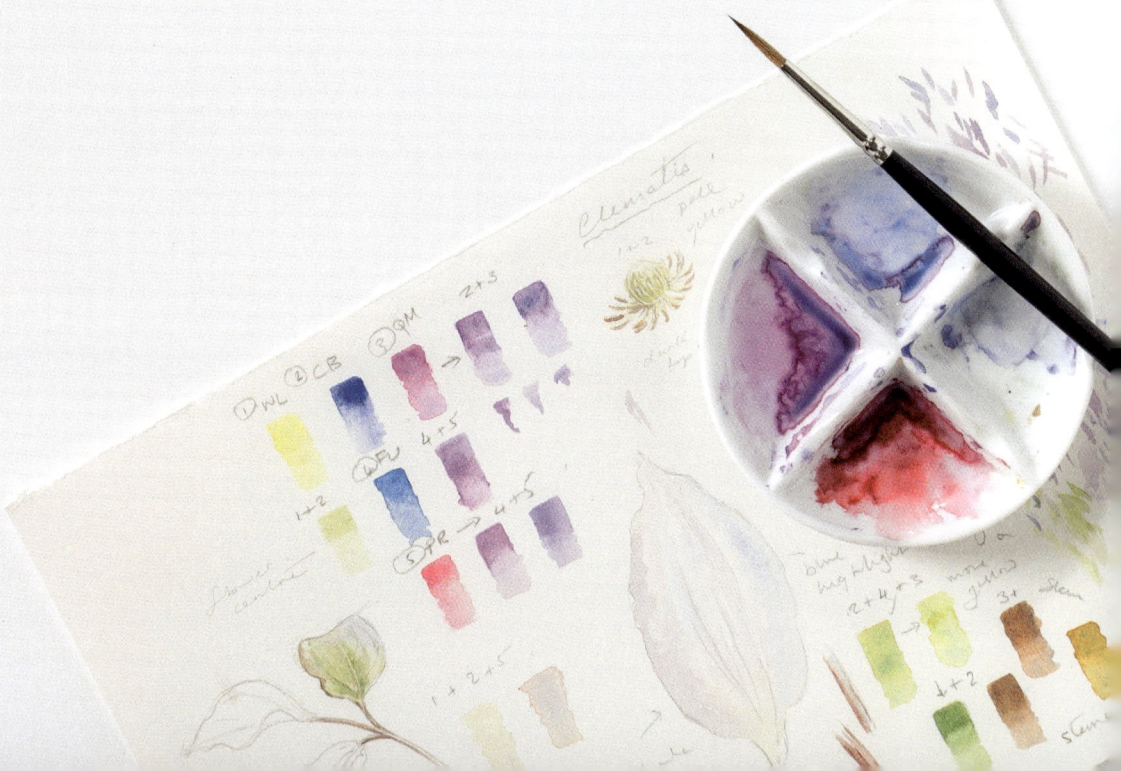

PAINTING

Begin the painting with pale, dilute mixes of colour variations to establish a little form, structure, and underlying colour on the main flower, painting directly onto the dry paper or into lightly dampened areas. It's important to build the colour gradually and not to use too much water or paint at this early stage as there are lots of subtle variations. Using too much paint will homogenize all parts and will likely mean you lose the effect of light and shade, creating a flat appearance later. Use the same approach on the side-facing flower – remember to take note of the light direction here too.

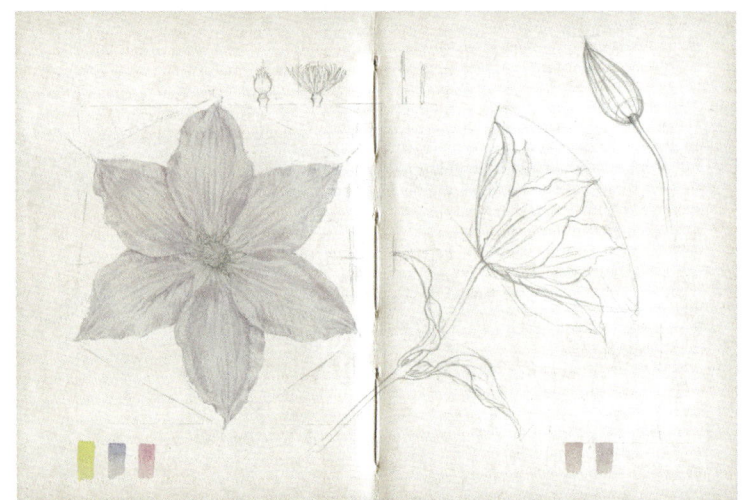

Use the diluted pale violet mix of Cobalt Blue and Quinacridone Magenta to paint the underlying structure of each sepal. This is not an outline painting but more about creating the rippled, veiny form on each sepal with an underlying colour. You can paint it with a larger brush, such as a size 4.

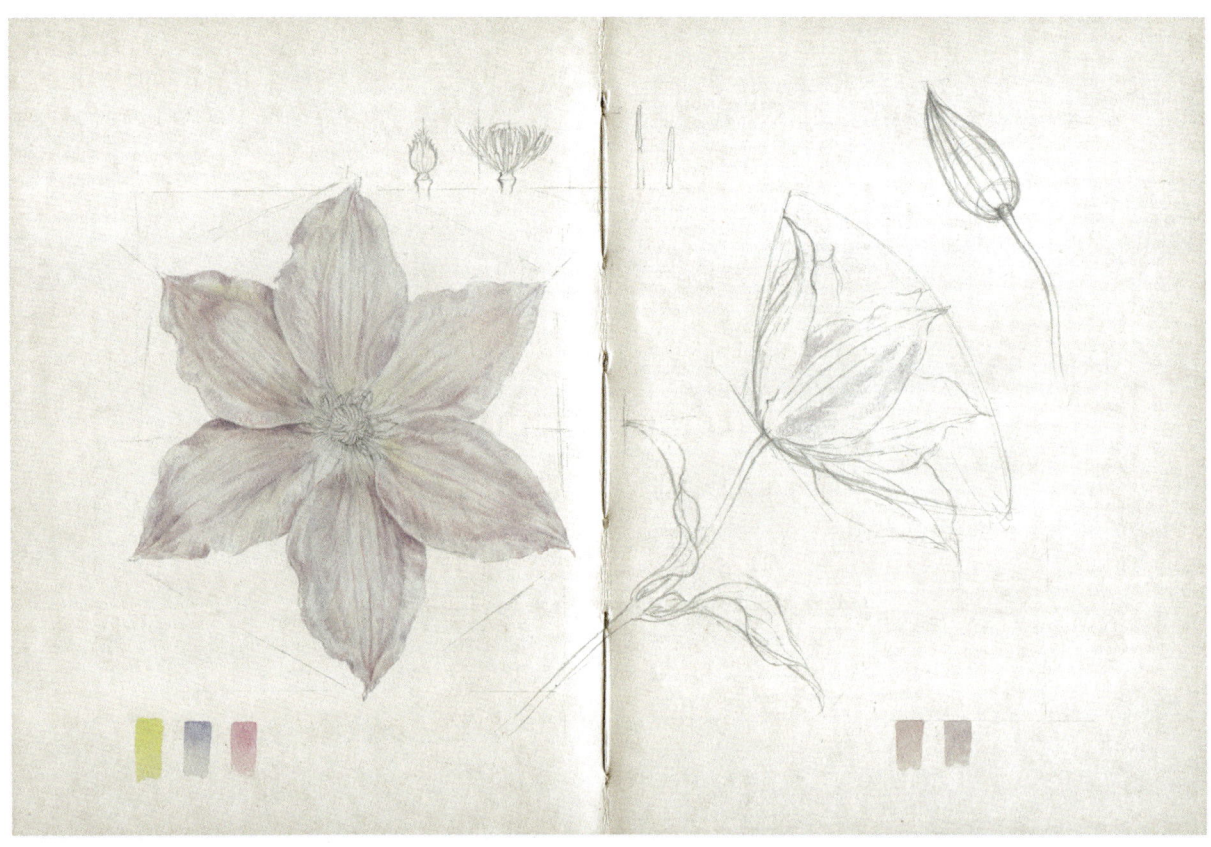

Next, I applied the warmer colours to the sepals. These are made with the addition of Winsor Lemon and by increasing the amount of Quinacridone Magenta to make a warmer violet colour.

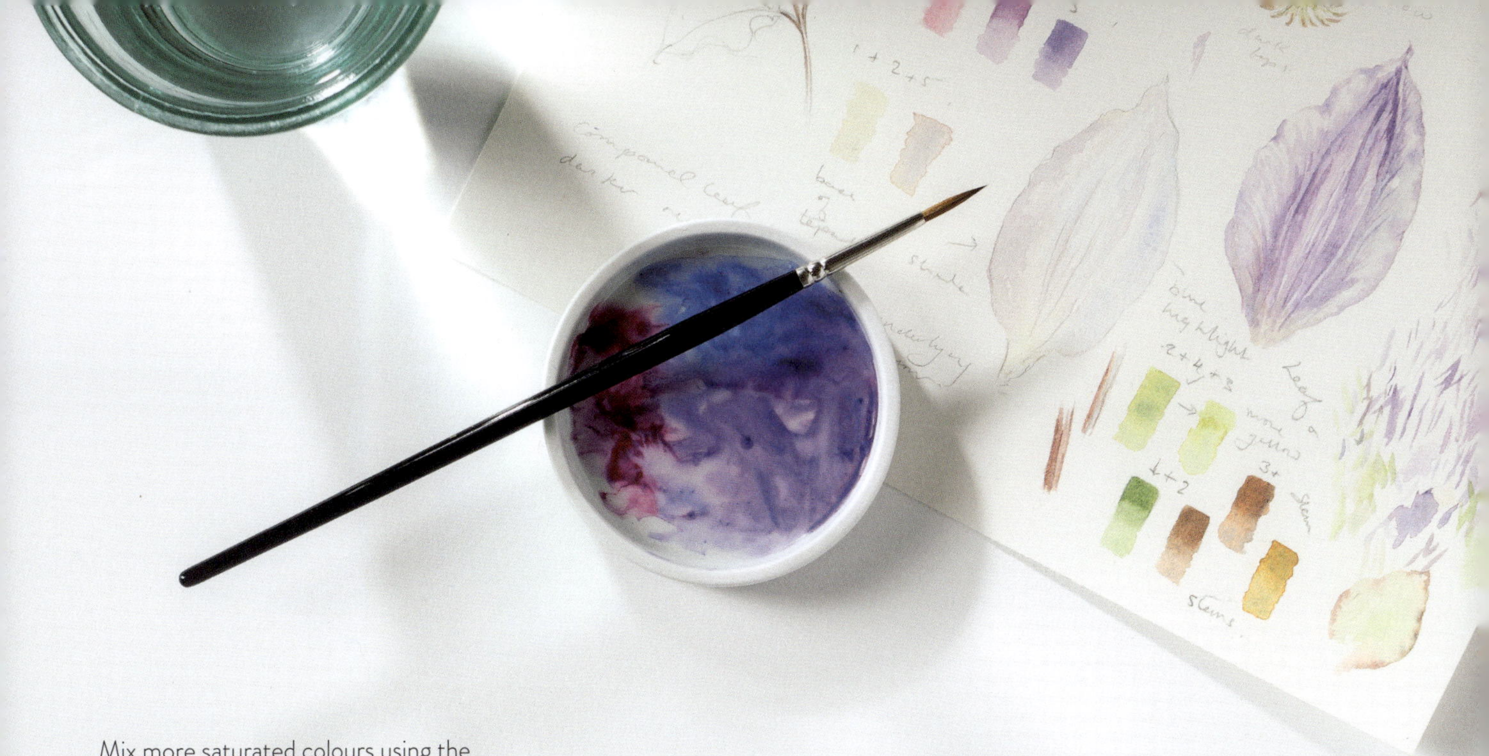

Mix more saturated colours using the same colours as previously used. For these mixes, less water and more paint is required. Practise painting swatches of each colour to achieve the correct saturation before adding the colour to the painting. Use a spare piece of paper to use as a scribble sheet for testing the colours.

Add the new mixes to the painting once the initial stage of the painting is dry, but note that the application should be quite selective and more like drawing strokes with a brush rather than using larger washes that cover whole areas. Clematis can have an element of transparency, so painting an indication of the sepal behind helps to give an impression of the light shining through the flower. You can also introduce a yellow-biased green on the underside of the sepals in the side view. Always take care to preserve lighter areas.

The colour palette and swatches shown are more intense colours mixed for the next stage of the painting. You can use the same three colours for these mixes but with less water added so that the paint is more saturated in colour and a slightly creamier consistency.

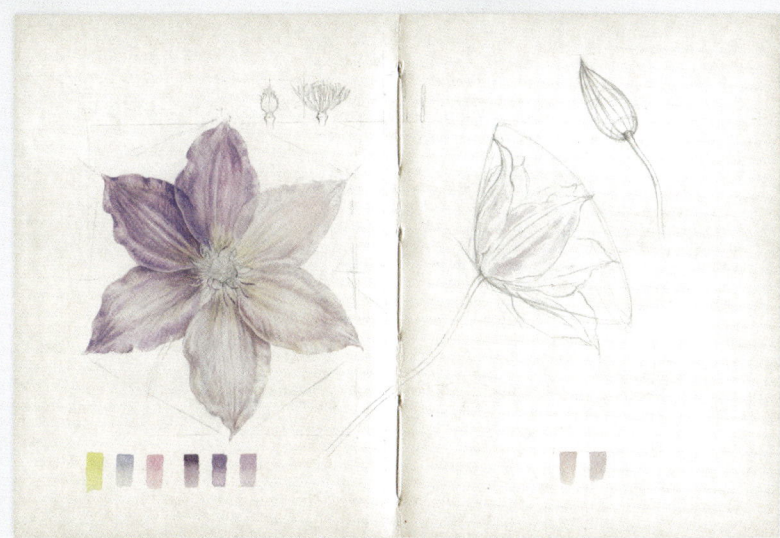

Here you can see the beginning of the process of adding more colour as I work around the flower. To build the colour in this way, dampen lightly with clean water first in selected areas, then add small amounts of saturated paint in a very controlled way, which will help you to create the puckered effect on the sepals, too. I also add the sepal transparency by painting the shadow edge of the petal behind.

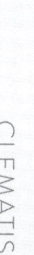

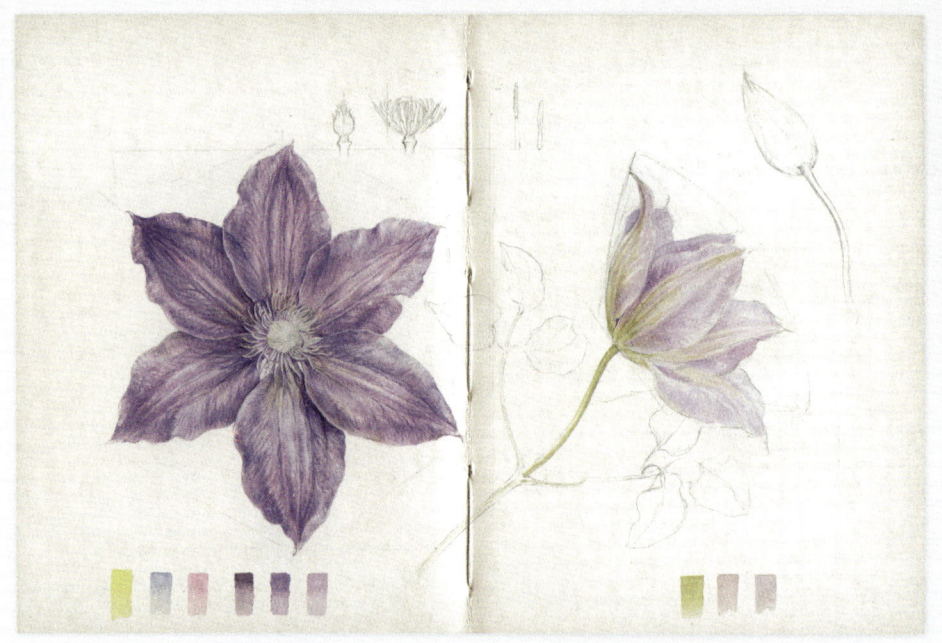

←

With each layer of paint, I covered less area and added finer details to the sepals, using a drawing style technique and a slightly thicker paint mix. This approach gave the sepals a realistic, vibrant appearance. The side view highlights the underside of the sepal, with more yellow applied.

Green mixes are usually made with three primary colours, and this is no exception. Mix the blue and yellow with a tiny amount of the same red that is used in the flower. The introduction of red makes a more natural green but add too much and it will turn brown, so it really must be a tiny amount of red.

Add the greens and browns to the leaves and stems, which will complete the basic layers in flower sepals, stems, and leaves. Next, turn your attention to adding more detail to the pages, starting with some definition around the anthers and in the centre of the flower.

You may be surprised to know that the yellow-biased green colour for the stem and centre of the rear of the sepals was mixed using the same three primary colours as used previously, but this time the blue and yellow are the dominant colours, with just a very small amount of the magenta added, as shown on the palette. However, the addition of Transparent Yellow to the palette creates a slightly stronger transparent green and this is the fourth colour used.

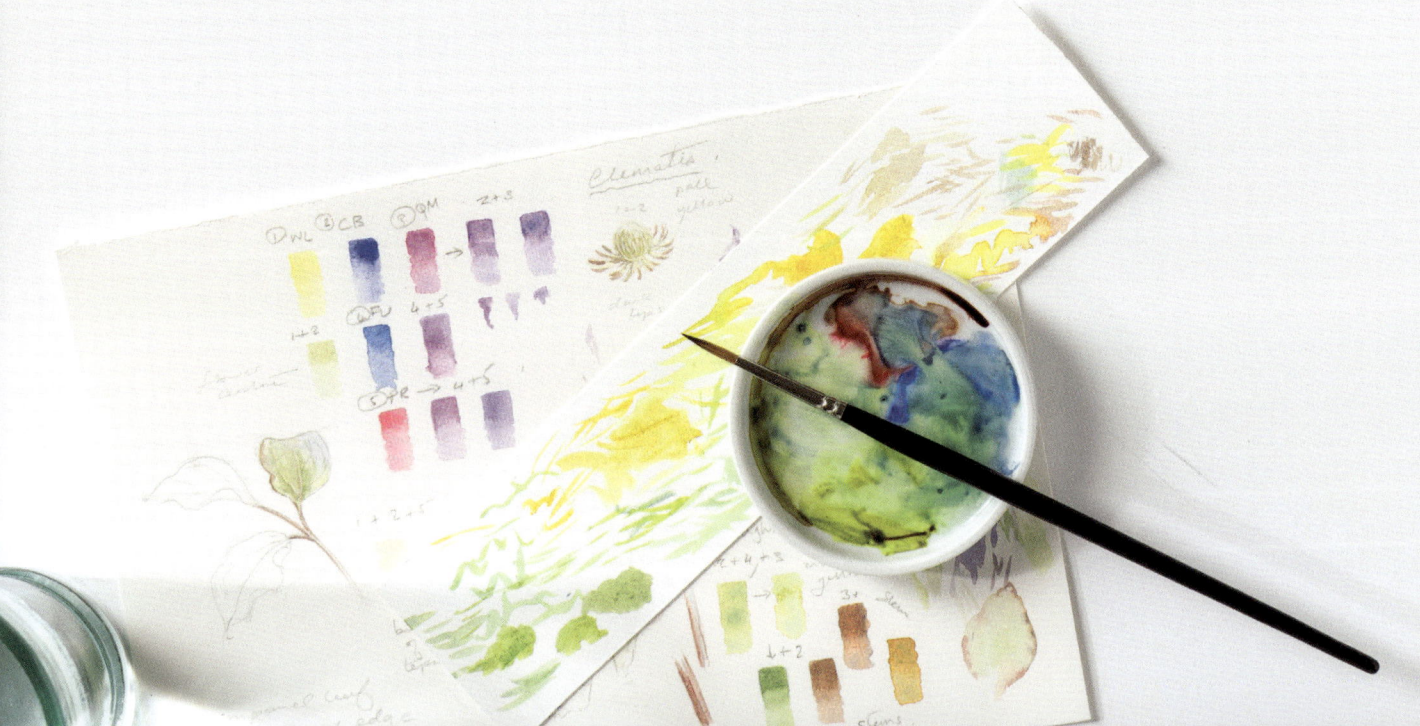

Although it may not be obvious, most green mixes will benefit from a very small addition of red in them. As you will know from the colour wheels in the Colours and Mixing section, different blues and yellows can be mixed to create a range of different greens, and those greens may be what you need, but very often a tiny amount of red can be added to make a more natural green.

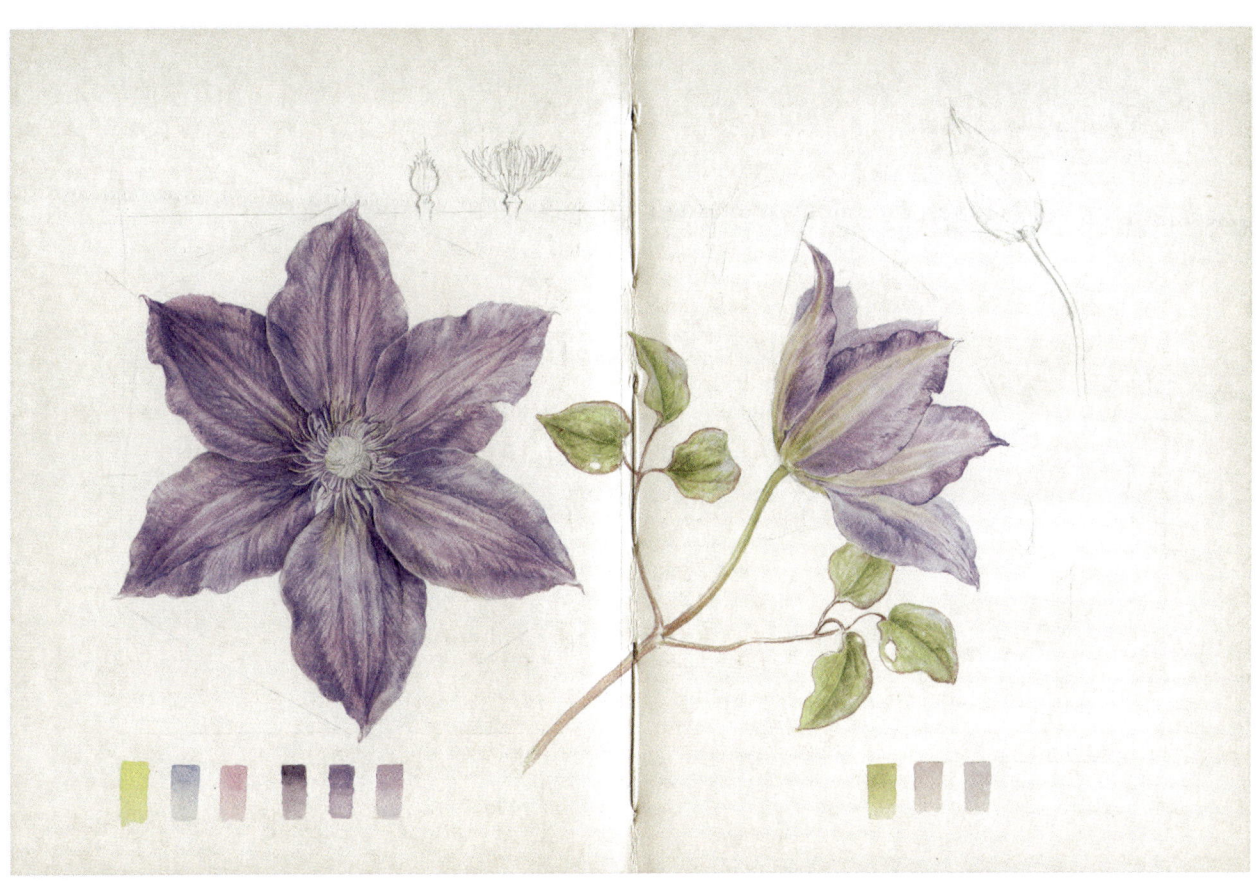

Next, lightly add the leaves and stems. The red-brown edges are mixed using the three primary colours. Avoid wet washes; instead, dampen the leaf surface with clean water and apply green paint into it. Add a touch of blue for sheen and paint the dark edges into the damp surface for a natural line. Use a small brush (size 1) with a creamy violet mix to add subtle definition to the flower centre.

The buds can now be added. Fortunately, Clematis have many flowers and so there are usually buds and flowers available at the same time. However, if there is a shortage of flowers, add the bud at an earlier stage. Add more detail to the flower centre to define the anthers.

Add colour to the remaining reproductive parts, including the central female pistil. For the separate illustrations showing reproductive structures with surrounding male anthers, I applied a pale wash first, followed by some definition and detail. For smaller parts such as these, you can use a smaller brush.

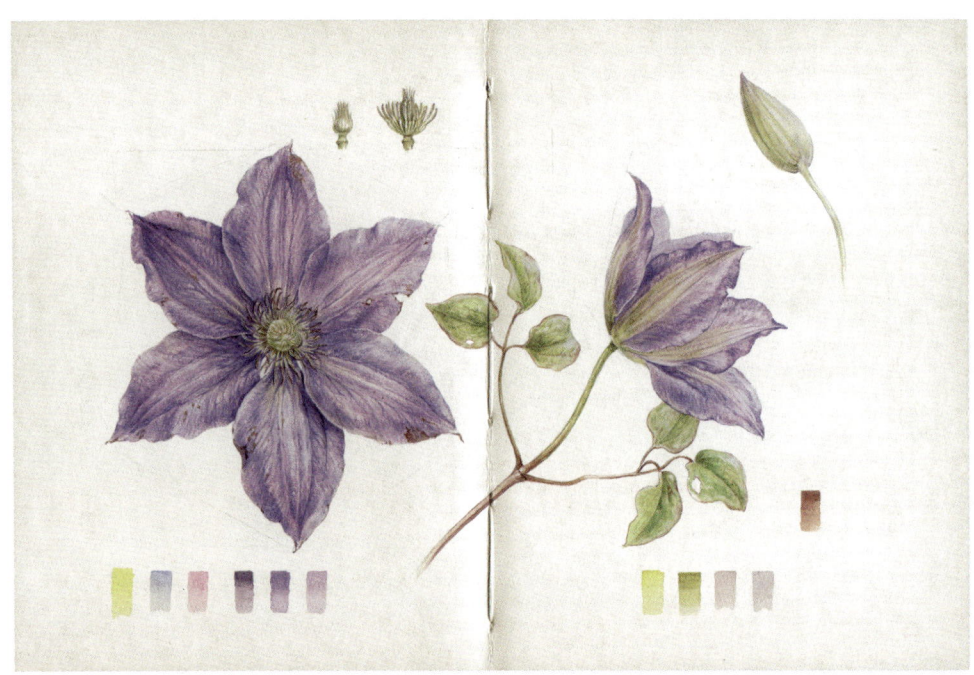

Now it's time to add the remaining parts, i.e. the bud and flower centre parts. You can use the pale yellow-biased green wash on the bud, with violet added at the tip of the bud. You can also use violet on the centre parts and, using a small brush (size 1 or 2), outline the anthers and other parts with a little of the red-brown mix that was used on the stem and leaf edges.

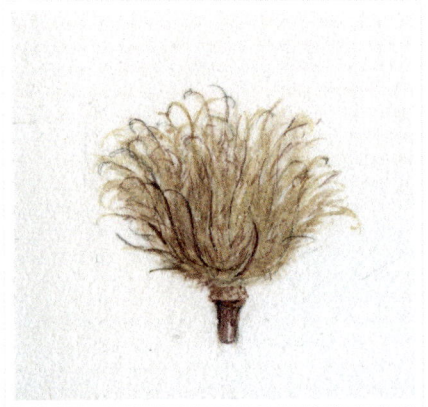

The final addition to the spread is the fruit or seed capsules, which have now developed from the carpels and have a feathery appearance at their tips, requiring tapering soft brush strokes. I used a pale wash of brown and violet first to establish the subject.

In the final stage, add the finishing touches with slightly thicker paint, and add fine detail using small drawing brush strokes. Carefully define the reproductive parts; strengthen the stem; add small hairs to the stems with a pale grey mix using the same three primary colours; also add short hairs to the bud. Add brown blemishes to the sepals and finish the feathery seed capsules. Finally, you can add additional notes to the spread to complete it.

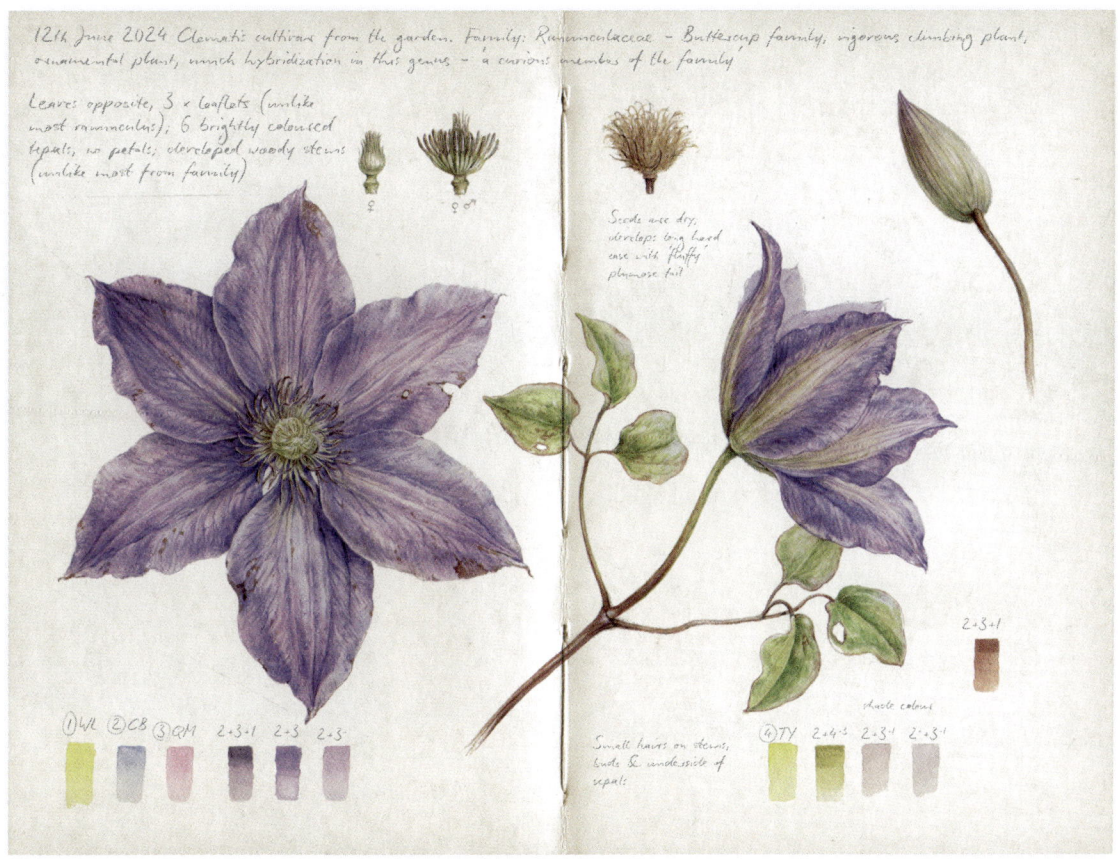

Finally, add finishing touches to dissections and the flower centre with a small brush, using creamier consistencies of paint, intensifying colour with violet and brown where needed. Use a diluted pale grey mix for tiny stem hairs, painting outward strokes to taper at the tips. Add brown blemishes to the sepals and refine details. Complete the spread with annotations, varying the ratio and dilution notes for how three primary colours create different hues.

Poppy *(Papaver somniferum)*

An upright composition in graphite and watercolour

Opium Poppies have beautiful flowers with crumpled petals that come in a variety of colours, including red, pink, mauve, and white. They are popular flowers that freely set seeds wherever they land, usually on poor soil. They also have attractive rounded seed capsules that can be kept and dried. Because their growth habit is upright, Poppies make a perfect choice for pages where you don't necessarily want to cross the centre pages or gutter of the book.

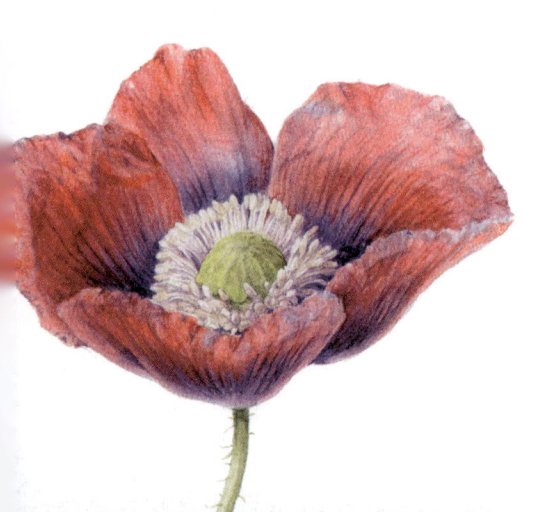

Finished sketchbook spread of a Poppy, with materials and equipment.

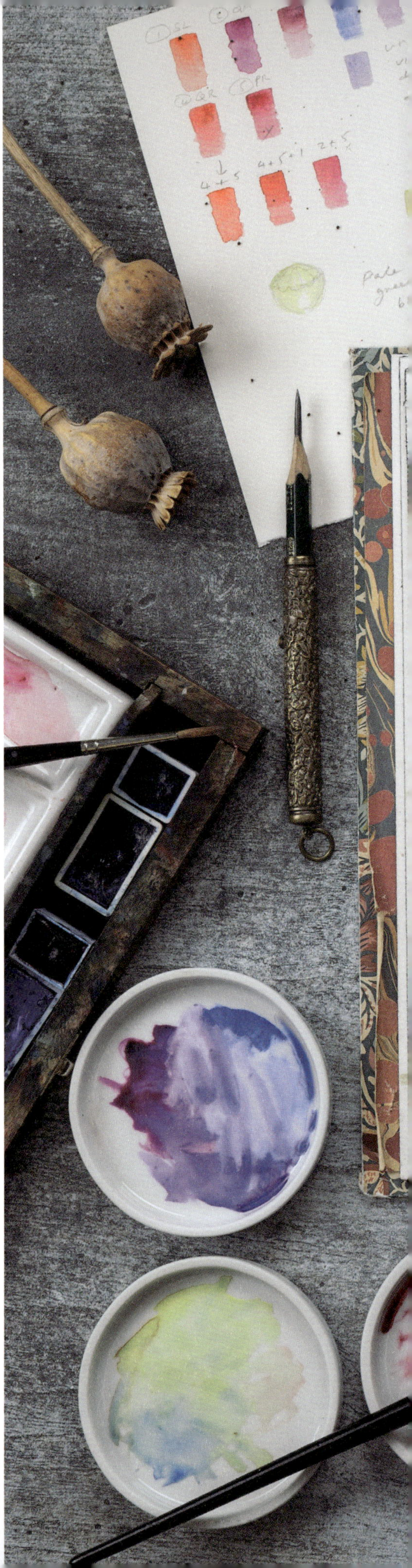

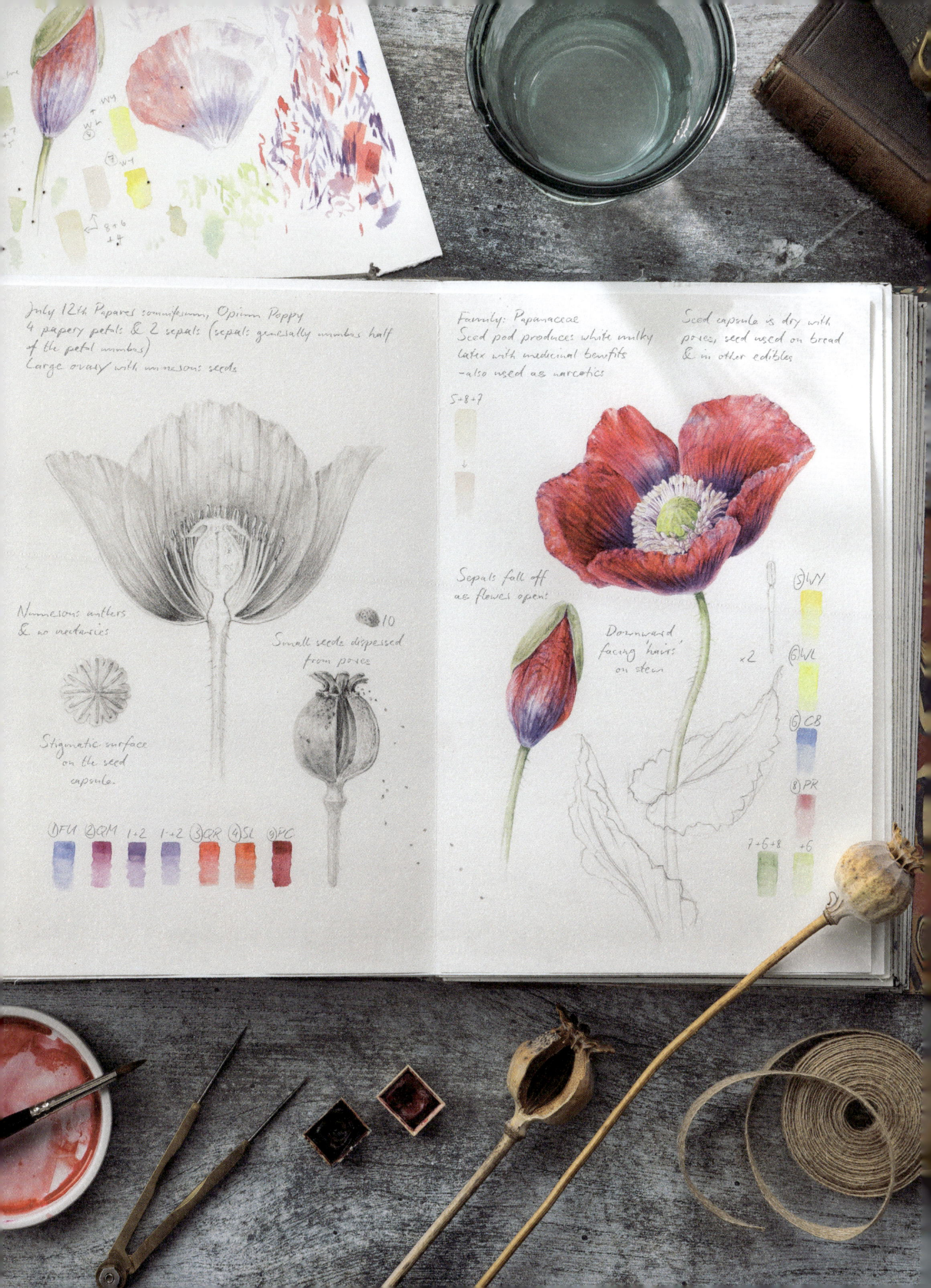

RESEARCH AND OBSERVATION

The Opium Poppy belongs to the Papavaceae family, otherwise known as the Poppy family. These plants have fairly large showy flowers. They are pollinated by insects yet have no nectaries. However, they do have a very large number of stamens, the carpel comprises a compound pistil (meaning it has many carpels), and the ovary has chambers that contain many ovules, which develop into numerous small dark seeds before escaping via the pores at the top of the dry capsule. These seeds are often used in the making of poppy-seed bread.

The sepals are usually half the number of petals, so for a Poppy with four petals, there will be two sepals. The plants are also known for containing latex, which is a milky sap. In Opium Poppies, this has been used historically in pharmaceuticals for the production of morphine and codeine, as the name *somniferum* indicates, meaning 'sleep bringing' in Latin.

COMPOSITION

As mentioned, the growth habit of the plant means that this subject works well on two separate pages. Sometimes students of botanical art find it challenging to work across the gutter of the book, and so if this is the case, the gutter can be avoided with this type of arrangement. Collectively, the two pages sit together and provide much information about the plant in an attractive way.

After learning about the plant, I wanted the content of the spread to focus primarily on the flowers and fruits as I found these aspects most interesting. I began by experimenting with the layout, and included one flowering stem and a bud with the two sepals on the right-hand page. Then, on the opposite page, I added a dissection drawing, for which I took a photograph to work from, alongside a study of the seed capsule that shows the internal chambers. Some aspects of this plant are quite challenging to paint, such as the complex centre of the flower and the crumpled petals, and you will need to plan your approach.

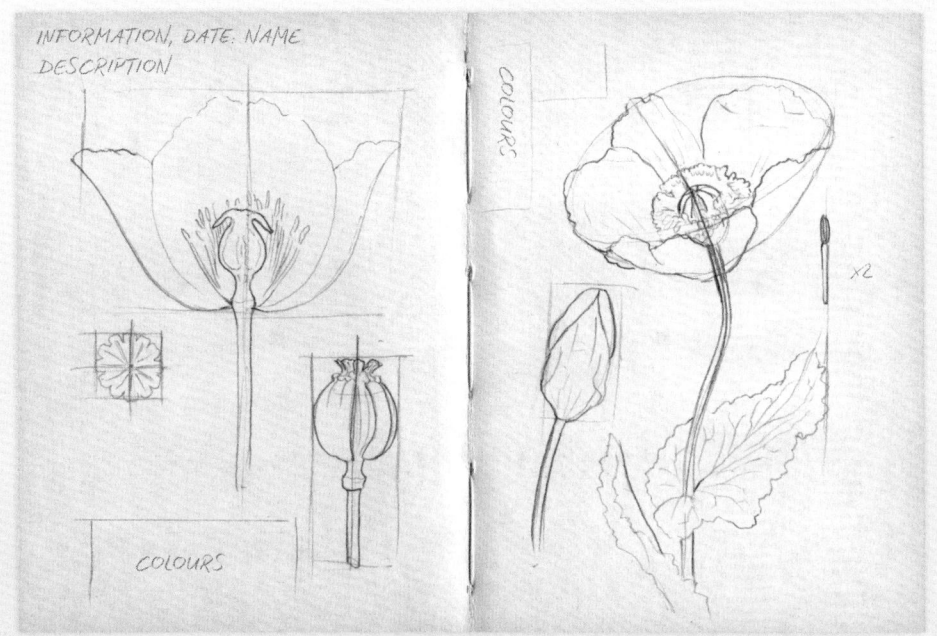

Sketch a rough graphite layout first with all of the elements that are to be included on the two-page spread; in this case, create two distinct pages. The colour elements will be on the right-hand page and the left side will be graphite. You can construct the sketch using an H or HB pencil. Sketch the basic shapes found within the plant parts directly into the sketchbook and refine them as a lightweight drawing.

←

SKETCHING

From your rough layout, refine the drawing by lightly drawing the structure of the flower stem into position, as this is the main focal point of the two pages. I like to think about the pages as having a 'main act' and a supporting cast, so I usually start with the position of the focal feature. The flower sits at an angle, so is roughly cup-shaped. Position the bud sitting lower down the page to make best use of the space by staggering the parts.

Keep just enough line work to be able to see the parts and erase anything not needed, because once painted over, it is not possible to remove the graphite.

COLOUR AND GRAPHITE

I suggest beginning with the watercolour flowers because once these flowers open, they soon fade and die. Identify the colours and note that there are underlying violets. You will need a number of reds to create the bright colour. Thereafter, work out the colours for the remaining elements.

Colours used: Quinacridone Magenta, Quinacridone Red, Scarlet Lake, Permanent Rose, Permanent Carmine, French Ultramarine, Cobalt Blue, Winsor Lemon, and Winsor Yellow.

The remainder of the double-page spread will be completed in graphite, using pencil grades 4H–HB. It is better to complete all of the base-layer work with harder grades of pencil to establish a smooth base first. Hard pencils (H grades) have more of the smaller clay particles in the pencil lead, which fill the paper surface, whereas softer pencils (B grades) have more of the large graphite particles in the lead, which can create a grainy appearance that is more easily smudged. This is why harder grades are used first.

The colour palette shows the range of colours and mixes I used; you can also see the same colours on the scribble sheet, which is used for testing the colours.

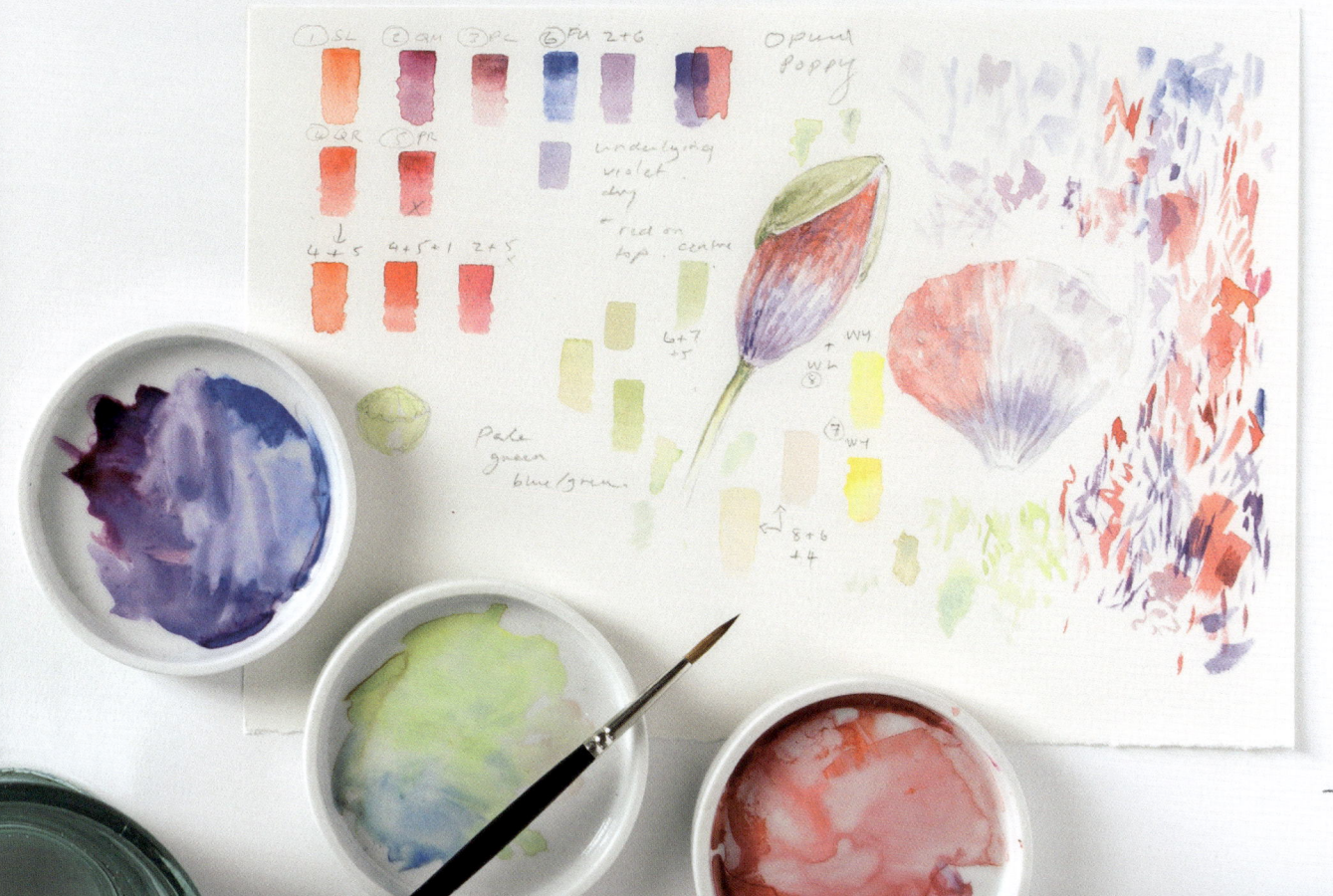

PAINTING

To begin the painting, add the underlying colour first. In this case, the colour is violet, which acts as a base for the darker purple centre of the flower. Once you have added the underlying colour, you can introduce the reds; it will take several layers of paint to achieve the desired saturation.

Add the reds gradually to the painting by layering. You will need to use several reds in the process. There is actually no need to use any other colours than reds to achieve the desired colour. It's worth experimenting with a range of reds and this is why a primary palette with several colours from each of the three primaries is more useful than a large palette of pre-mixed colours, which can become confusing.

Next, add the green centre, stem, and sepals using a pale green mix. Most green mixes are made with three primary colours and this is no exception: mix the blue and yellow and add a tiny amount of the same red that is used in the flower. As before, the introduction of red makes a more natural green but add too much and it will turn brown, so it really must be a tiny amount of red. You can adjust the green to make various colours by altering the ratio of the colours in the mix. This means the mix can be lighter or darker depending on the amount of water used or it could be blue- or yellow-biased, all of which is easily achieved with the same three colours.

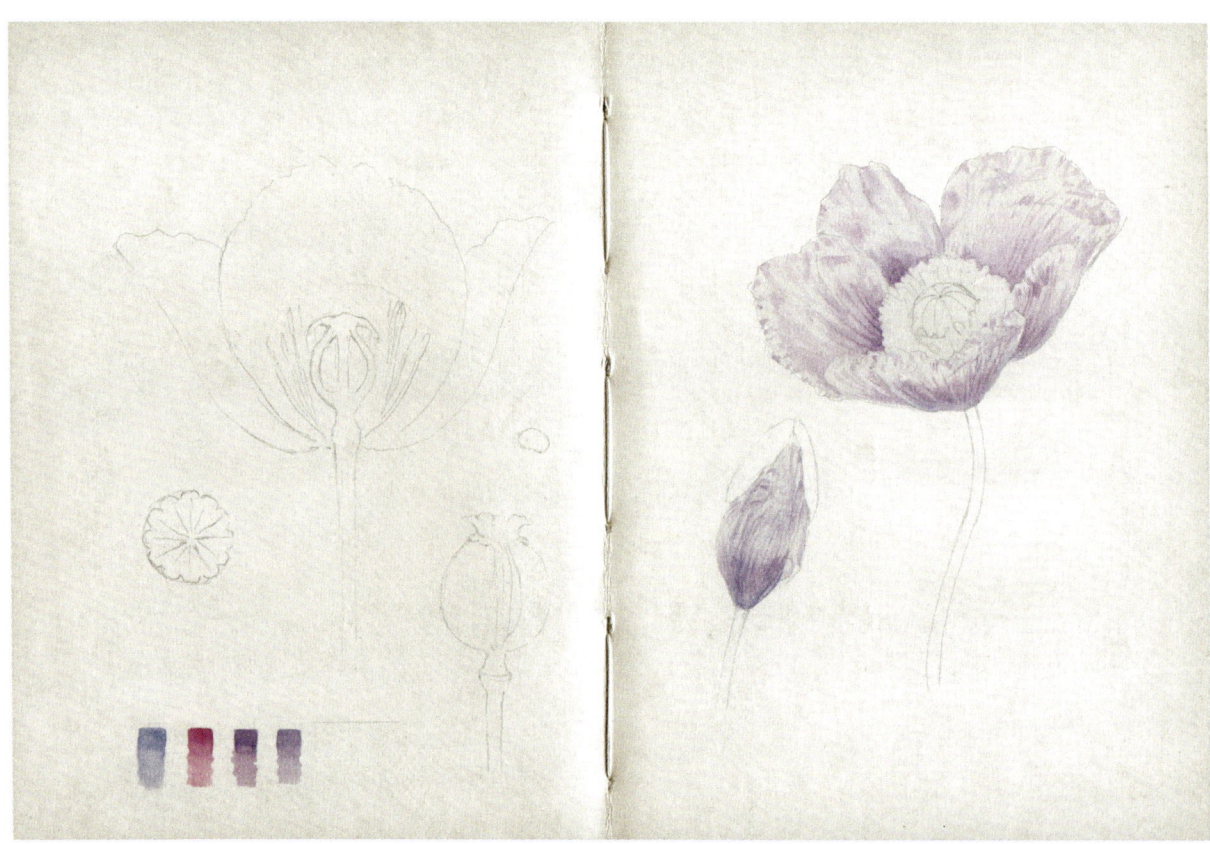

Begin with an underlying wash using a mix of French Ultramarine and Quinacridone Magenta and apply with a size 2 brush. It will help to dampen the area around the central anthers first using clean water, then add the colour. Brush strokes should extend upwards from the centre directly onto the dry paper to create the crisp creases and lines. Add the same colour to the bud.

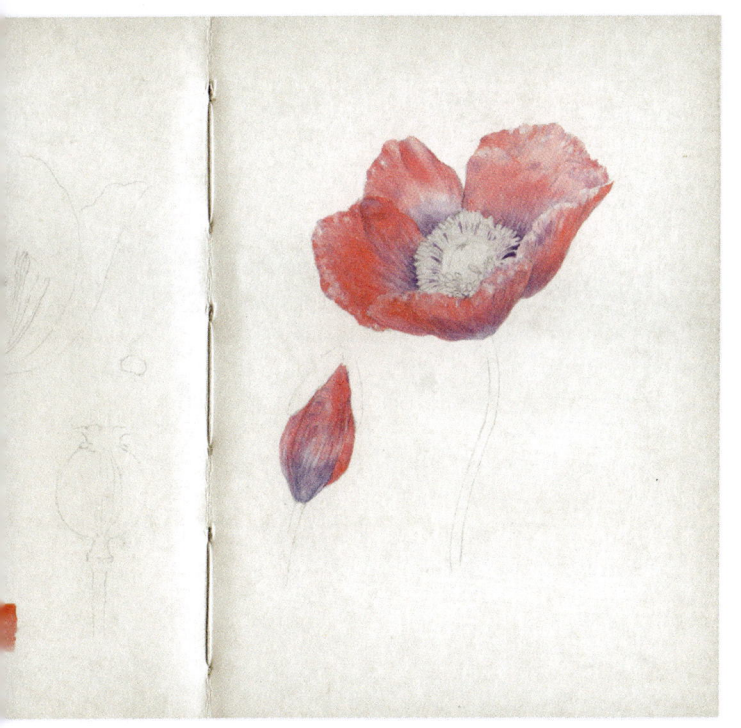

Add the first layer of red to the flower using a size 4 brush and the wet-in-wet technique, and Quinacridone Red and a small amount of Scarlet Lake for warmer areas of colour. Wet the area first and add the red while it is still wet. Drop the Scarlet Lake into smaller areas. Work on one petal at a time, painting the alternate petals to avoid colour merging while still wet. You can achieve the effect of transparency in the petals by painting a faint indication of the petal lying behind wet-on-dry to create a sharp but pale edge of the petal. Leave small areas of white where the light catches the creased petals. Apply the same to the bud.

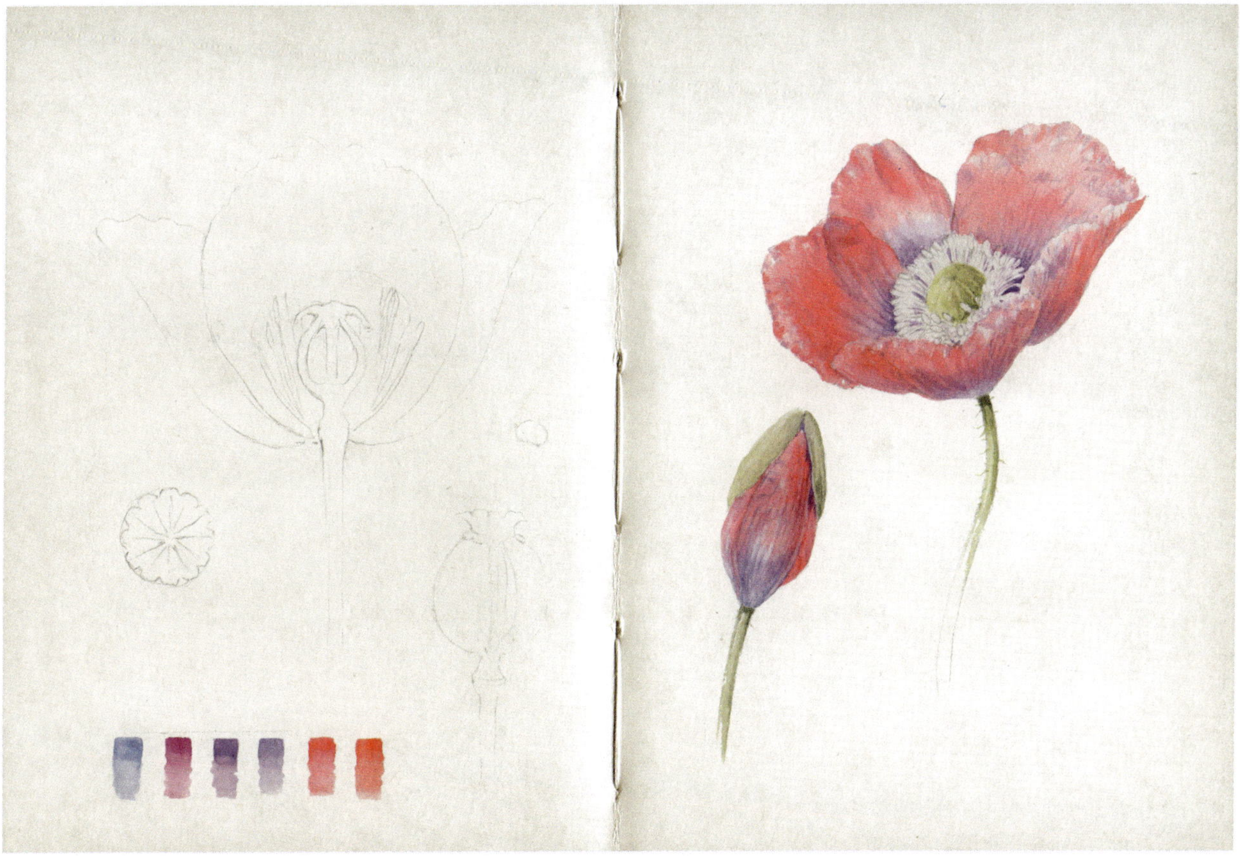

Add the green centre, stem, and sepals at this point using a mix of Cobalt Blue, Winsor Lemon, and a small quantity of Permanent Rose. Vary the mixes from a yellow-biased to a darker blue-biased green. Add the paler green as a light, graded wash, then use the blue-green for the darker areas, wet-on-dry.

The stamens, comprising anthers and filaments, are pale in colour and it's important not to overwork them – you need a dilute colour and this is mixed from the primaries. Often the mistake made with a complex flower centre is to outline or attempt to paint around too many of the anthers and filaments, which looks clumsy. Instead, treat them as a mass initially, with only small gaps in places. Later, use light and shade to separate parts where needed.

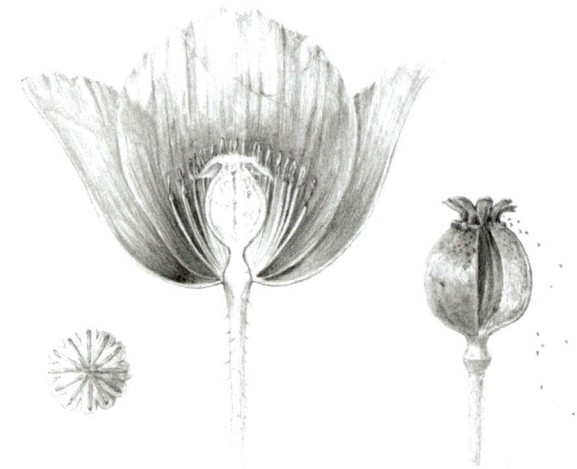

With the violet mix, add definition to the stamens where there are any obvious gaps or shadow. Be careful not to outline or use too much paint, and observe the light and shade. The anthers are a very pale colour so use a dilute mix of Permanent Rose, Winsor Lemon, and a minimal amount of Cobalt Blue as a light wash on them, leaving the filaments largely clear of colour.

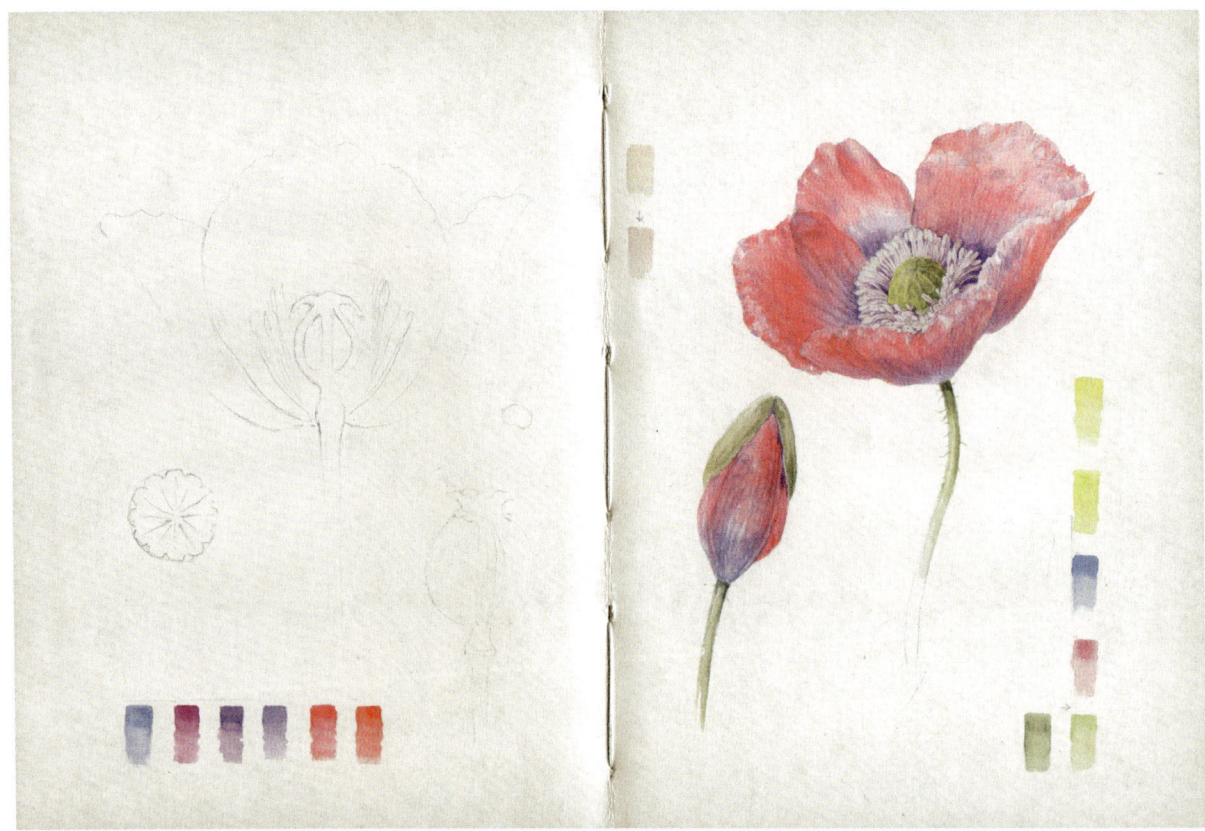

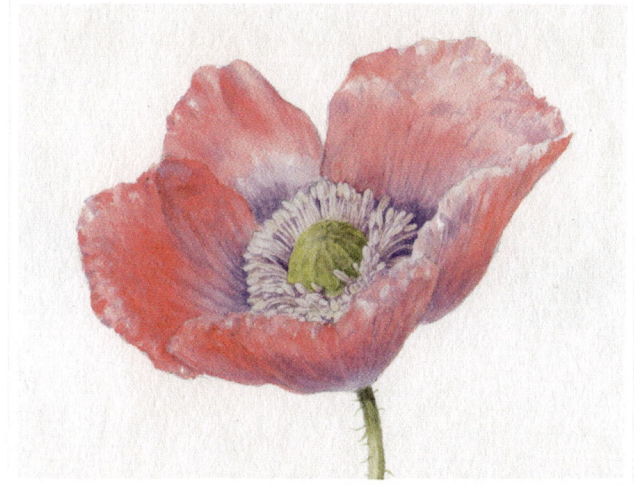

Here you can see how much, or little, detail is used in the centre. It's important not to overpaint this area; instead, deal with the whole area as a mass and then add a little definition and separation using light and shade with pale violet colours painted onto the dry surface where needed.

Building the reds can be more challenging because we also want to retain a little transparency and the creased appearance of the petals, so use layering with a number of different reds. Intensify colour in all parts and add more detail to complete the flower and the bud, which finishes this part of the sketchbook page.

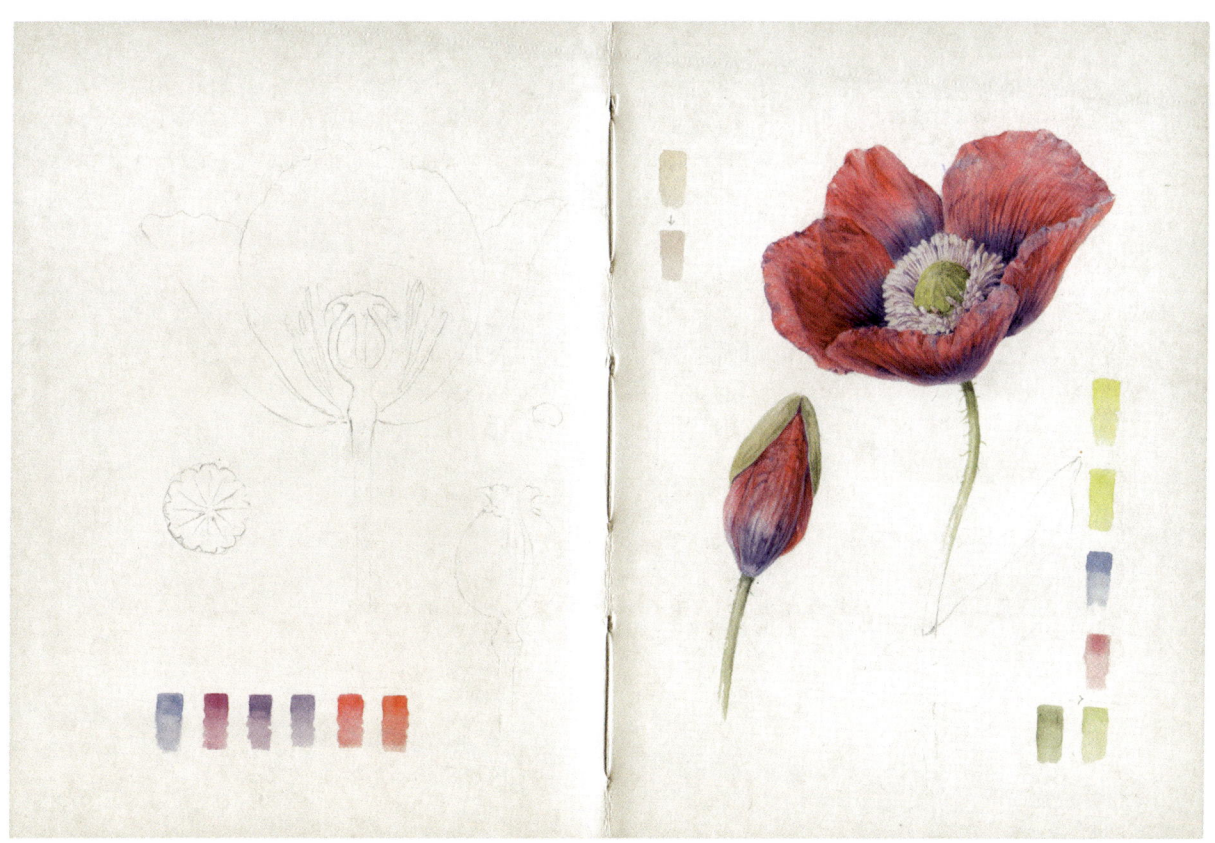

Strengthen the red with layering of colour, each time adding less and using increasingly dry techniques as the colour builds. Use two to three layers at this stage or until the colour is rich enough but not oversaturated; I used some glazing of colour too. Add Permanent Carmine in the last layer for the darker reds but be careful not to lose the transparency in the petals. I also strengthened the purple with a thicker mix of paint, and this made the centre parts appear brighter.

Complete the next stage of the illustration using graphite shading techniques. Using a range of grades to achieve the tonal variation and three-dimensional form in the subjects is required. If only one grade is used, such as an HB, the drawing will have less depth. Also, do not apply too much pressure as this can result in a shiny appearance, which spoils the drawing. Therefore, create the base layers first using the hard grades and add the soft grades as the drawing develops more form, meaning the soft grades generally cover a smaller area of the subject. Graphite will smudge in a sketchbook where pages are touching, so it is advisable to spray the page with fixative spray.

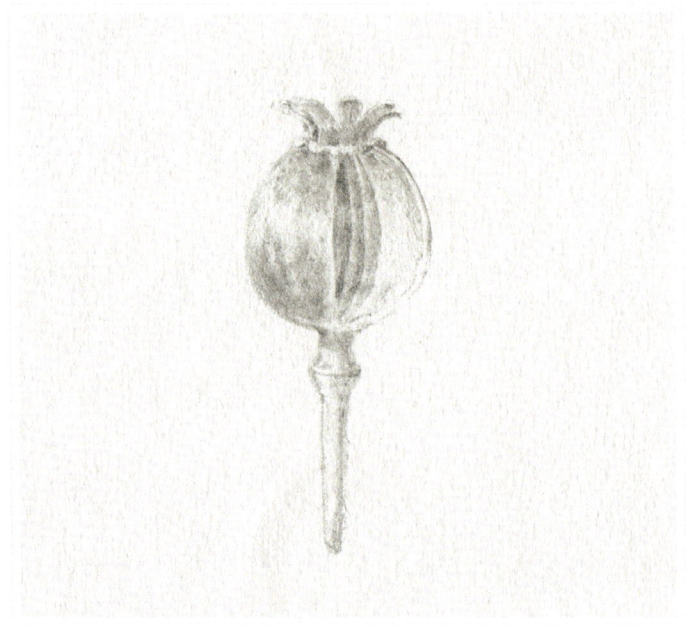

For the graphite element of the pages, use a range of pencils 4H to HB to achieve the variety of tone.

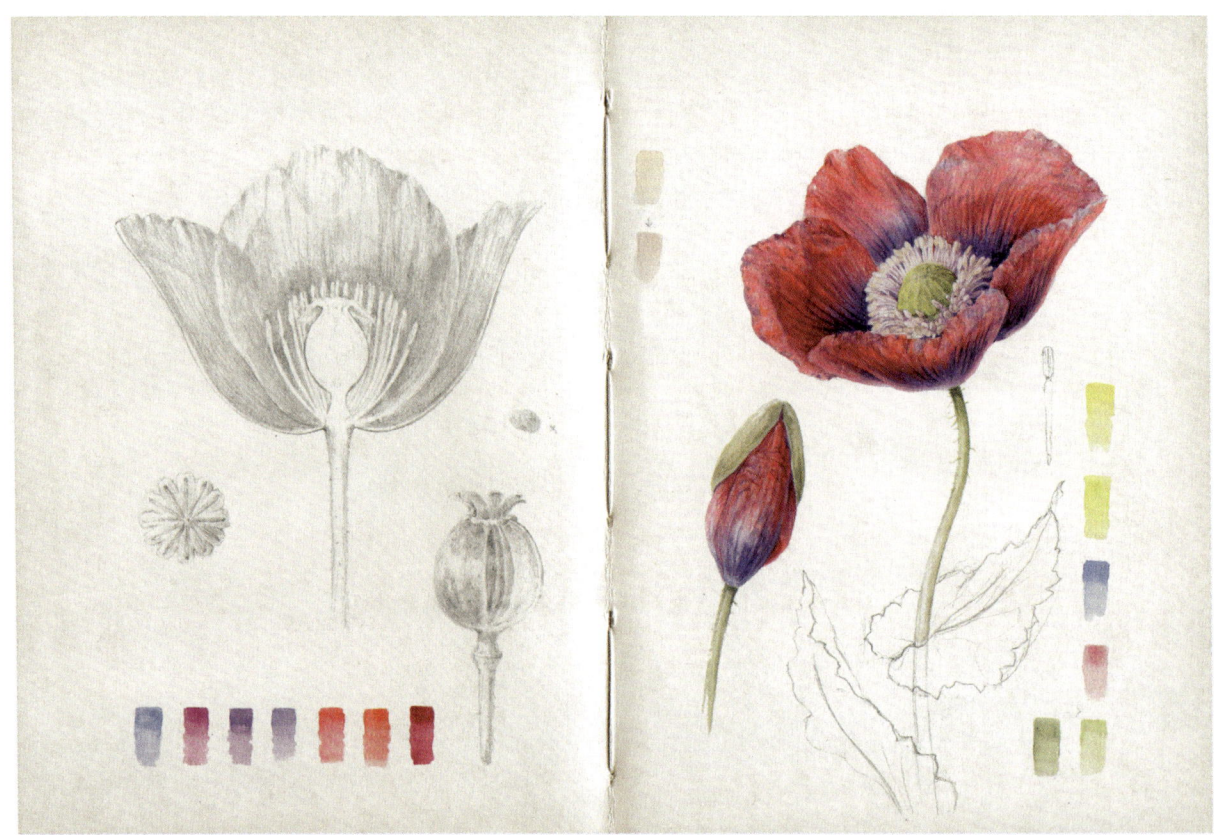

I added the initial layers of graphite to all parts using a 4H pencil, working carefully around the pale areas of the stamen and the pistil. I then used a 2H to create more tonal values. You can add transparency to the dissection petals by shading the petal lying behind the centre one.

For the final stages of the graphite, use the HB pencil for the darker areas of tone; you can also sharpen the lead to a finer point for small details around the anthers. I opted to leave the leaves on the colour page as rough line drawings, but you could either render these with graphite or paint them in watercolour.

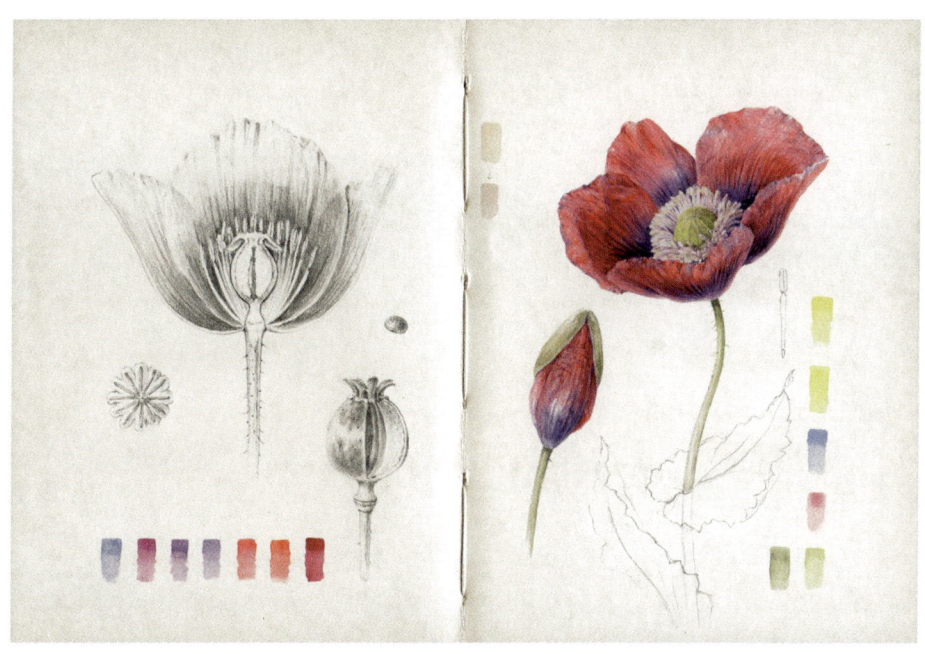

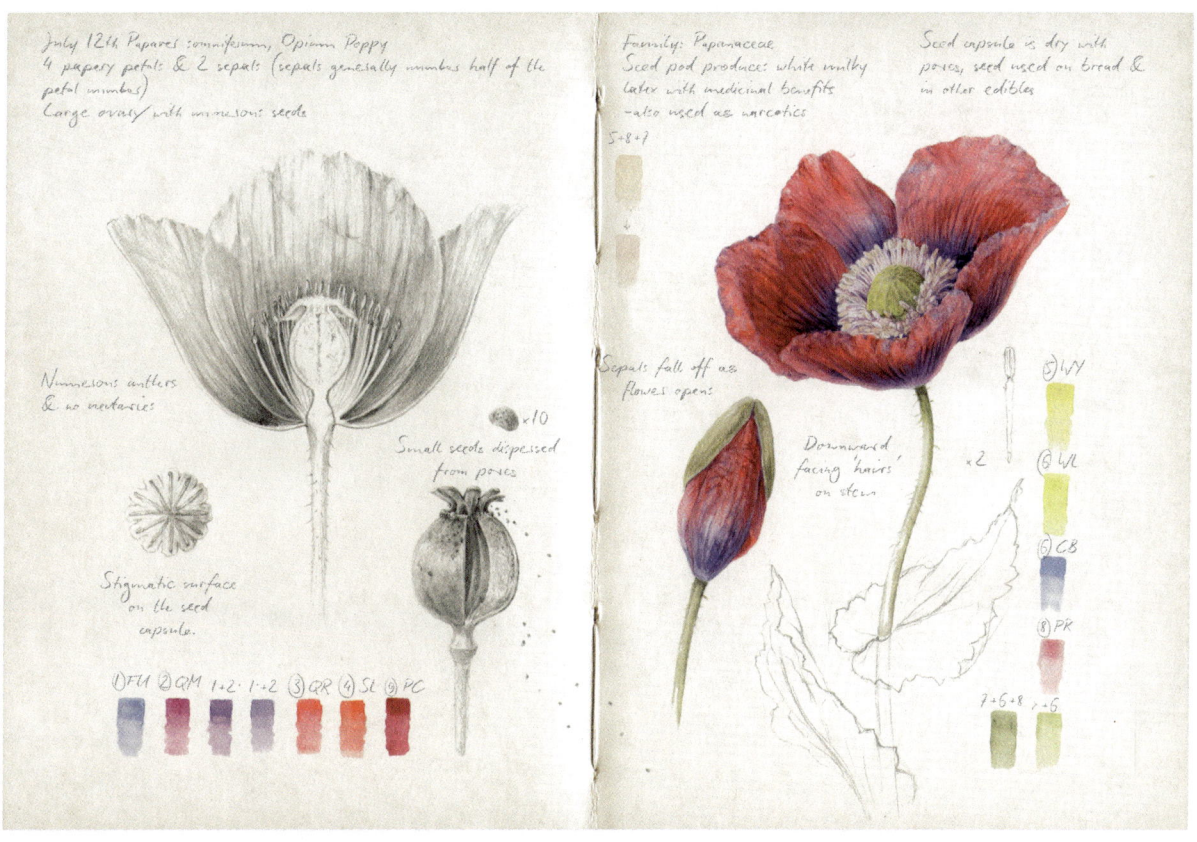

The two pages are complete and further notes are added. Always make sure that all colours used are noted for future reference should you decide to make a painting of the plant.

Viola (Viola tricolor)

A double-page spread

Violas are a good choice for a slightly more complex plant with multiple leaves. The flowers are brightly coloured and flat-faced, making them easy to draw. They continue to flower for many months, providing a constant supply of material. The leaves, although numerous, are relatively simple, being neither too large nor too small, and the plant can easily fit onto a double-page spread at its actual size, which means that the illustration will cross the gutter of the sketchbook.

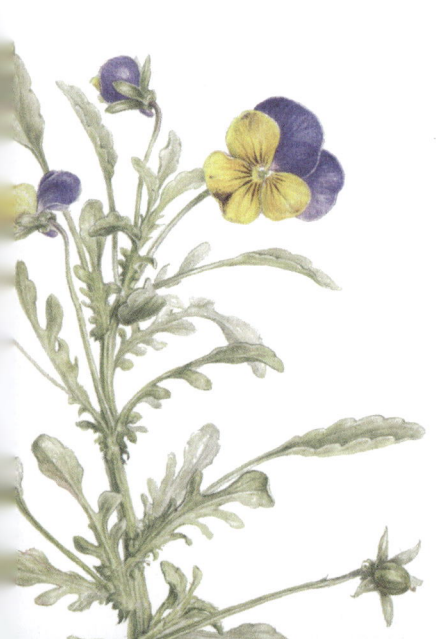

A sketchbook spread of a Viola tricolor from the garden, a work in progress in the studio.

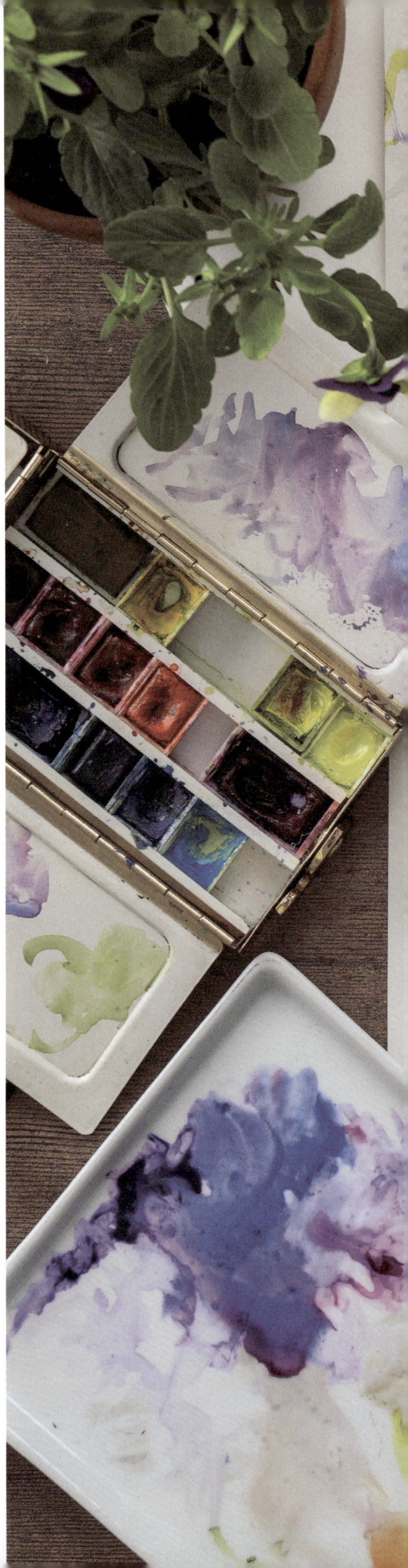

→

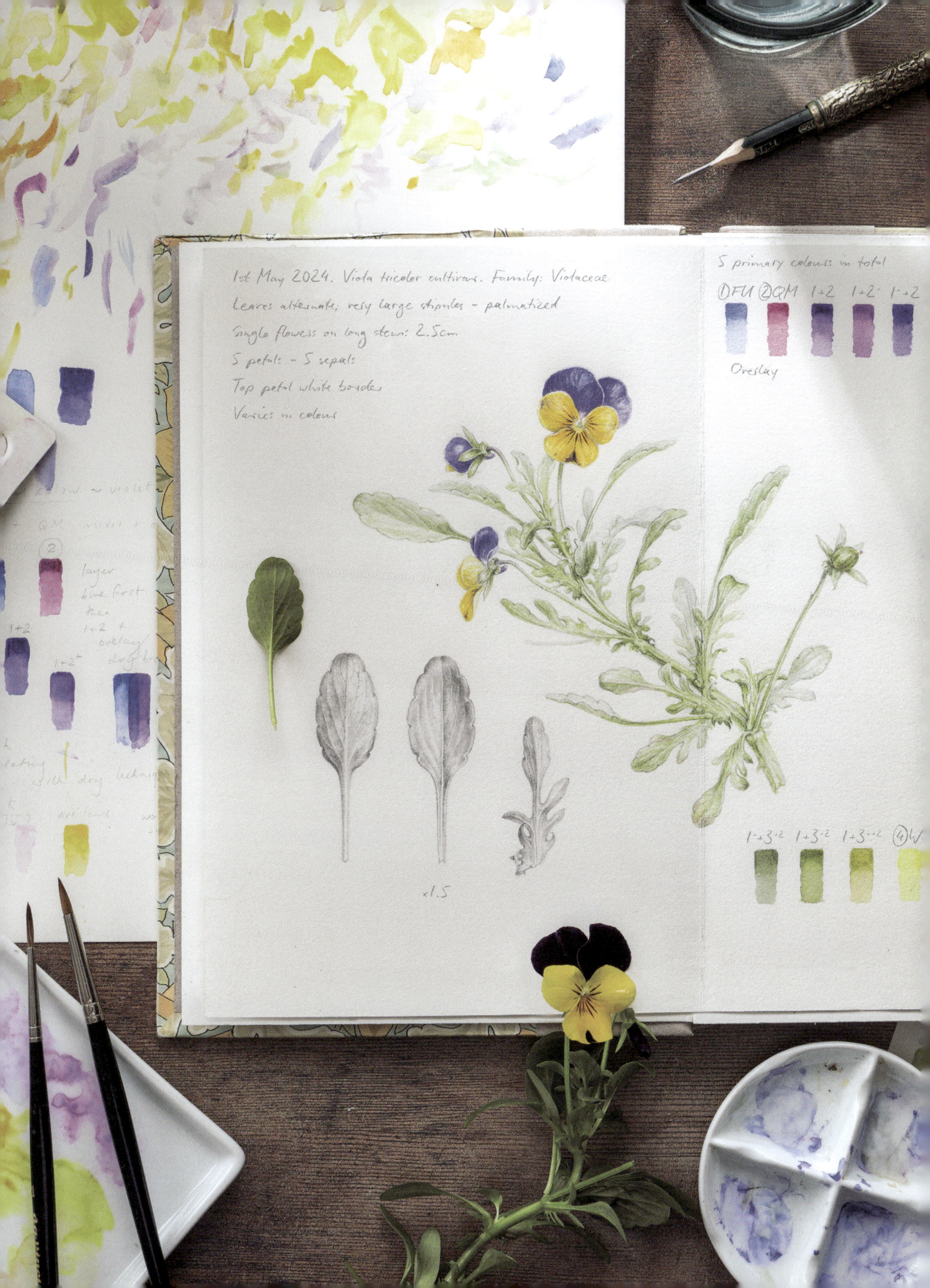

1st May 2024. *Viola tricolor cultivars.* Family: *Violaceae*

Leaves alternate; very large stipules – palmatized

Single flowers on long stem: 2.5cm

5 petals – 5 sepals

Top petal white border

Varies in colours

5 primary colours in total

① FU ② QM   1+2   1+2   1+2

Overlay

1+3·² 1+3·² 1+3·² ④W

x1.5

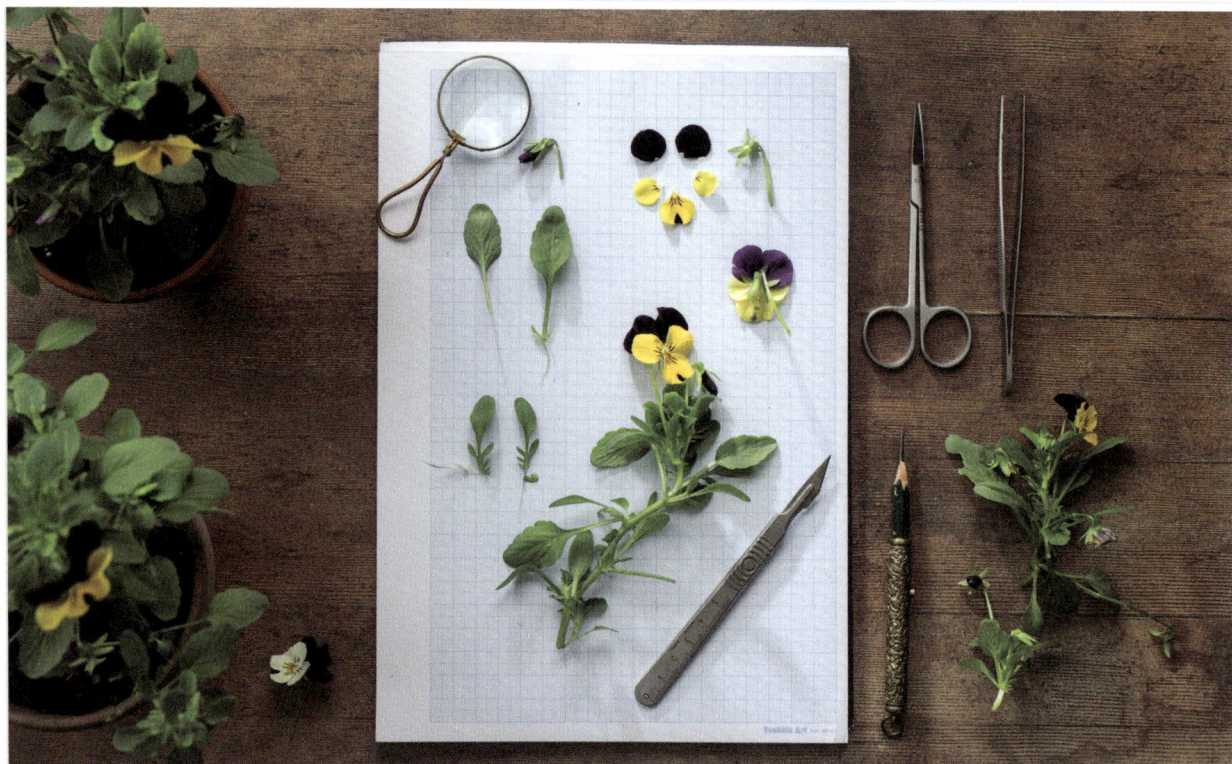

RESEARCH AND OBSERVATION

Violas are in the Violaceae family. They have simple alternate leaves with stipules. Flowers can be solitary and are bilateral with five petals and sepals.

This is a more complicated study because there are many leaves, flowers, buds, and seed capsules. A close look reveals the alternately arranged leaves on the stem and two large stipules are found at the base of each leaf. The stem is flattened on the sides and the flowers are bilateral. There is also a little nectar spur on the lowest petal. The ovary is superior, meaning it is positioned above all of the other floral parts (as opposed to an inferior ovary, which would be attached below the other floral parts).

All of these feature should be included in the sketch page, and I could also include a dissection; however, it is not easy to see the reproductive parts of the flower unless viewed with a hand lens or microscope, and so for this spread I decided not to include a dissection. The flower, once pollinated, quickly produces seeds in the swollen fruits, and this means I could also include these fruits on my final spread. Occasionally, I press a few sections of the plant for reference, and these make a nice addition to a sketchbook at a later date and replicate herbarium (a collection of dried and pressed plants used for study) specimens.

Various parts of the deconstructed plant parts placed on graph paper with a 1, 5 and 10mm grid for size reference.

The shape of the plant requires the composition to cross the gutter of the book. Begin the line drawing by measuring the height and width of parts and plotting onto paper using basic shapes, angles, and marks to establish the size and structure of the plant across the spread. Pencil marks should be light and made using an H or HB pencil, which can easily be altered or removed.

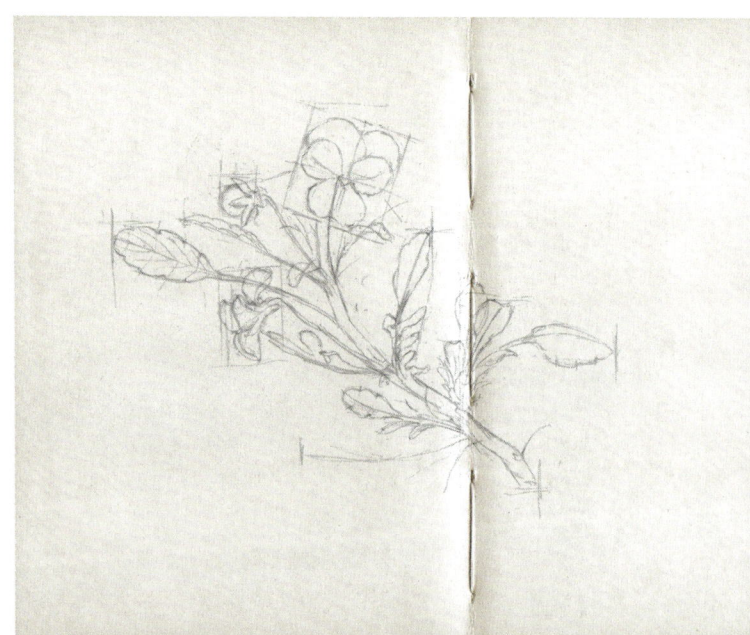

COMPOSITION

The growth-spreading habit of the plant means that this composition can span across the centre of the two pages. You can cut away some unnecessary parts from the chosen section of the plant, such as branched stems at the base of the main stem. This will remove some of the cluttered leaves and make it slightly easier to see the main stem; however, if you do this, be careful not to alter the arrangement of parts and ensure you still show how leaves and petioles are attached to the stems. The stem is quite sprawling and will sit comfortably across the pages.

As I was focusing on just one flower stem, I sketched it straight into the sketchbook (a planning page is only needed if you're struggling to fit everything on).

SKETCHING

Begin by lightly sketching the plant and working across the pages, which makes best use of the space. Lightly draw the stem in first to anchor the position on the spread and then begin to add the shapes of all the measured parts coming from the stem – so add the flowers, leaves, buds, and seed pod. Don't draw any part in detail but gradually add details as the whole drawing develops to a finished stage.

Next, plot the positions of all other details to be added, leaving a space with a ruled line for the seed capsules to be added later. Before painting, use a putty eraser to lighten the drawing, so that the line is not too heavy.

Add detail drawings of the leaves and stipules on the lower left. On the right-hand side of the spread, lightly rule a vertical line. This is where you can add the rear of the flower. Leave space for the fruit capsule and open seed pod, which can be added once it opens. Ruling a line means that parts can be aligned and neatly spaced.

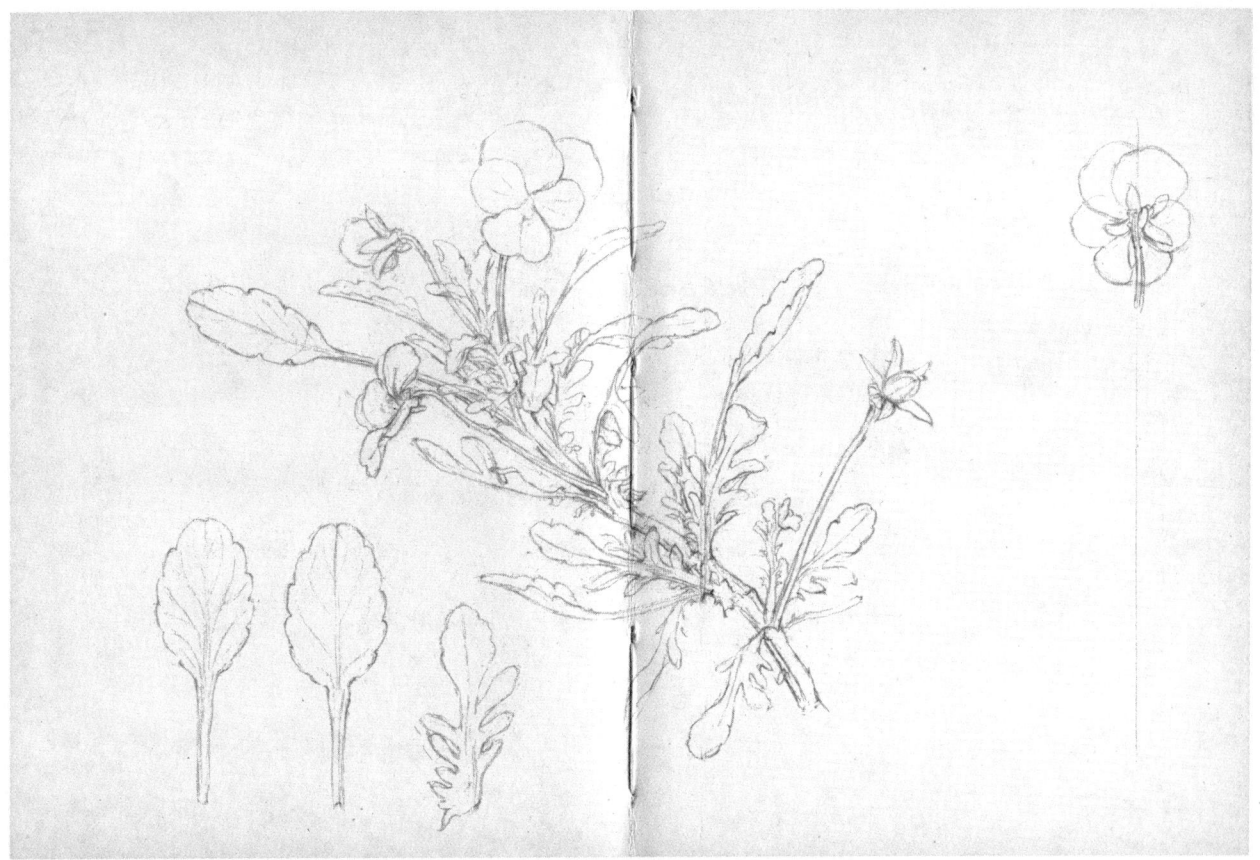

COLOUR STUDIES

I mostly work out colours in advance on spare paper, so that I know what will be used on the spread. For some colours, I mix two or three primary colours together and others are created by overlaying separate colours on the paper, which makes a third colour: this process is called optical mixing. This approach can be particularly useful when working with violets, when blues and pinks or reds can be overlaid, rather than mixed. Optical mixing gives a different outcome to mixing on the palette and is worth experimenting with.

Once the colours are decided upon, add painted swatches to the spread, using the most appropriate free space. Write down the primary colours and the mixes from those colours for reference. I used just five primary colours in the spread and all colours were mixed from these.

Colours used: Cobalt Blue, French Ultramarine, Quinacridone Magenta, Winsor Yellow, and Winsor Lemon.

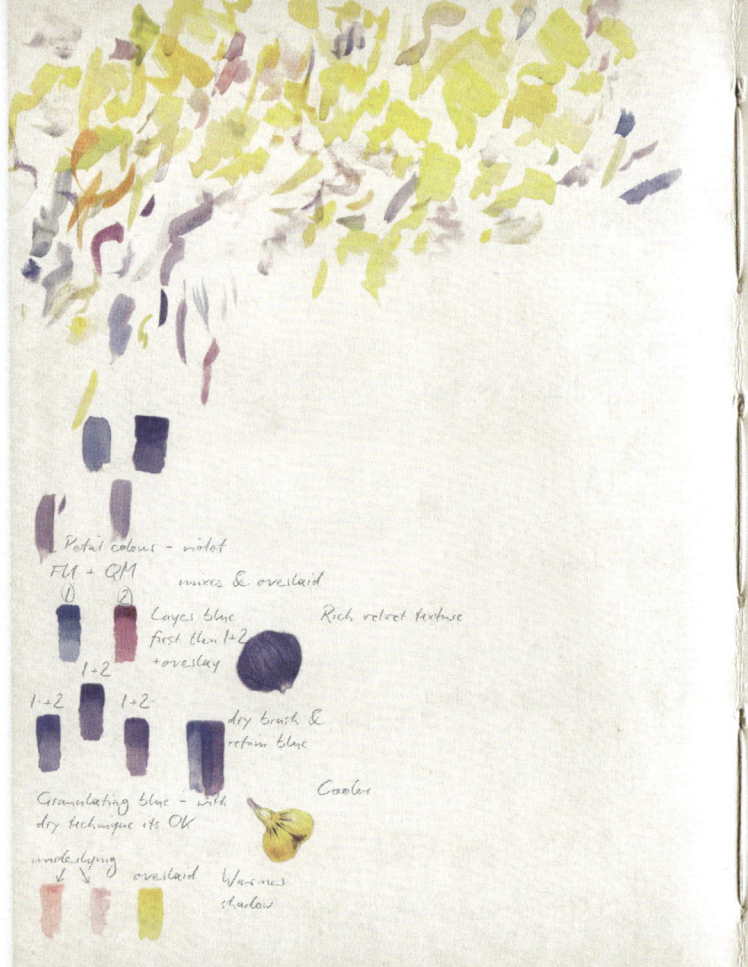

The ceramic watercolour palette shows the consistency of the paint and colour mixes alongside a practice page for testing colours on watercolour paper. Time spent testing colours in the initial stages can reduce any uncertainty over which colours to use during each stage of the painting.

Make a separate colour study. This is where you can work out the initial colours. I also made a small practice page of violet and yellow petals in advance of painting the sketchbook spread.

Distance and separation can be achieved by painting the parts further away paler and sometimes a pale blue or violet in colour. This technique is called aerial perspective and is commonly used in landscapes but can be used in botanical work too.

PAINTING

First, paint in the underlying violet colours with a mix of blue and pink using French Ultramarine and Quinacridone Magenta. Apply this violet mix on the flowers where the darker upper petals are. Apply a very dilute shadow colour, made with the same colours but much more pink in appearance, to the lower lemon petals.

Next, turn your attention to the leaves: in this case, there are many leaves and so to avoid confusion, paint the elements that are further back paler and less saturated; using the aerial perspective technique in this way will enable you to create visual separation between overlapping parts and also create depth. For this dilute colour, I used Cobalt Blue, Winsor Lemon, and a very small amount of Quinacridone Magenta.

Next, add the stem colour, using the same colours but with more Winsor Lemon in the green mix. Keep colour light at this stage of the painting; remember that it's easy to add more paint but it's not so easy to remove paint if applied too heavily.

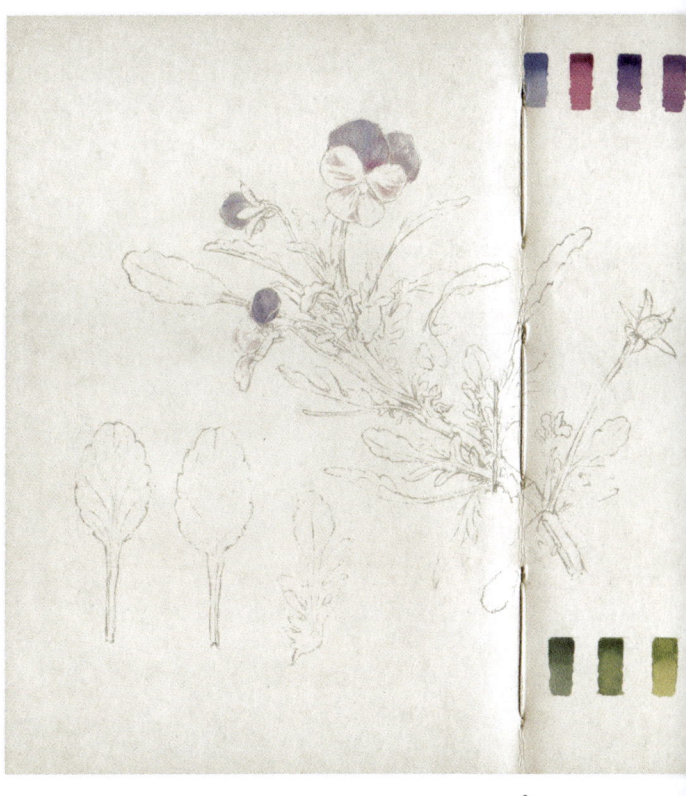

Begin the painting, using a size 2 or 3 brush for most of the work as the subject is fairly small.

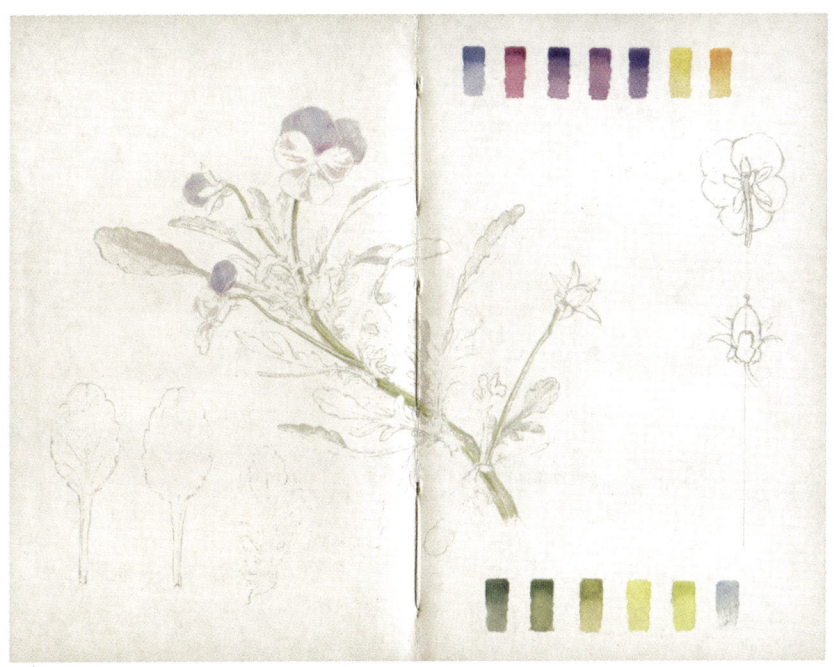

Add a very pale wash of colour to the leaves at the rear of the stem. This will create the effect of them being more distant and will help separate them from the more strongly painted leaves in the foreground. Paint the stem using a pale green mix but note there needs to be some variation where it is slightly darker on the underside of the stem in the shaded areas.

Next, focus on building up the leaf colour in stages. The nearer leaves require a more saturated green and more detail than those further away. For this part, use French Ultramarine to make a stronger green mix, which can be combined with the same lemon colour and small amount of magenta. Continue building up the violet on the upper petals. On the yellow flower petal, add Winsor Lemon and Winsor Yellow over the initial shade colour.

Add dry brush details on leaves and flowers, such as the markings at the centre of the flower, using more creamy mixes of paint.

Then finish the additional details. I opted to include the front and back view of the leaves and one stipule in graphite, so as not to clutter the spread and to keep the focus on the main stem. I painted the rear of the flower and fruit. The fruit, which had now opened to reveal the seeds, was the last part to be added in watercolour. This balanced the spread and provided additional information about the plant. Finally, I made an additional colour swatch of the mix for the seed pods.

Paint the leaves nearer to the front a more saturated green. It is important to observe the light direction on all parts of the plant and this is particularly important on the leaves.

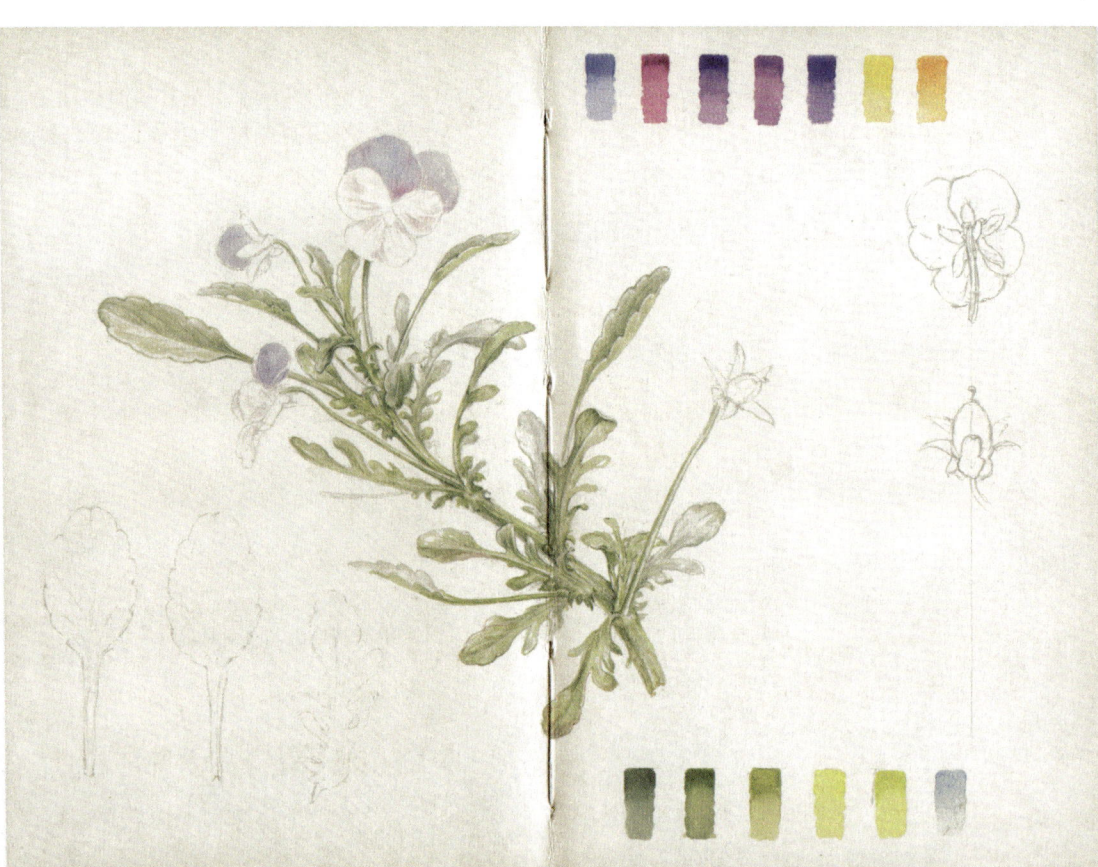

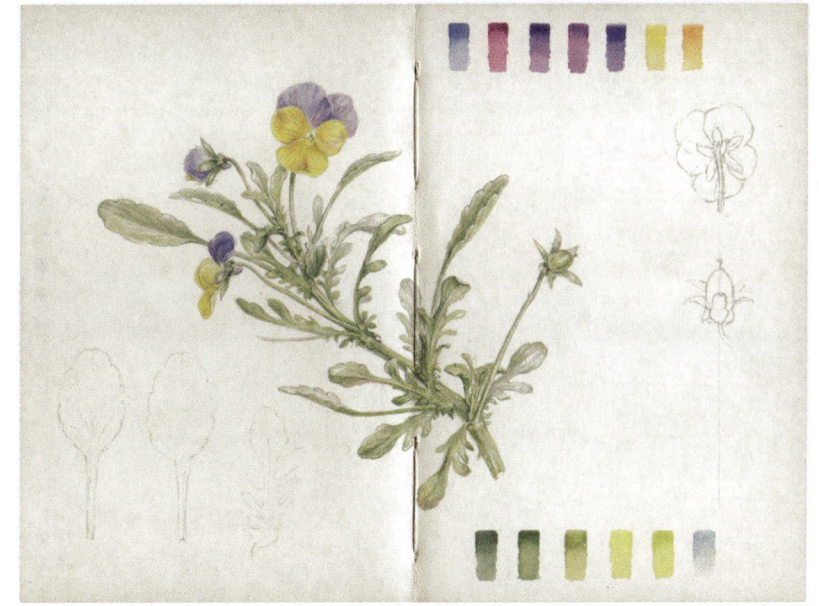

On the flower, add layers of the blue-violet to the upper petals and Winsor Lemon and Winsor Yellow to the lower petals. Use Winsor Lemon in the cooler-looking areas and Winsor Yellow in the warmer areas near to the flower centre.

In the final stages, add extra details. Shade the leaves with continuous tone using an HB pencil. Paint the back of the flower slightly paler than the front, as the petal undersides are less intense in colour. Add the fruit and open pod in watercolour, deepen colour and detail with dry brushwork, and use a size 1 brush with a dark violet mix for the flower markings.

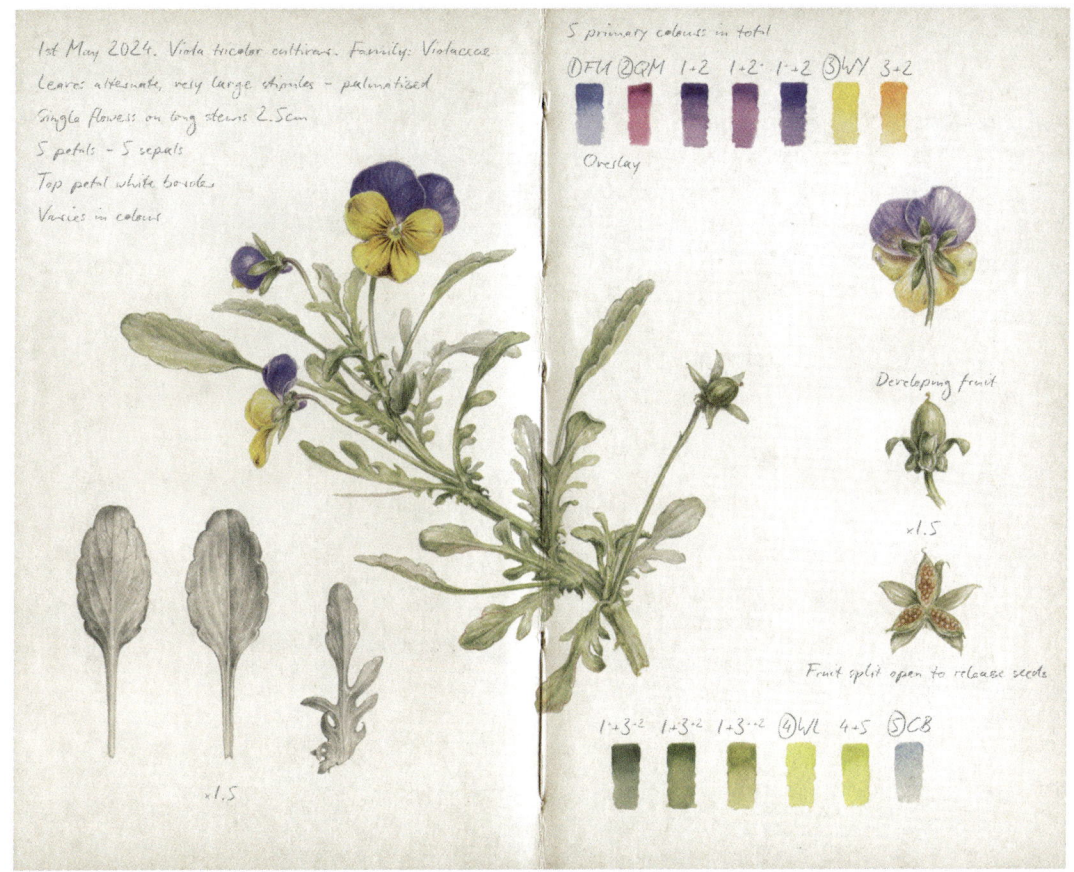

ALTERNATIVE FLOWER SKETCHBOOK PAGE

Intrigued by the diversity in Violas, I made an additional collection-style page of the flowers, showing differently positioned flowers, colour variations, and seed pods. Collection-style pages are revisited in a later project.

This style of page may be easier for a complete beginner or could be an addition to the previous page. The approach in drawing and painting is much the same but there are few key differences.

Before beginning, I drew and painted a single flower as preparation and this allowed me to establish a successful approach to the drawing, tonal values, and the painting. Next, I started work on the sketchbook page. I painted my palette of colours at the left side and numbered them. I made a note using the number system next to each flower to indicate the colours used, otherwise the page would have been cluttered with too many swatches. I also added a range of possible mixes beneath the primary palette.

Most importantly, the layout needed to be well spaced. I dropped the flowers on the page and made rough marks showing position. Finally, I completed one flower at a time. This approach can feel less daunting for beginners and makes an attractive collection.

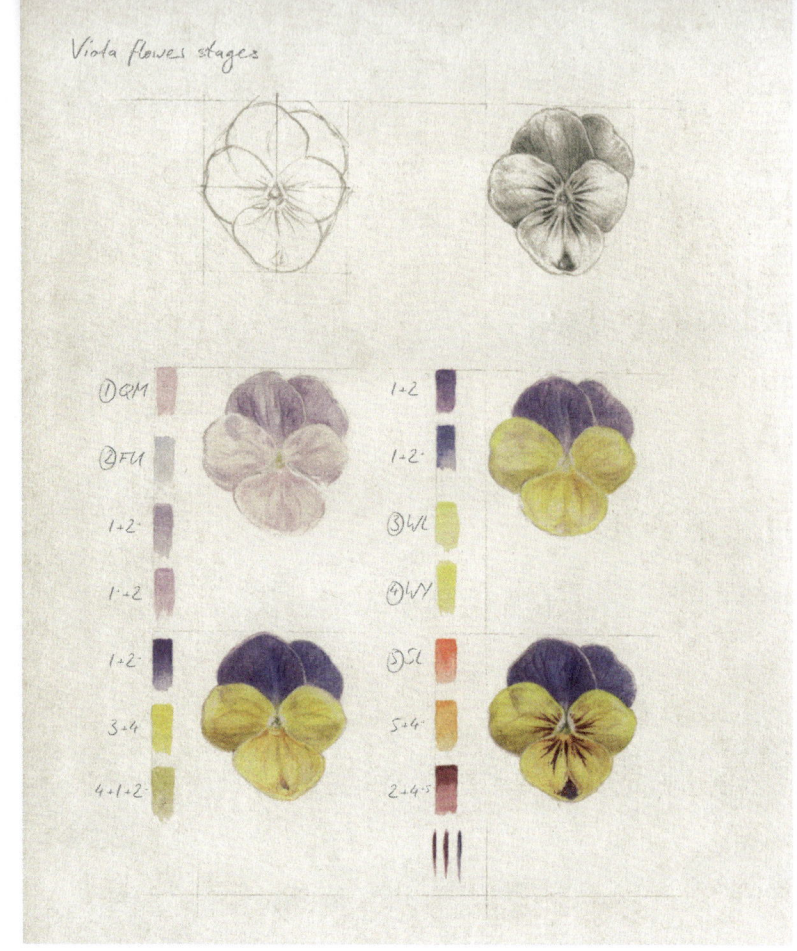

A flower study made in advance is useful. It can establish how to draw the flower and how to render it using tonal values in graphite. Thereafter, the approach with the watercolour techniques and mixes can be worked out until the flower is finished, as shown here. This helps with understanding the steps required to get to the end point when painting a detailed flower.

Adjust the placement and choice of flowers until a well-spaced and colour-balanced arrangement is achieved. Such a study can be less daunting than painting the larger section of stem with many leaves, but simple leaves could also be added to this page.

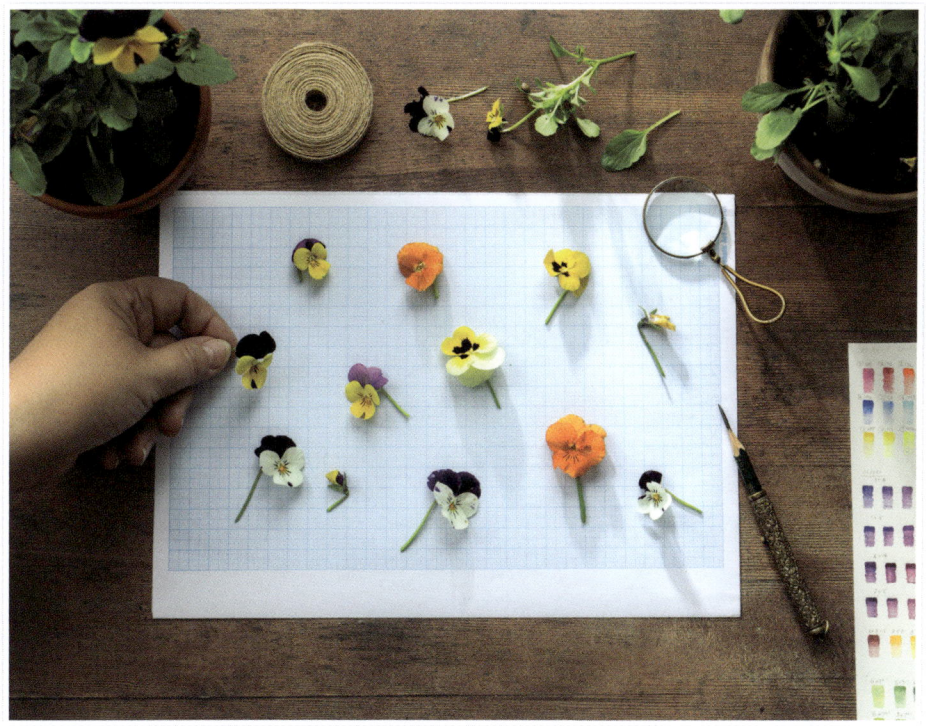

This simplified page shows how the flowers can be evenly spaced to create an aesthetically pleasing arrangement showing different types of flower patterns, colours, flower positions, and buds.

The finished sketchbook page with a range of simple Viola flowers and a fruit makes an excellent project for a complete beginner.

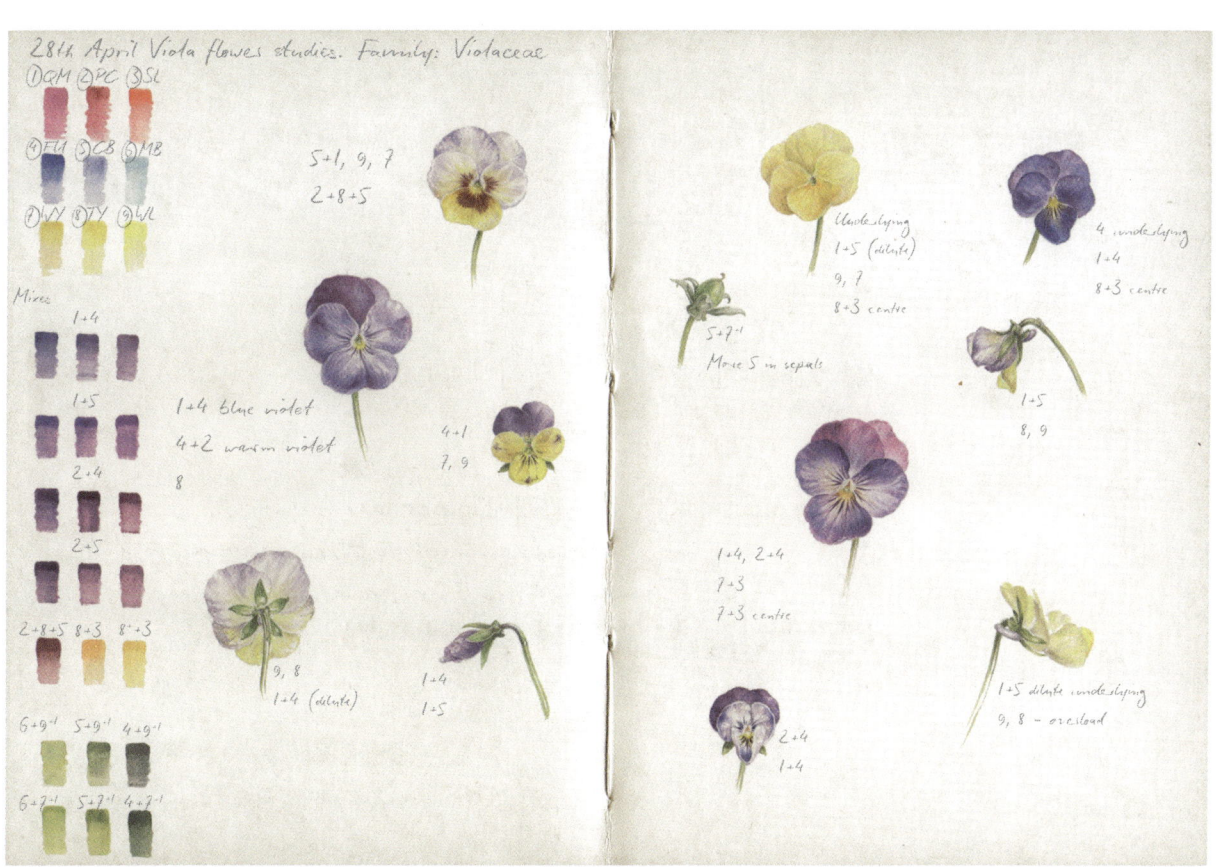

Primula *(Primula vulgaris)*

A view from above

The wild *Primula vulgaris* is often found in woodland and this species is the subject of this sketchbook spread. If you don't have the species, there are also many cultivated varieties of Primroses that are easily obtained from garden centres. Primulas begin flowering early in the year or even in December, and continue to flower for several months, making them relatively easily to source and an abundant source of plant material. The Primula has a low-growing rosette of leaves, with multiple flowers, and makes an excellent subject to illustrate from above.

Having the leaves surrounding the pale flowers makes it easier to paint the flowers against the darker green background because it helps them to stand out. Many low-growing or clump-forming plants can be painted from above and this makes an attractive composition, albeit a slightly more challenging one.

The finished sketchbook spread of Primula vulgaris on the desk, alongside a range of materials and equipment used in the project.

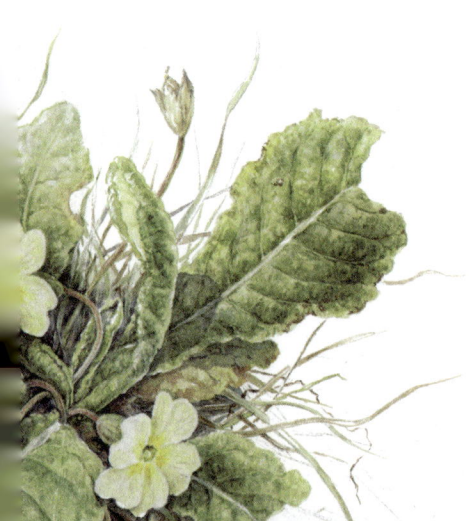

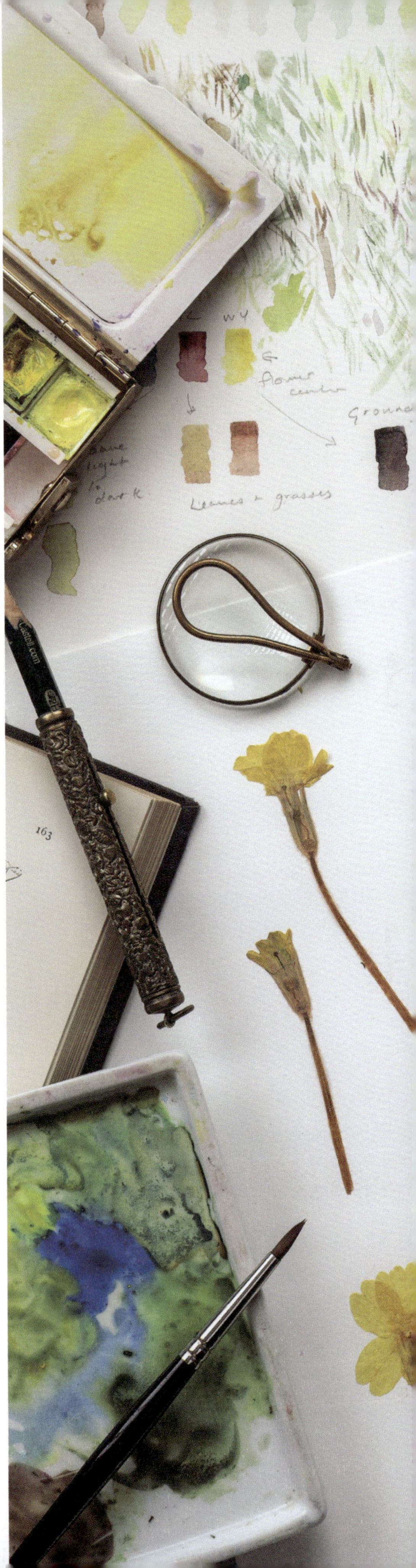

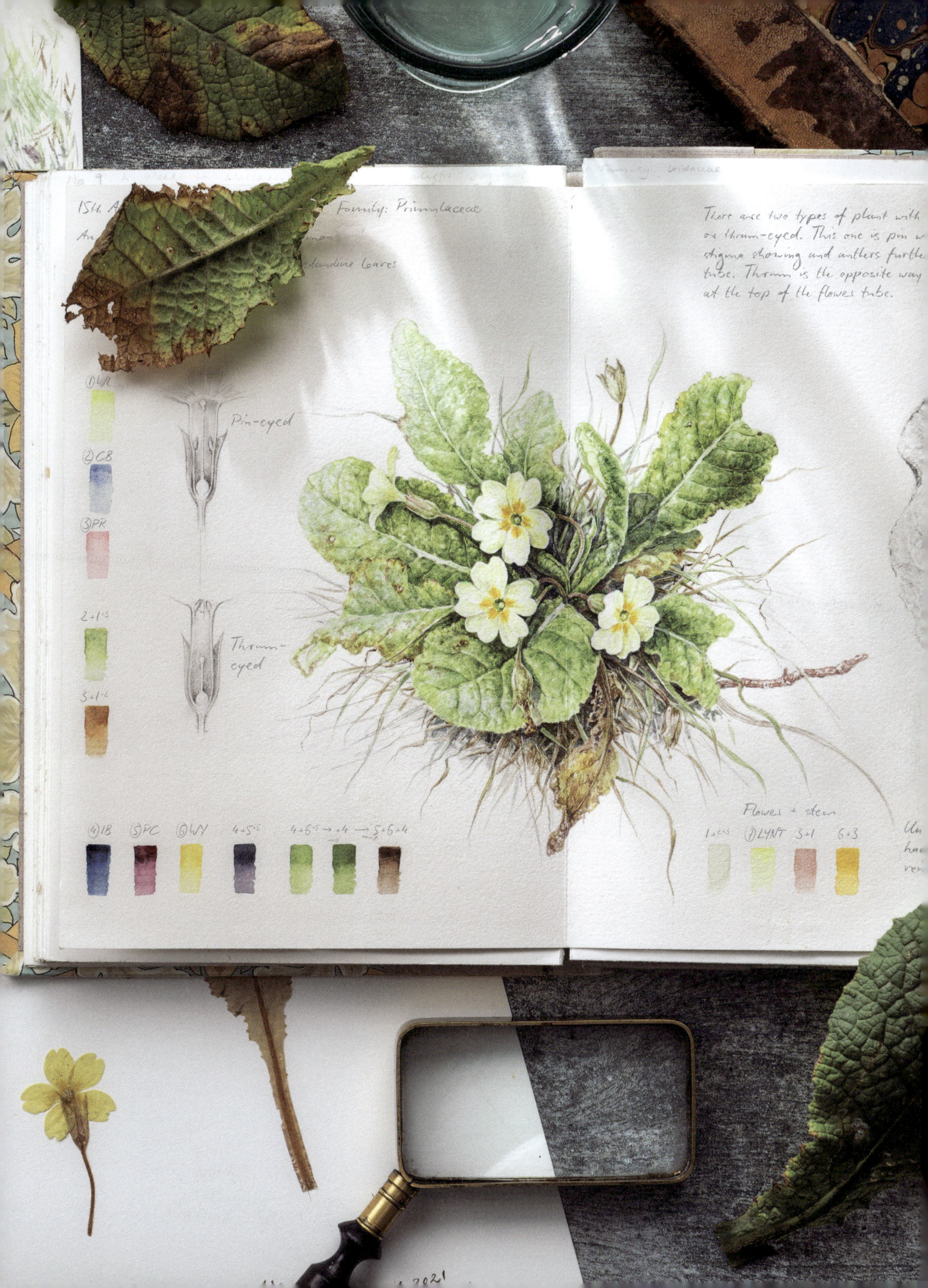

RESEARCH AND OBSERVATION

Primulas are members of the Primulaceae family and *Primula vulgaris* is a low-growing perennial plant with crinkled leaves that are hairy on the underside. Flower stalks are also hairy, with single flowers at the top of the stem. The pale lemon flower has five notched petals with a darker yellow marking at the centre. Interestingly, there are two different forms of flowers found on different plants and these are known as 'pin-' and 'thrum-' eyed flowers. Pin-eyed flowers have a long stigma visible at the opening of the corolla tube, and in thrum-eyed flowers the stigma is short and the anthers are positioned at the opening. This 'arrangement' helps to promote cross-pollination.

COMPOSITION

For this sketch spread, I took the decision to illustrate the whole plant from an aerial viewpoint, with a little of the habitat beneath the plant included too. This approach is well suited to lots of clump-forming plants or those where leaves grow in a rosette-type arrangement near to the ground (known as a basal rosette). The drawing for the plant is quite complex as there are many overlapping leaves and lots of grasses beneath, and the pale flowers sit in the centre of the plant above the leaf rosette.

The drawing will sit in the centre of the double page. Two flower dissections will be added to the left side and a drawing of the leaf underside will be included.

SKETCHING

Begin by making very rough sketches, plotting in the position of all the various parts almost in a schematic style with no detail, instead using angles and shapes. This makes the drawing process much easier as it allows you to make sense of the parts in relation to each other. Think about the leaves emerging from the centre as though they are arranged on a clock face.

Once this is complete, you can refine the drawing. At this point, there is no need to sketch in the grasses as it may confuse the drawing at this stage; it is better to move swiftly to the painting of the Primula in the next step. If the plant has been uplifted from the garden with roots, it may deteriorate, so no time should be wasted; it can be replanted as soon as the painting is complete.

Make a rough schematic drawing using an HB pencil. Mark the overall height and width measurements on the spread to contain the entire subject. Position the subject in the middle of the two pages, leaving sufficient white space above and below the drawing. Next, plot the angles of leaves with the midrib first, and draw the shapes of the various parts as they are positioned.

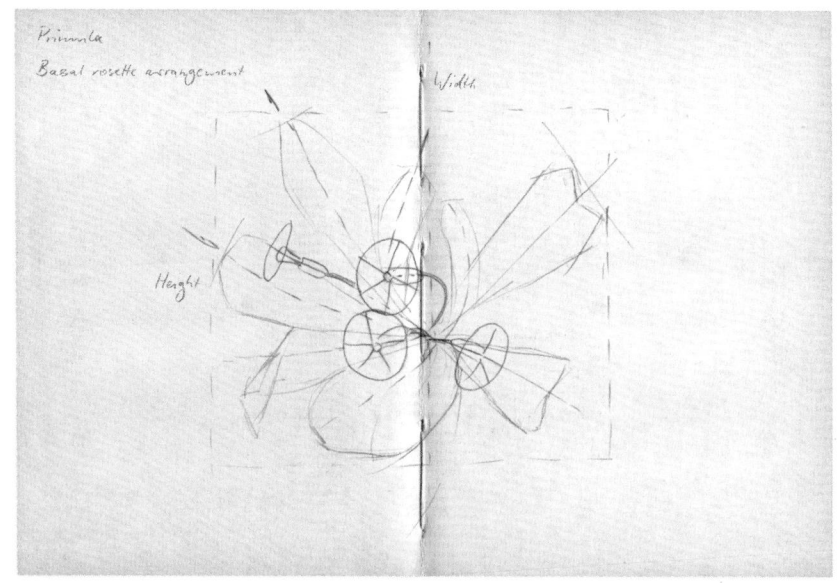

Refine the drawing to include more detail in the flowers by adding the petals. Draw the leaves in more detail with the vein pattern drawn in lightly. Plot the position of the flower dissections and the leaf underside.

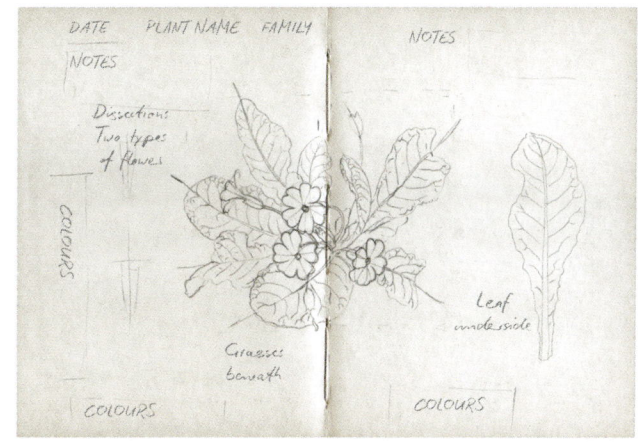

COLOUR

Colours used: Permanent Rose, Permanent Carmine, Lemon Yellow Nickel Titanate, Winsor Yellow, Cobalt Blue, Indanthrene Blue, and a small amount of white gouache.

The remainder of the double-page spread will be completed in graphite, using pencil grades 4H–2H.

PAINTING

To begin the painting, lightly outline the leaves and veins by painting wet-on-dry. This makes it easy to see the flowers and also makes sense of the complicated venation in the leaves. Follow this by adding light washes of blue to indicate highlights on the leaves, after which you can add green to a lightly dampened surface.

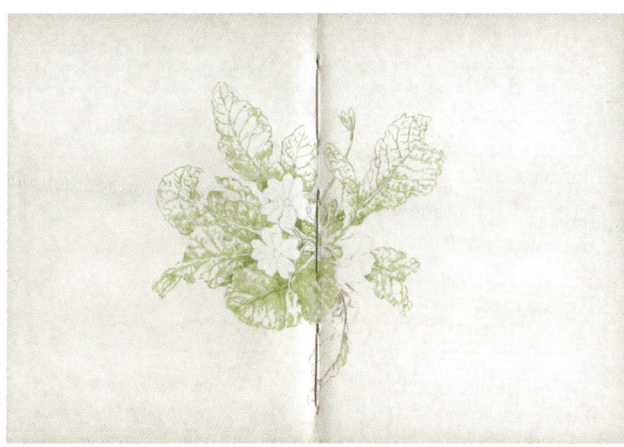

With a pale green mix of Cobalt Blue, Winsor Lemon, and a small amount of Permanent Rose, lightly outline the leaves on dry paper, using a size 2 brush. Use the same three colours to mix the brown colour for the decaying leaves, mixing Permanent Rose and Winsor Lemon first, then adding Cobalt Blue until the colour becomes brown. In some areas, I added a wash of the pale green, which made the pale flowers stand out.

Add a pale wash of Cobalt Blue to the highlighted areas on the leaves and, once dry, add more green to the leaves to build up the colour. Use brown for the leaf blemishes. In the centre of the flowers, add Winsor Lemon to create definition, leaving the stigma the white of the paper.

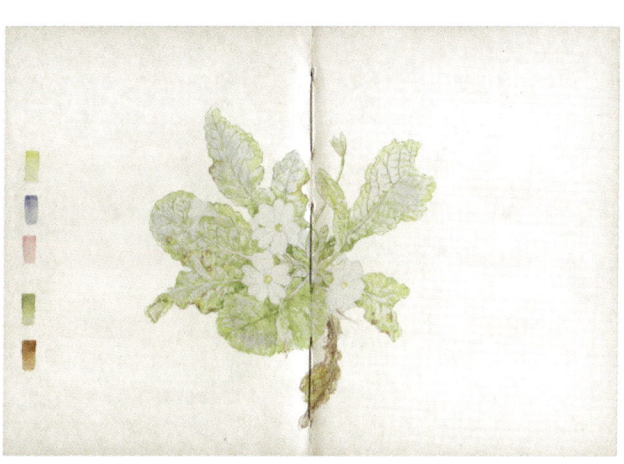

Apply a dark colour onto the dry paper in the negative space between the plant parts at the base of the plant, which will give the painting more depth and create the illusion of the ground beneath. This must be very dark nearest to the centre and should fade out further from the centre. In the faded-out parts, the area should be dampened with clean water to create a soft edge.

Build up the greens and make the leaves into more solid forms while preserving highlights by painting areas selectively. Dampening with clean water first can make this process easier to manage. Add some colour variation to the leaves with yellowing edges and introduce a darker green mix to create depth in the colour; paint all of this into a dampened surface.

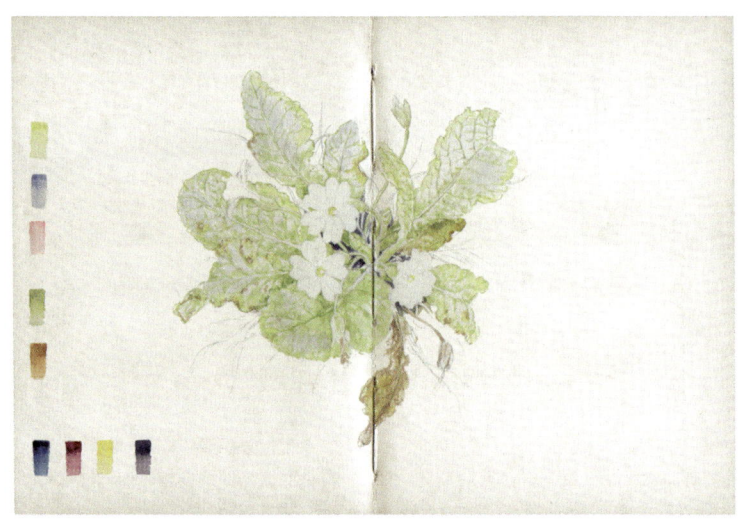

Lightly sketch in a few of the grasses underneath the plant. Next, mix Indanthrene Blue, Permanent Carmine, and a small amount of Winsor Yellow in a creamy consistency to make a very dark blue-purple colour. Begin to paint the negative space between the leaves and flower stems in the centre of the plant.

I intensified the green on the leaves using a second green mix; this time, I used Indanthrene Blue, Winsor Yellow, and a small quantity of Permanent Carmine to create a darker green that was gradually added to the leaves, painting in small sections of the leaf. This approach ensured that the lighter areas were maintained. I added Winsor Lemon to yellowing areas of the leaf and also deepened the aged brown leaves.

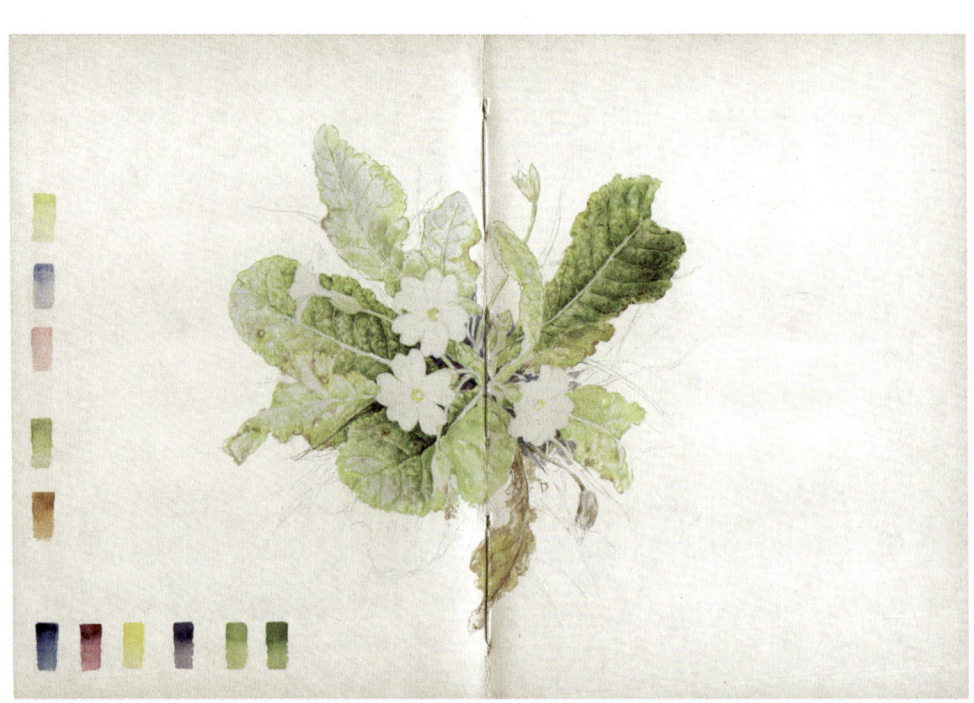

When the greens are well established, it's time to add the flowers with very soft shadows first, which can be painted onto the dry white paper. Once dry, overlay the pale yellow wash. The colour of the Primula can be difficult and often turns dirty-looking if shadow colours are too heavy; or, if too much yellow is added, the colour will be overly bright and not typical of the flower. The yellow is very soft and subtle, and this is why it's best to paint the leaves around the flowers first and to be cautious with adding the flower colour. Remember that it's better to add too little than too much.

Here you can see the colour palette and the saturations of colour, as well as the swatches and scribble sheet where colour is tested before application.

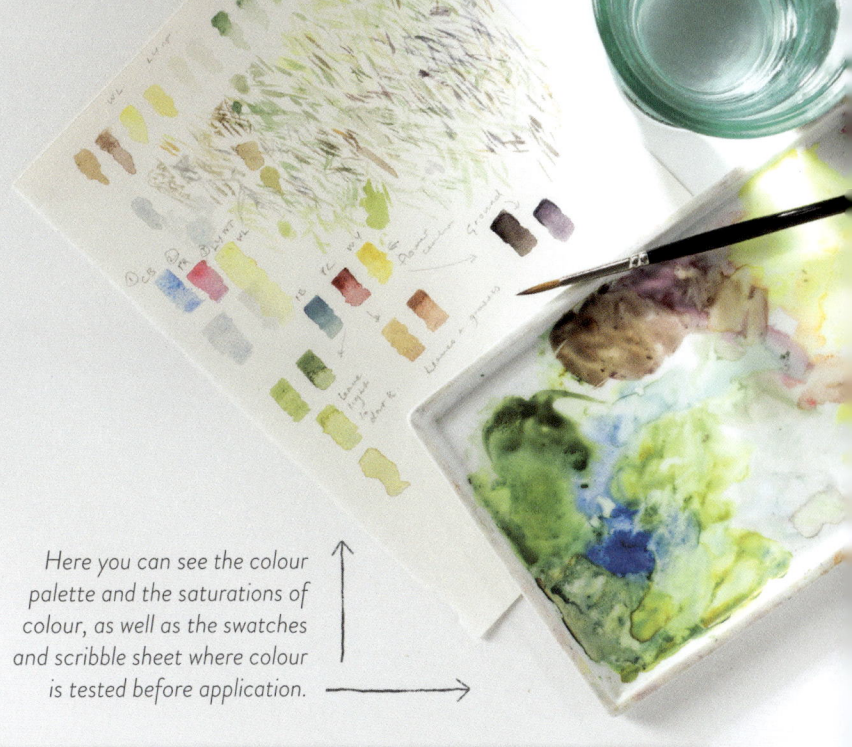

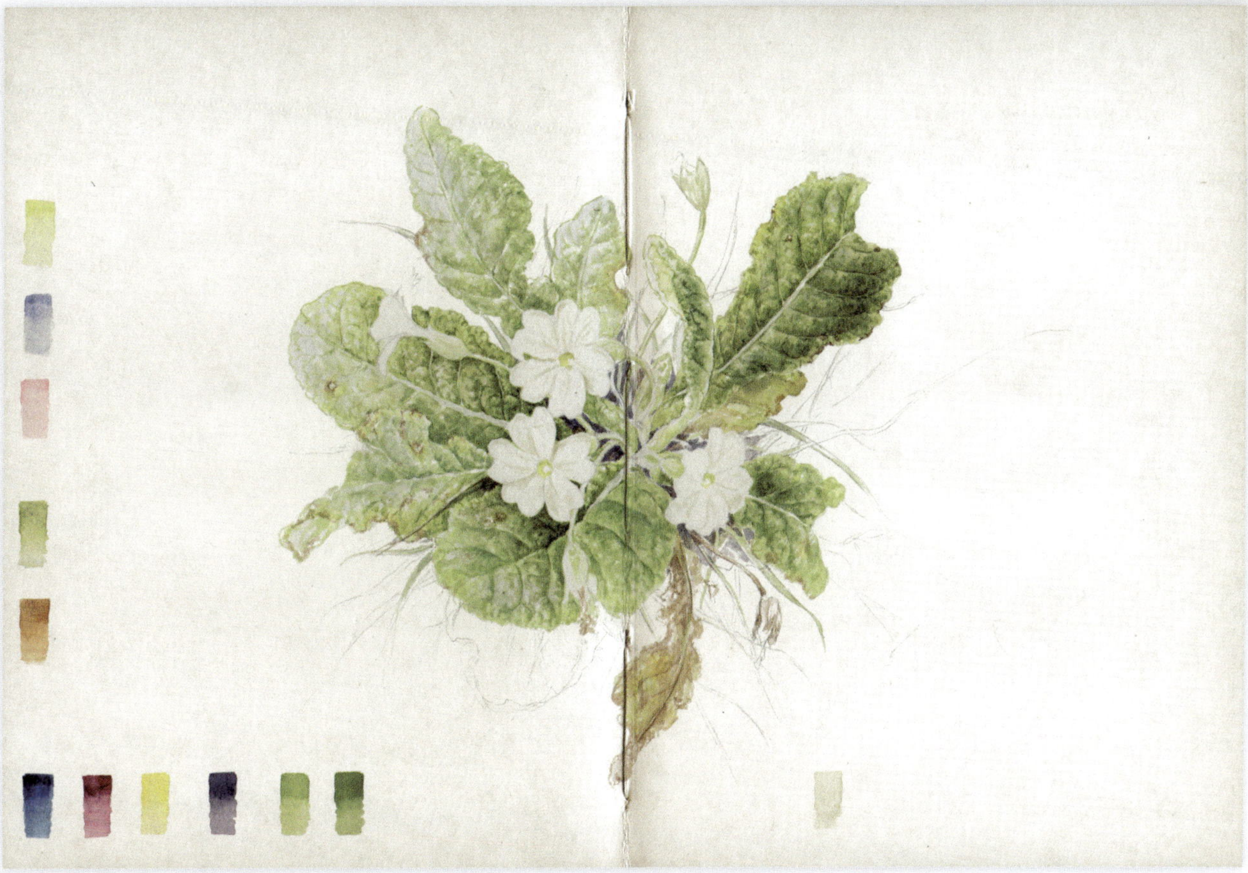

Add a very dilute shadow colour to the palette using a mix of Winsor Lemon, Cobalt Blue, and Permanent Rose. The mix is a pale yellow-biased grey and you can use it as a shadow colour in the flowers, applying it sparingly with a small size 2 brush. Be very cautious with how much is used; I used it mostly for shadows between petal overlaps and the venation and indents. Be sure to carefully observe the light and shade and don't overdo it.

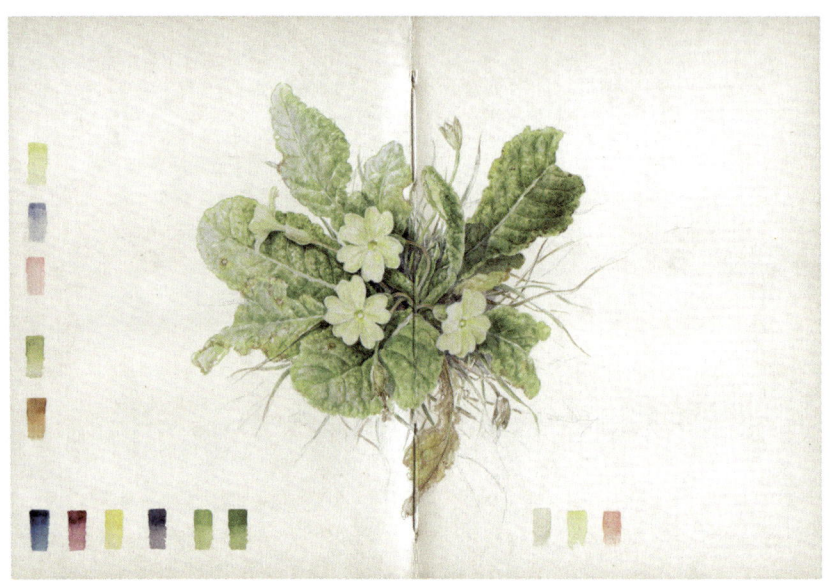

←

Apply pale lemon to the flowers using Lemon Yellow Nickel Titanate in dilute washes, as its softer colour suits the pale petals. Paint over the shadow colour with the yellow, but avoid any highlights, which can be left white; add Winsor Lemon if needed to brighten.

Add greens for the grasses and extend the dark blue negative painting between them. Finish with a pale mix of Permanent Rose and Winsor Lemon on the flower stems.

Extend the grasses beneath the plant to create a naturalistic-looking habitat with darker shadows between the grasses.

In the final stages, finish off all parts. Add the darker yellow centre markings to the flowers. Deepen the colour in the leaves and intensify blemishes by drawing with a dry brush into lightly dampened areas. Further intensify the darks in the negative space and add small white hairs to the stems with white gouache, using a size 1 brush, to finish the painting.

→

Intensify the colour all over to finish the flower, and add the darker yellow markings near to the centre using Winsor Yellow mixed with Permanent Rose. Darken the flower centre with green and add some pale Winsor Lemon to the stigma. Add detail to the grasses as they extend beneath the flower. I drew the flower dissections on as outline drawings, enlarged x1.5. I also added the underside of the leaf as an outline.

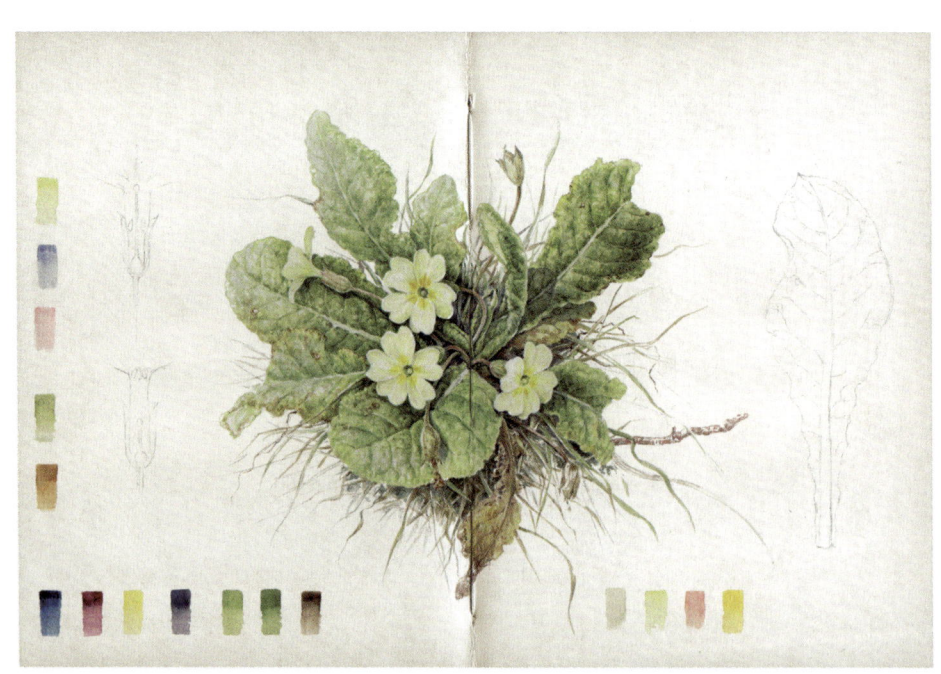

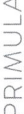

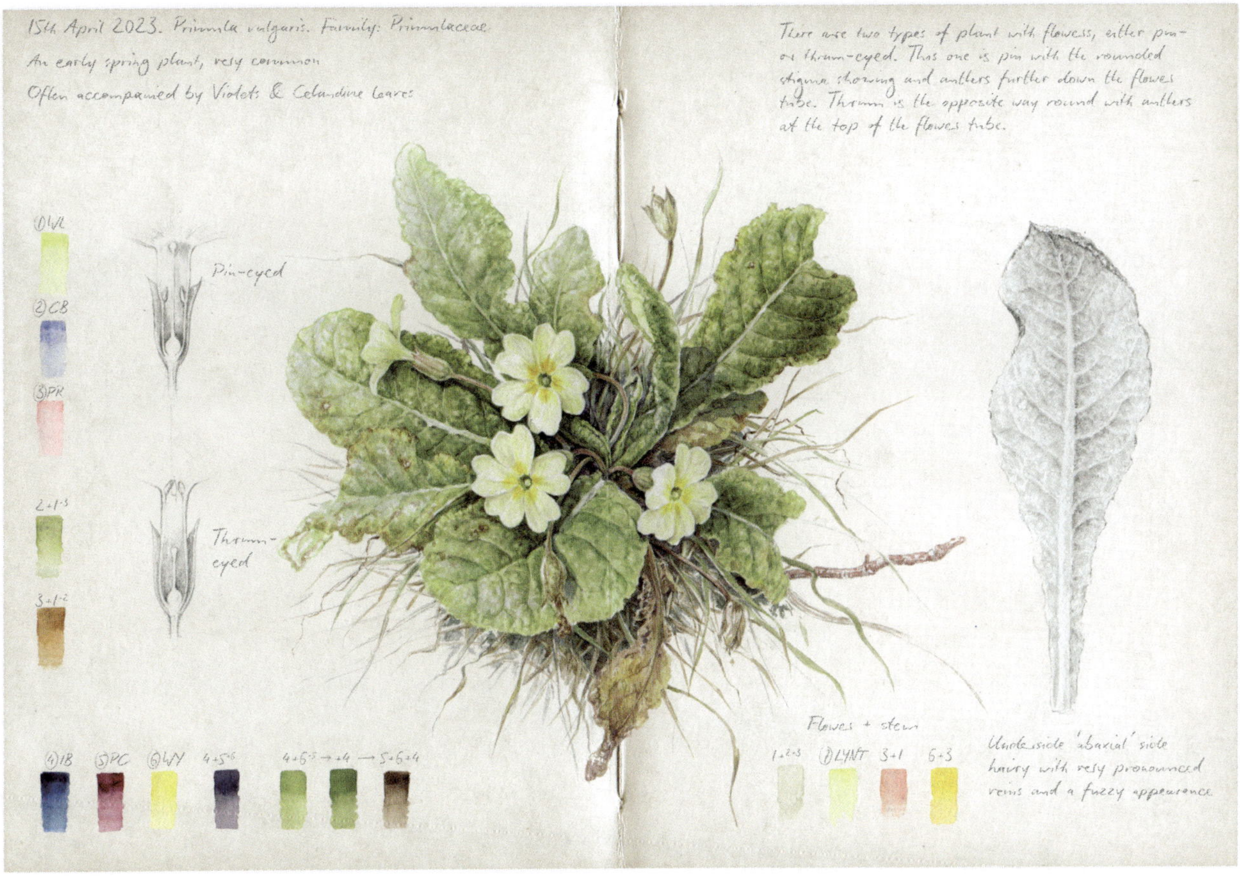

I rendered the flower dissections using graphite with 4H and 2H pencils and continuous tone shading. To complete the page, I rendered the underside of the leaf using a scumble and small hatching technique with the same pencils, and added more notes about the plant.

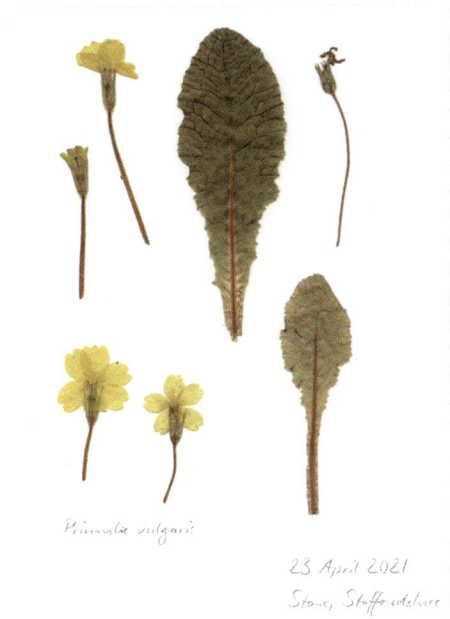

You can also press and dry the plant parts, which can then be either added to the sketchbook or kept separately.

A Collection of Found Objects

This sketchbook spread is somewhat different than others in the book because it is a collection of natural objects rather than a study of one subject. This type of spread was explored earlier with the Viola flowers, and there are many different options for collections of subjects. The collection makes a good spread for beginners because each subject is small and manageable. Subjects can be added gradually on an individual basis, or planned as a whole composition in advance. In this step-by-step project, the latter approach is used.

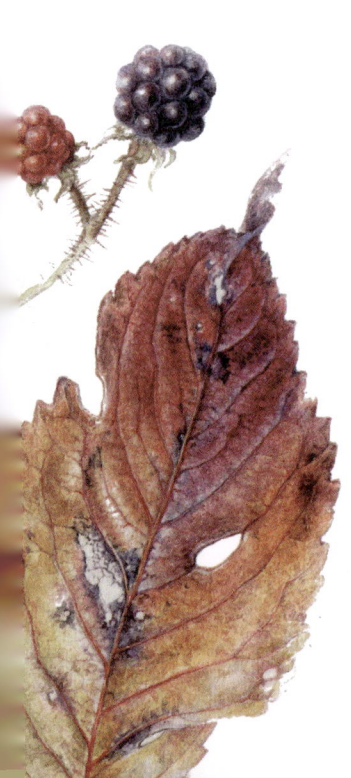

A finished collection on my desk, surrounded with materials, equipment, and some of the subjects.

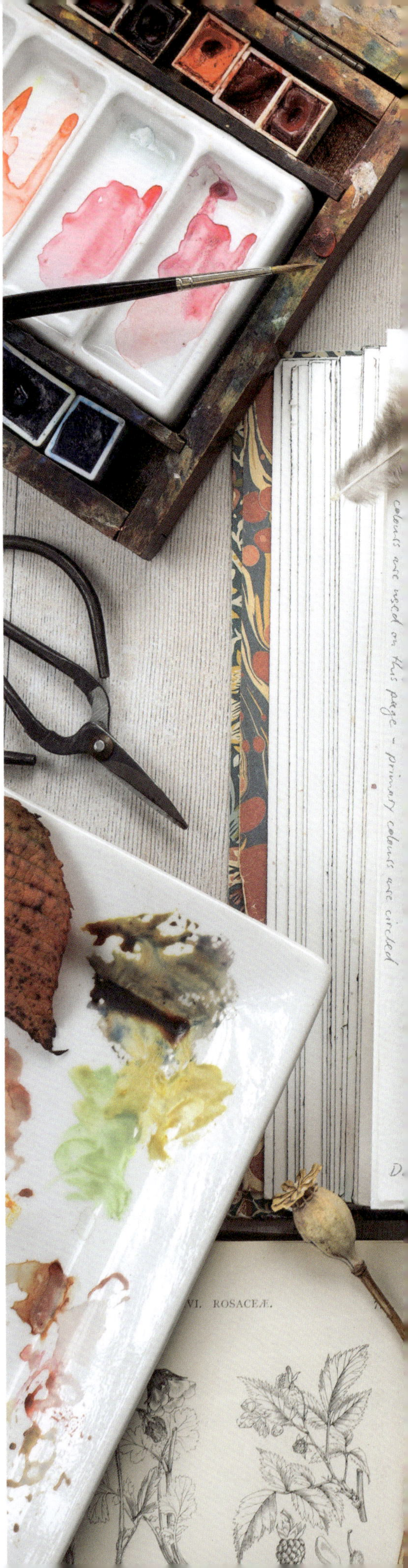

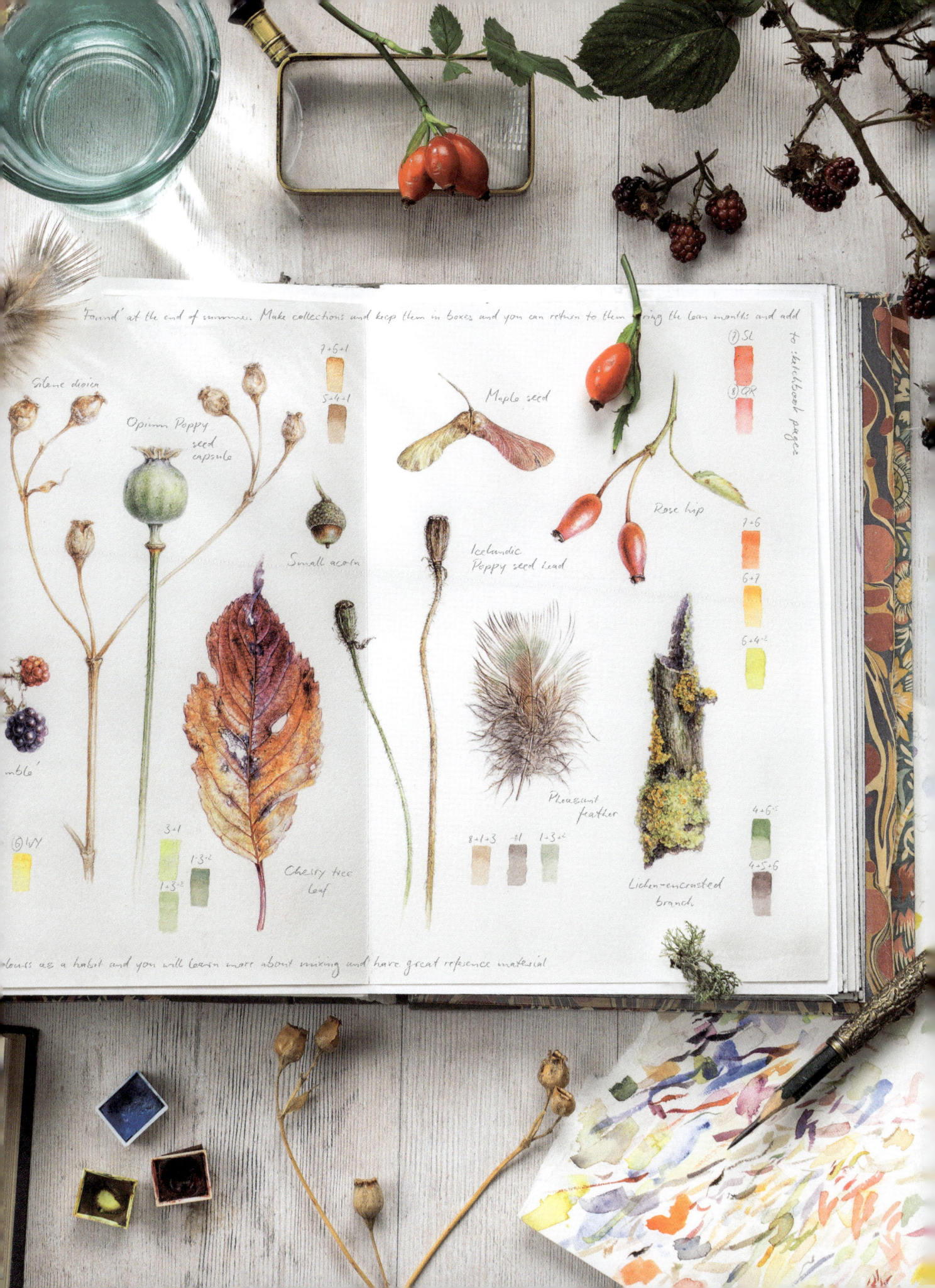

'Found' at the end of summer. Make collections and keep them in boxes and you can return to them during the lean months and add

to sketchbook pages

Silene dioica

Opium Poppy
seed
capsule

7+6+1

5+4+1

Maple seed

⑦ SL

⑧ QR

Small acorn

Icelandic
Poppy seed head

Rose hip

1+6

6+7

6+4+?

3+1

1+3+?

1+3+?

Cherry tree
leaf

Pheasant
feather

Lichen-encrusted
branch

4+6+?

4+5+6

mble'

⑥ IVY

8+1+3

⑦1

1+3+?

colours as a habit and you will learn more about mixing and have great reference material

COMPOSITION

The first stage is to look at what subjects you may want to include on the spread. It's a good idea to lay the elements on a sheet of paper or table top, to explore which arrangement works. Take photographs to see what looks best, as viewing a photograph can really help to spot the things that don't look right. Think about the size and shape of the individual components as well as the colour balance. For example, if there are red subjects, such as small fruits, they will be a dominant colour and will need to be balanced on the spread with other strongly coloured subjects.

Natural objects can be collected and stored in boxes for such studies. These can be botanical or other nature-based subjects that complement botanical work, such as feathers, insects, or shells. Botanical subjects include dried seed capsules; other elements can be picked fresh, such as small autumnal fruits and leaves, and lichens.

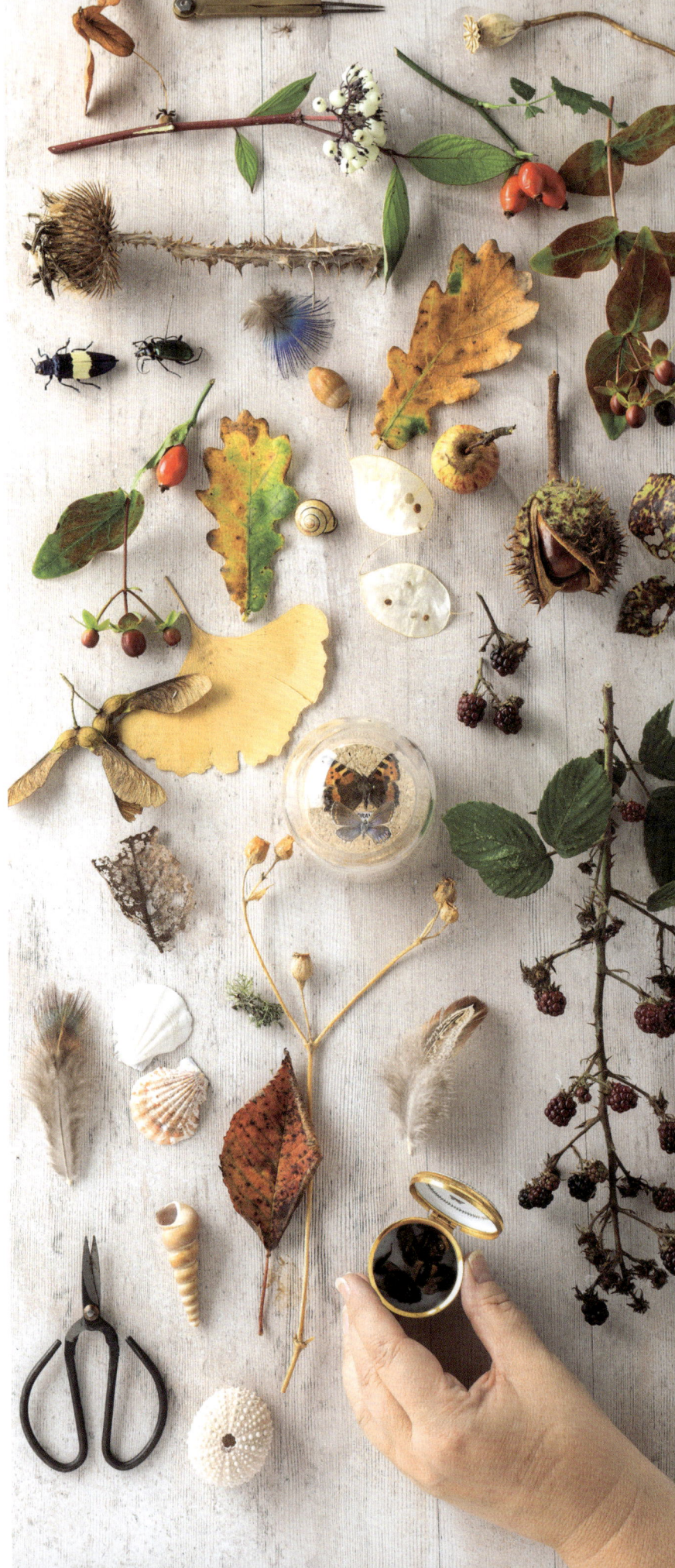

In this example, the rose hips are balanced with the brightly coloured leaf and red fruit on the blackberries at the other side of the pages. Similarly, a dark woody subject placed at the top of the page on its own would not look right, but when placed at the bottom of the page opposite a dark blackberry, the spread becomes more balanced when viewed from a distance. It is better to add the heavier weight of colour at the bottom of the page to anchor it.

If you don't feel comfortable drawing directly in your book, you can play around sketching the individual subjects first and also play around on tracing paper first to work out the best options. This allows some freedom to change things before committing to a composition in your sketchbook.

You will need to carefully consider the space between the subjects. Objects need to be placed in an arrangement that balances on the spread. The negative space between subjects should be comfortable, neither too close nor too far apart. Check with photographs, as this records each arrangement and facilitates many different options. You can then recreate the arrangement that works for the final drawing.

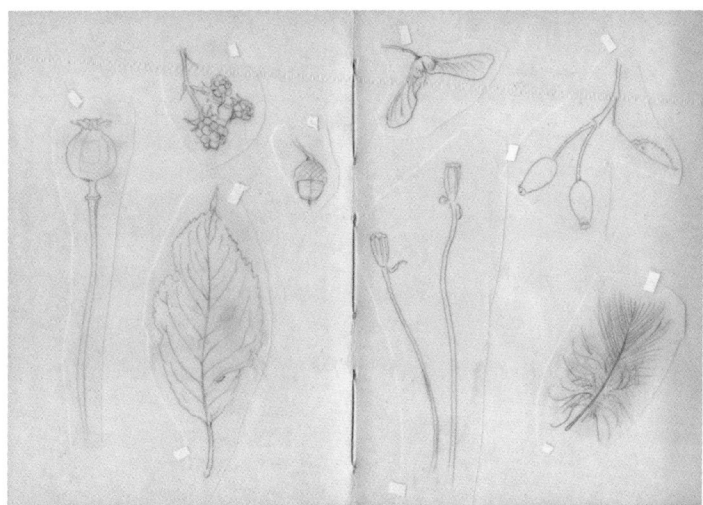

I sketched a possible arrangement of subjects onto tracing paper. In this case, it initially looked slightly sparse so I added more subjects to fill the spread, taking into consideration the space between subjects and the space to the outer edge of the spread. Remember that the spread should be well balanced.

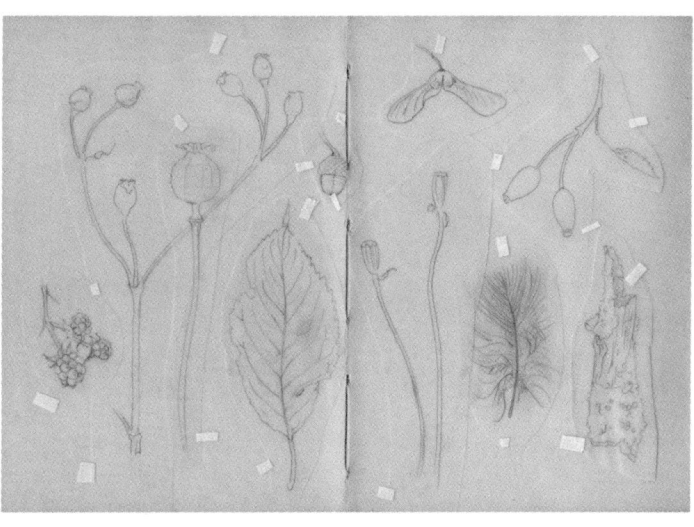

PAINTING

You can now lightly outline the subjects in watercolour directly onto dry paper with a colour that will easily blend in with what will be the final colour. Violets and blues can work for many subjects, and if the painted outline is pale enough, spot colour can be added where there is underlying colour, such as in the yellow on the hips. Once this outline is complete, begin work on individual subjects; I worked on several at a time. Most of the subjects will last for a long time so there is no rush.

I suggest making colour swatches for each subject on a separate page as you progress; otherwise there may be far too many colour swatches on the spread, in which case the pages will quickly become cluttered and disorganized with so many subjects. Once you have decided on the colours, you can add them to the spread for reference.

I decided to paint the first light layers of colours on all subjects to establish a base and get a feel for how the finished spread might look. This also gave me the opportunity to work out the colours for everything on my separate sheet. This doesn't mean you can't add more colours as each subject develops.

Choose a colour for each subject if needed. I adjusted the violet colour from a pink-biased violet to a blue-biased violet and added a touch of Winsor Lemon on the brown and red subjects.

Keep your subjects in the same position on a separate sheet and have a lamp on them to ensure that the light is consistent across the spread. This is important because if light comes from the left on one subject and the right on another, the spread will look very disjointed and will lack consistency. Having a lamp positioned on the subject also creates good highlight and shadows on each individual subject, and it is important to establish this form at the early stages of the painting.

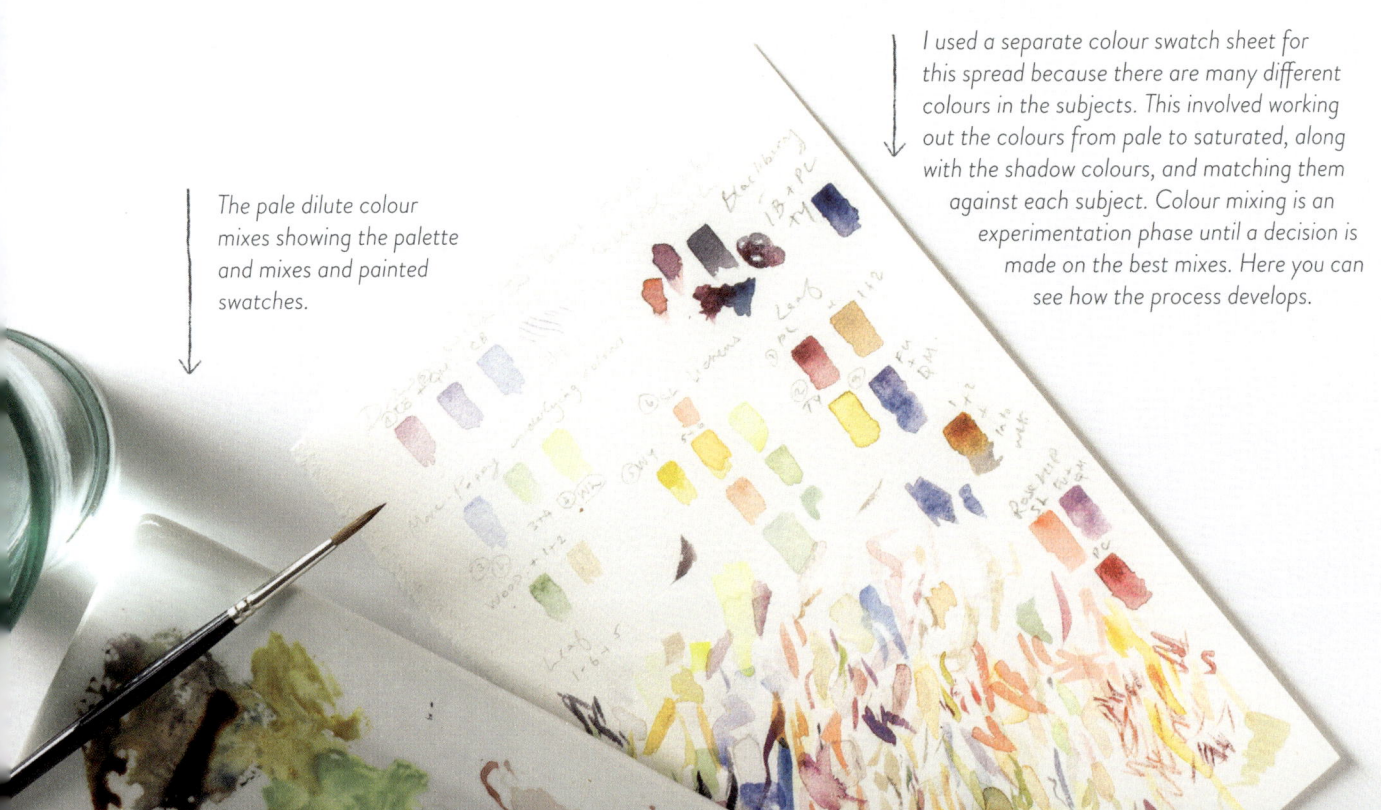

The pale dilute colour mixes showing the palette and mixes and painted swatches.

I used a separate colour swatch sheet for this spread because there are many different colours in the subjects. This involved working out the colours from pale to saturated, along with the shadow colours, and matching them against each subject. Colour mixing is an experimentation phase until a decision is made on the best mixes. Here you can see how the process develops.

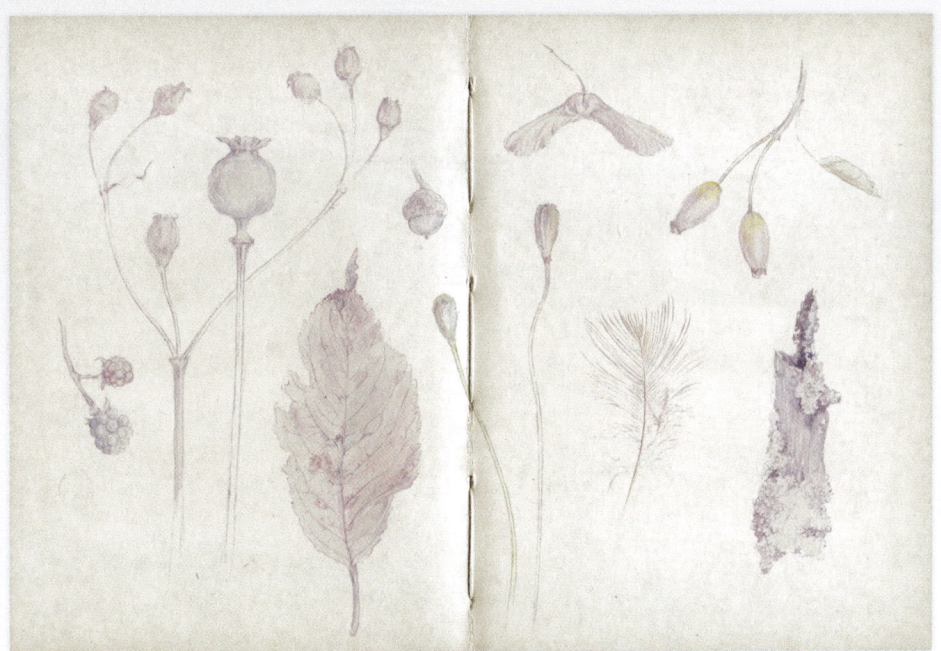

Make an outline painting of the subjects using a warm violet mix of Quinacridone Magenta and Cobalt Blue. This outline should be very pale, which means that the paint is dilute enough to merge with the painting.

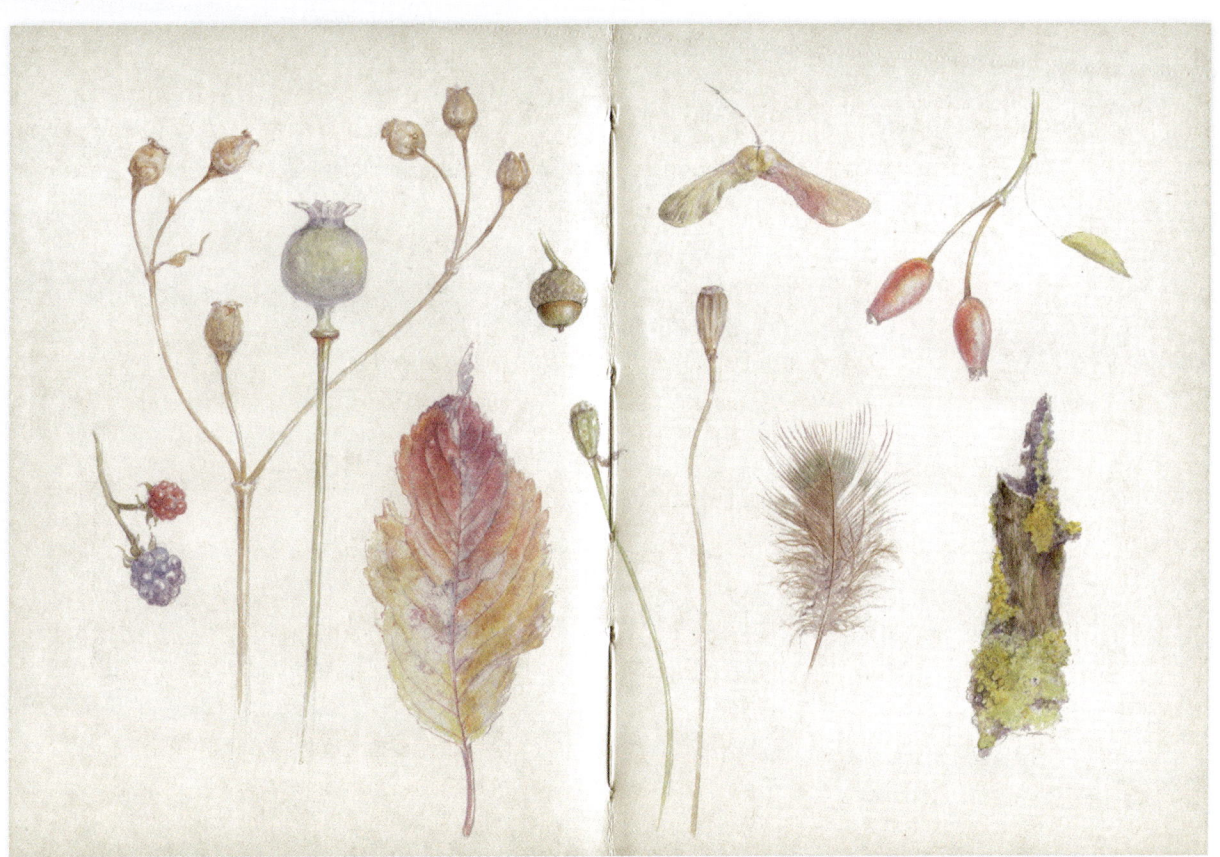

In this next stage, lightly add to the colours with additional layers in areas that are lightly dampened with clean water. I painted all subjects one at a time, using the colour reference on the separate colour swatch sheet. No subject is painted to a finished level, otherwise the spread could end up unbalanced.

The first layers should have established a good base for all of the subjects and you can begin to increase the saturation on individual subjects next. Here you can again work one at a time but can also move between them, which can help keep your interest from waning.

For example, I painted some detail in the lichen-encrusted branch but also intensified the colour of the yellow lichen; also, on the rose hips, I increased the saturation by painting into a lightly dampened surface with bright reds. I added a rich brown to the acorn, intensified the colour on the autumnal leaf, and added a glaucous green to the Poppy seed head. This stage is very much about establishing more saturated colours. Add the swatches of these colours to the spread so that you don't forget what you did at each stage.

Increase the saturation on most parts of the elements. Again, this is about balance of colour, although some subjects are naturally more dominant than others, such as the reds and dark colours. However, the composition planning stage should mean that this balance is to some extent dealt with earlier.

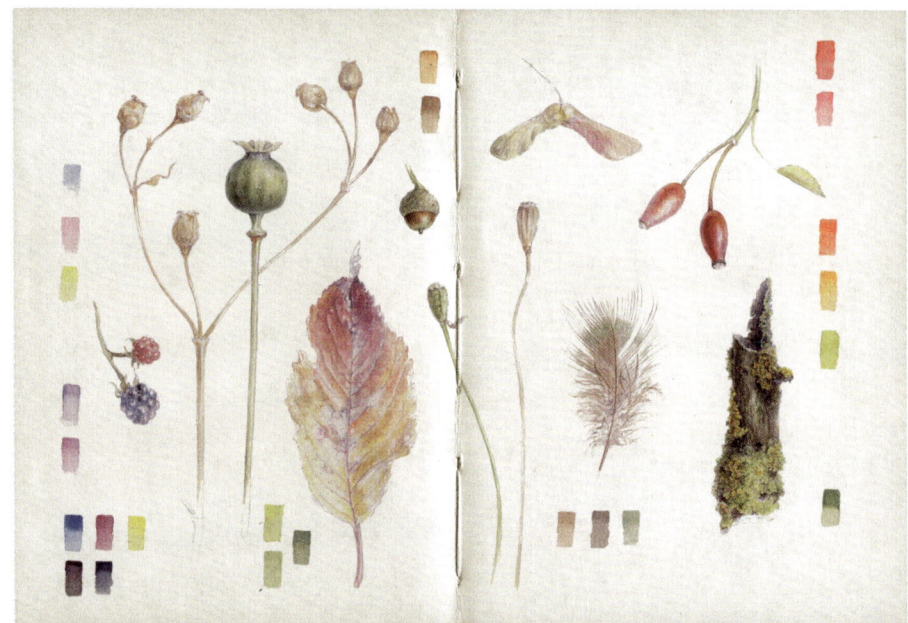

In the final stage, increase the form, colour, and detail. In subjects such as the veins in the maple seed, paint very fine veins onto the dry surface with a small size 1 or 2 brush; there is little point in using a smaller brush as it won't hold enough paint and smooth lines are very difficult to achieve with such small brushes.

There is a lot of fine detail in this particular stage and you will find that the process slows. Add feathery parts with soft, tapering, fine, dry strokes; draw small networks of veins with the paintbrush on the leaf; draw the pattern on the cap of the acorn and draw the fine hairs on the poppies with the tip of the brush. You can apply all of these with a very fine drawing brush technique. It takes time to achieve the small details, which make all the difference to the final outcome. Take a close look at the final painting to see what detail I added.

Lastly, add the names of the subjects, the final colour notes, and notes detailing other information to complete the spread. You could also use the border of the spread to write around.

I highly recommend this type of collection-style page, especially if you feel slightly stuck in a rut or can't settle on a larger subject to paint. You can paint a collection of anything you like – seed pods, leaves, petals, flowers, or, like this spread, a mixture of found objects.

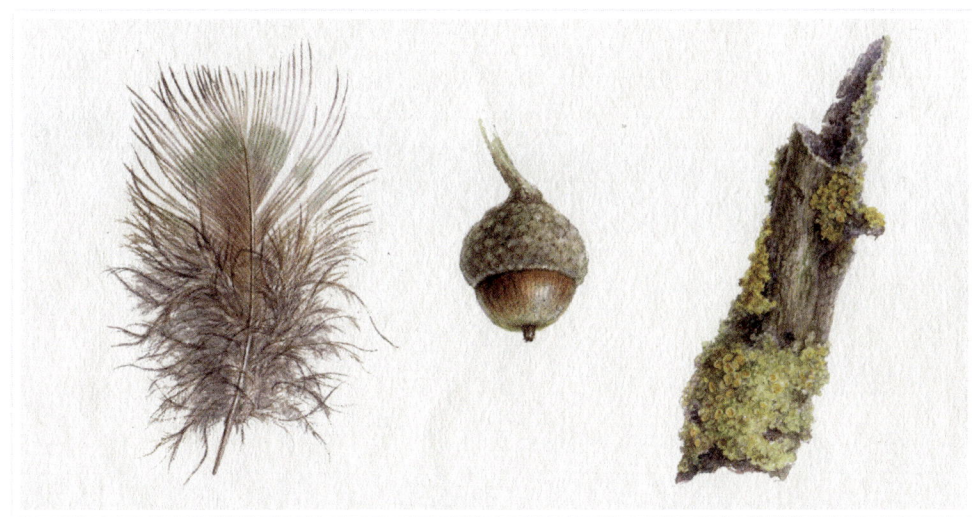

In these close-up images, you can see the fine detailed brush work in the final stages of the pages. I painted this detail with a small size 1 or 2 brush to create fine lines.

Complete the pages by increasing the colour saturations and detail across the whole two-page spread. Thereafter, complete the remaining colour notes and add the names of plants and other relevant information. Due to lack of space, I chose to write the additional notes around the edge of the spread.

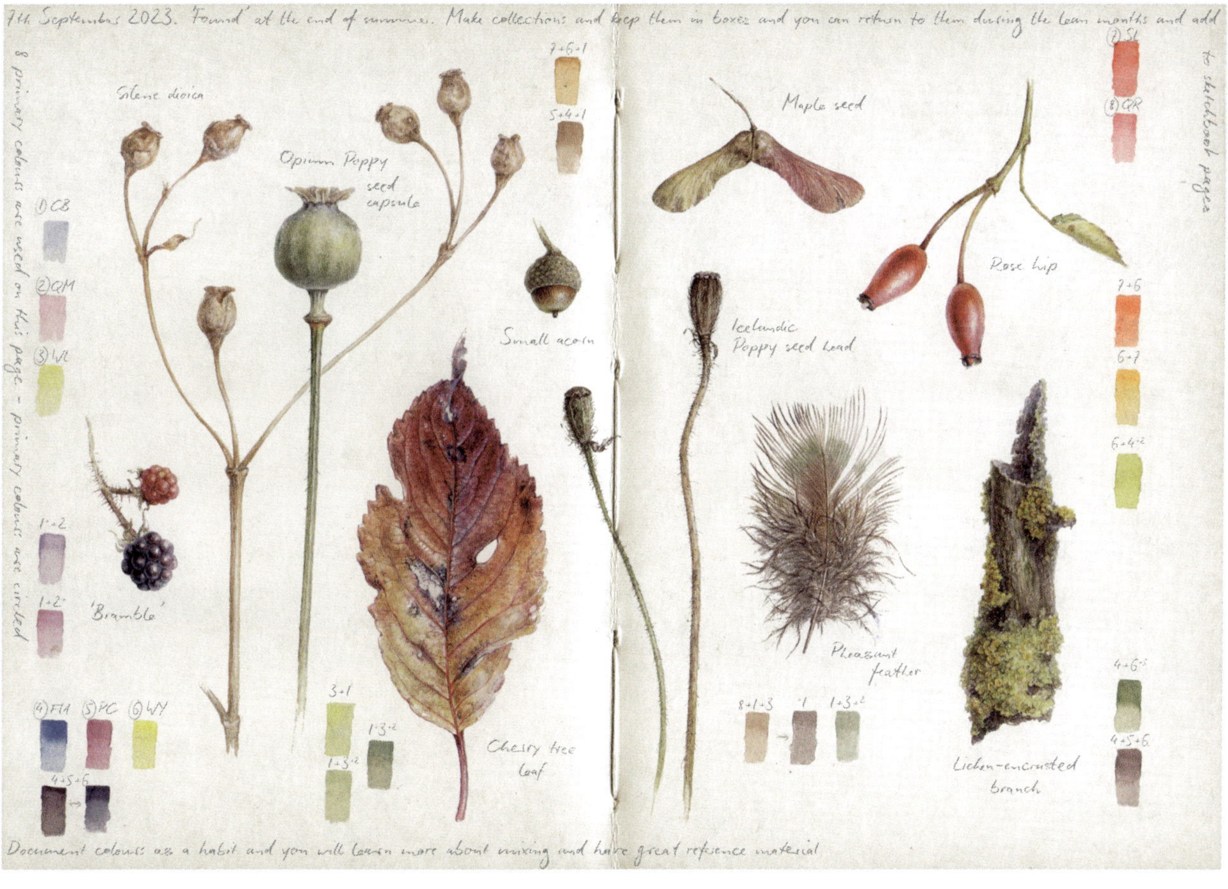

7th September 2023. 'Found' at the end of summer. Make collections and keep them in boxes and you can return to them during the lean months and add

Silene dioica

Opium Poppy seed capsule

Small acorn

'Bramble'

Cherry tree leaf

Maple seed

Rose hip

Icelandic Poppy seed head

Pheasant feather

Lichen-encrusted branch

8 primary colours are used on this page — primary colours are circled

Document colours as a habit and you will learn more about mixing and have great reference material

Lupin *(Lupinus hybrid)*

Tall plants using a large leaf background

Tall plants such as the Lupin can present the sketchbook artist with quite a few challenges. You might think that it's not possible to illustrate such large plants on the relatively small pages without greatly reducing the drawing. However, it is perfectly possible and is a case of figuring out and organizing the plant into its parts, which can be overlaid using different strategies.

A Lupin is illustrated in such a way in this project, and part of the process is to use a drawing of a large leaf in the background. In addition, the various stages of the flower are included and quite a few approaches are used to deal with illustrating a larger plant and overlaying parts.

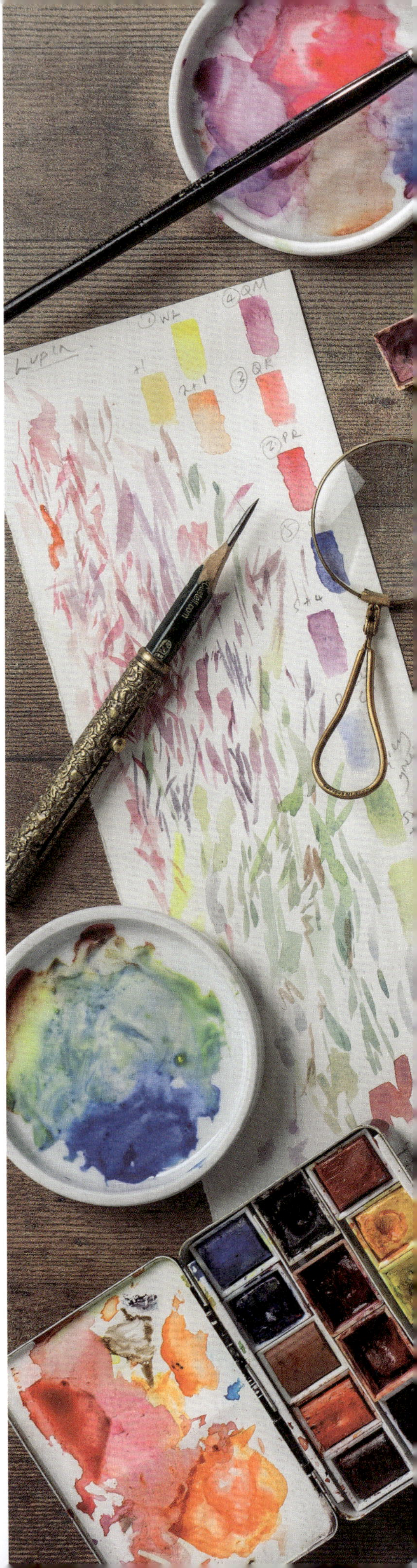

Finished sketchbook page of the Lupin with materials and reference photographs.

→

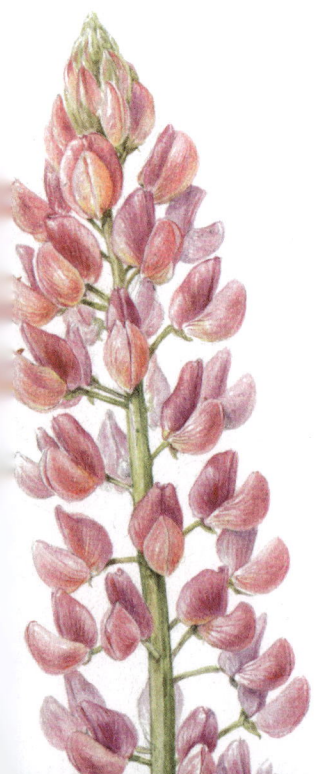

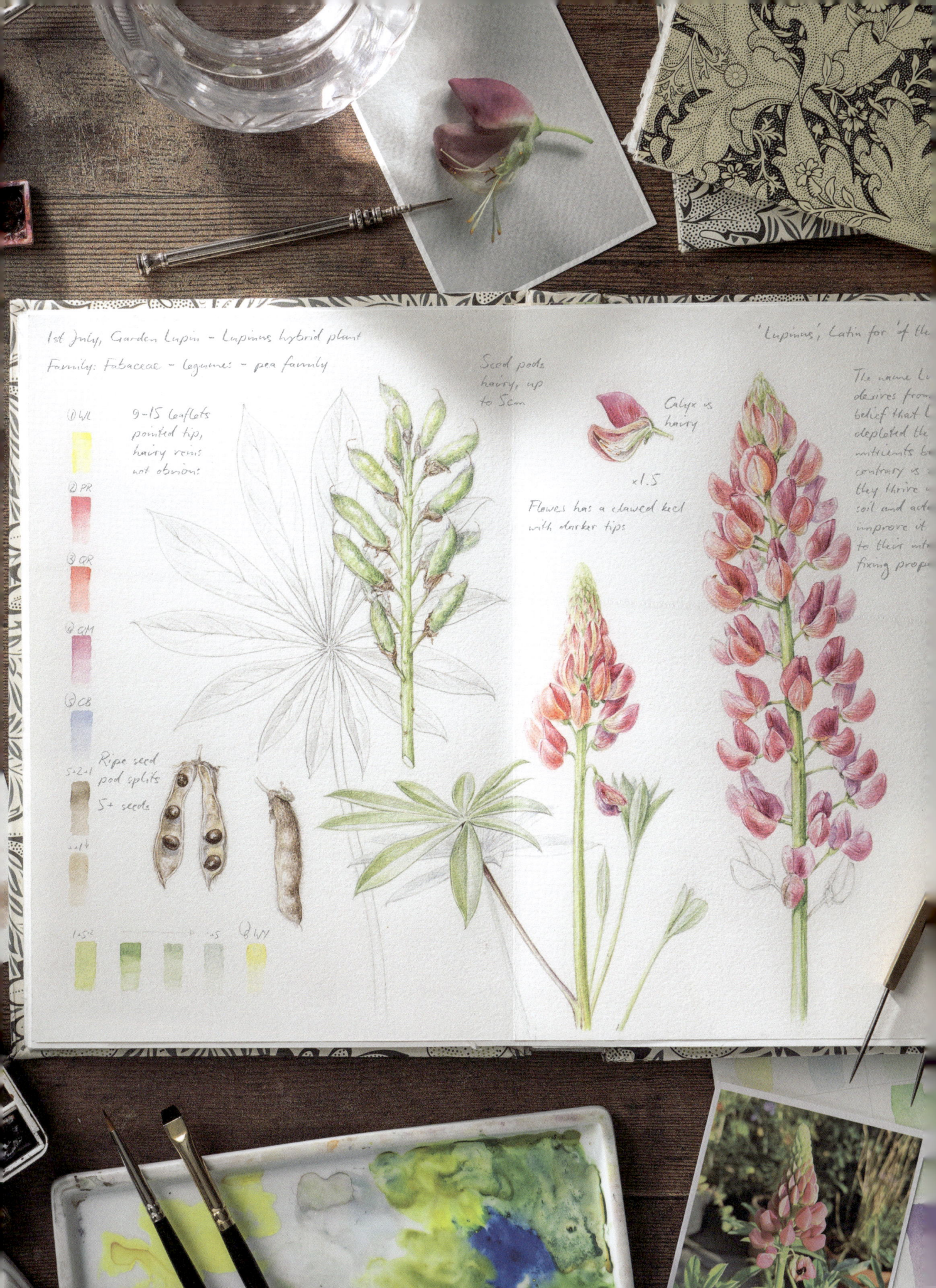

1st July, Garden Lupin - Lupinus hybrid plant
Family: Fabaceae - legume - pea family

'Lupinus', Latin for 'of the

① WL

② PR

③ QR

④ QM

⑤ CB

9-15 leaflets
pointed tip,
hairy veins
not obvious

Seed pods
hairy, up
to 5cm

Calyx is
hairy

x1.5

Flower has a clawed keel
with darker tips

The name L
derives from
belief that l
depleted the
nutrients be
contrary is
they thrive
soil and act
improve it
to their ni
fixing prop

5+2+1

Ripe seed
pod splits
5+ seeds

1+b

1+5+2   +5   ⑥ WY

RESEARCH AND OBSERVATION

Lupins are members of the Fabaceae or Pea family and have a characteristic fruit, which are legumes or pods that split open to release seeds. They also have bilateral flowers with five petals. Leaves on this Lupin are palmately compound (i.e. palm-like with several leaflets on a single stem).

COMPOSITION

The first stage is to make a rough layout planning the drawing. I began with the tall flower spikes, in which the flowers spiral around the stem. Make a very rough drawing, initially using the various parts of the plant and the shapes within it. Begin with a mature flower spike and a second spike that is just coming into flower, with leaves. In addition, there is a stem that has developing fruits and a large leaf.

This type of drawing doesn't take very long, perhaps 15–20 minutes at most, because there is no detail in the drawing, but it is incredibly useful in planning the page. It is advisable to try a few different arrangements before deciding on the final composition. Using overlaps will be necessary and so place the large leaf behind the stem with the developing fruit capsules.

SKETCHING

Thereafter, refine the drawing on the spread, with a lightweight pencil line of the two flower spikes first. From your initial sketch, you should already know where the other parts might fit on the spread.

COLOURS

The flowers are bright pink but vary in colour; from the top and at the bud stage they are pale green; further down there is a bright, warm pink with a cooler pink on the upper banner petal. As flowers age, the colour becomes cooler, almost purple.

The leaves are pale to mid-green and hairy on the underside, which adds a silvery appearance on the edges.

Colours used: Winsor Lemon, Winsor Yellow, Permanent Rose, Quinacridone Magenta, and Cobalt Blue.

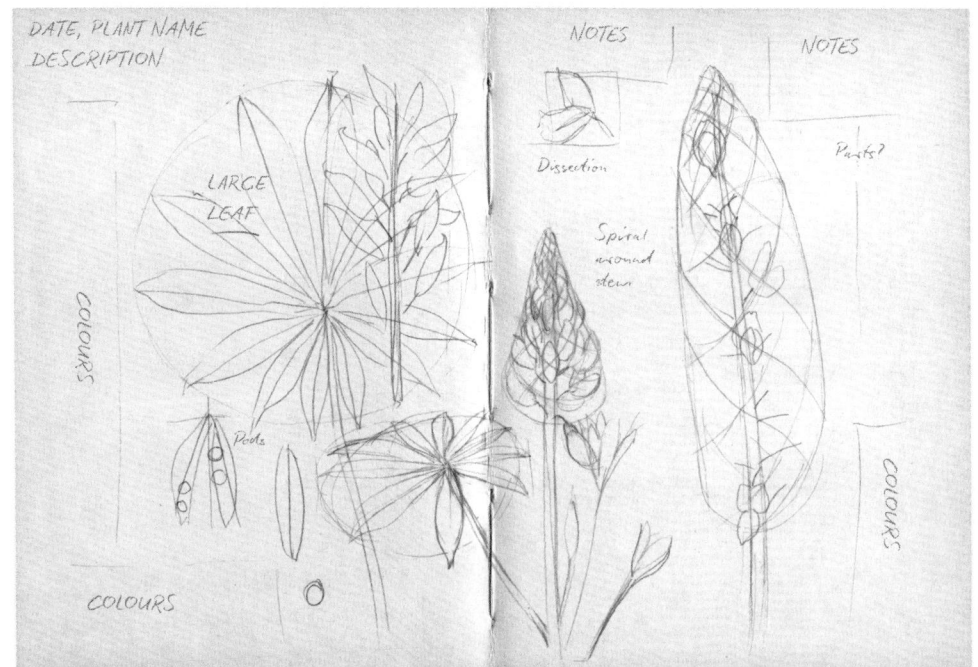

Draw a rough composition using an HB pencil. Use basic shapes and angles within the plant to construct the drawing and the arrangement of the parts in order to fit them on the spread.

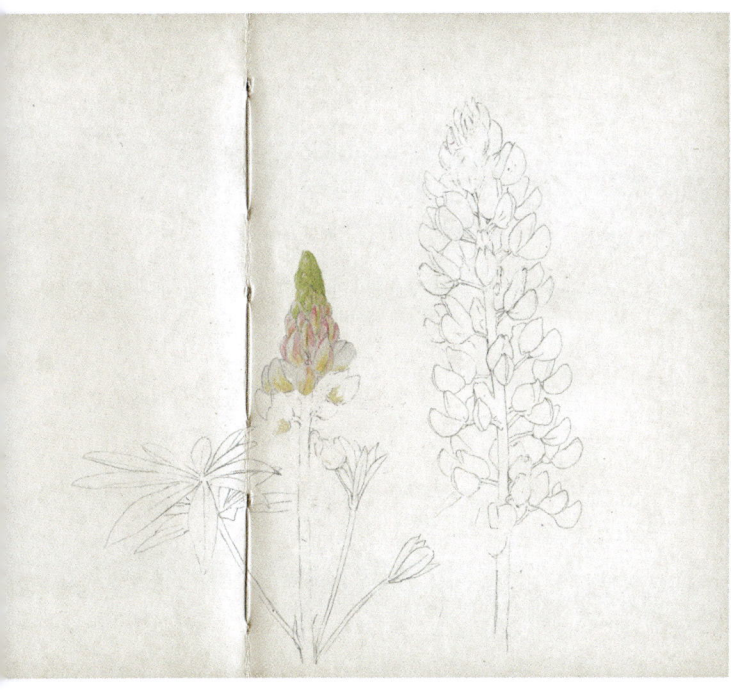

PAINTING

Next, start to work on the flower colours because the flowers are the first to fade and time is of the essence when working on plants. You can use a combination of several reds but first underlying yellows on the near and upper flowers; add greens at the top of the flower spike and yellows to establish the bright flower colour by underlying the pinks. Towards the base, the mature flower spike flowers are cooler in colour as they fade with age.

The effect of adding yellow underneath the pink creates a brightness of colour that couldn't be achieved otherwise. This is the effect of optical mixing, which is the strategy of overlaying one colour over another to create a third colour. This type of overlaying has a different outcome compared to mixing the same two colours.

Using a size 4 brush, add Winsor Lemon directly to the paper on the upper and nearest flowers. At the top of the flower spike, add a pale yellow-biased green colour using Winsor Lemon mixed with Cobalt Blue, plus a tiny amount of Permanent Rose to make a more neutral colour (but being careful not to add too much of the red).

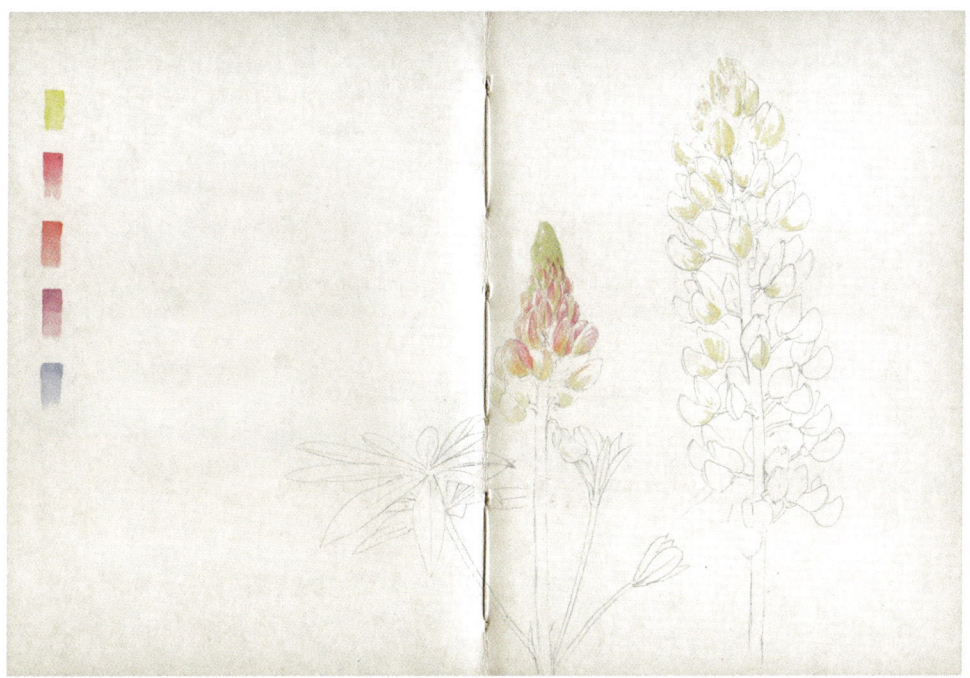

Add Winsor Lemon on the lower parts of most of the upper flowers, particularly those nearest to the front of the stems, as nearer parts will be the most saturated or brightest in colour.

Add the reds or pinks on top of the initial yellows but only on certain parts of the plant where the flowers are brighter – this is usually the parts that are nearest to view; those that are further away can be less saturated and paler.

Add greens to the stem and the flower stalks (pedicels), which helps to visually clarify the flower spikes. Paint the leaves with a dilute blue, keeping the rear one pale to create distance. Next, add green to the nearer leaves,

taking care to always observe the light and shade falling on the leaf. Again, this use of more saturated colour in the nearer part and less saturated in the distance creates depth and separation between those parts. This is the aerial perspective technique and can be used very effectively in sketchbooks.

Add Quinacridone Magenta and Permanent Rose to the top/upper petals on the flowers, and Quinacridone Red and Permanent Rose to the lower petals of the flowers.

→

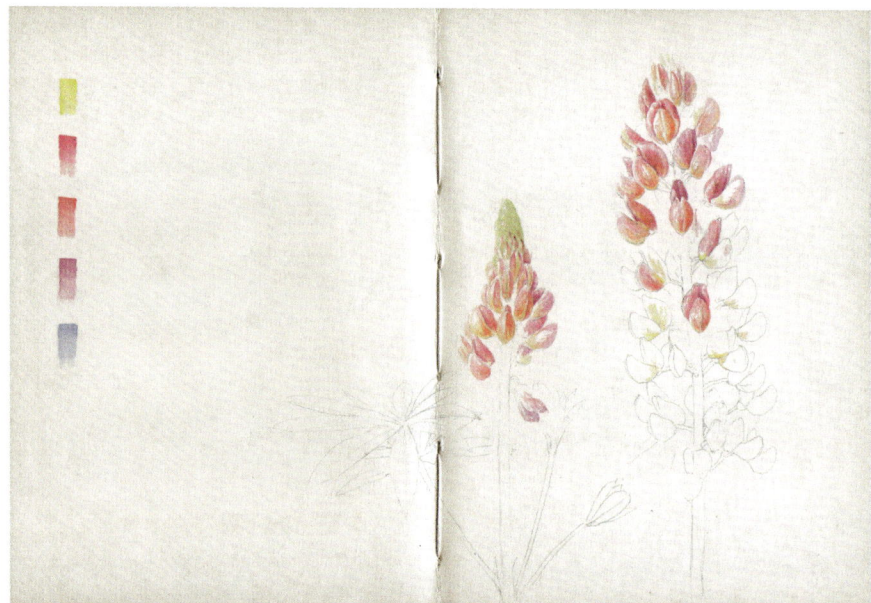

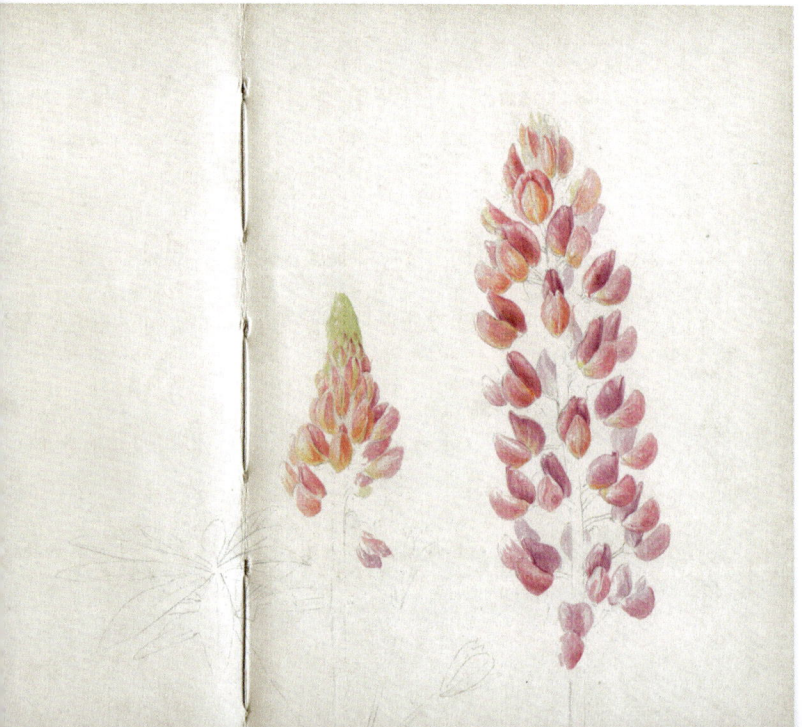

←

Nearer to the base of the more mature spike on the far right of the page, use the cooler pink, Quinacridone Magenta, to create the colour of the older petals. Also, paint the flowers at the rear of the tall flower stem with a dilute version of the colour and a touch of Cobalt Blue; this gives the impression of the flowers being further away and avoids any merging of tonally similar parts that may be touching.

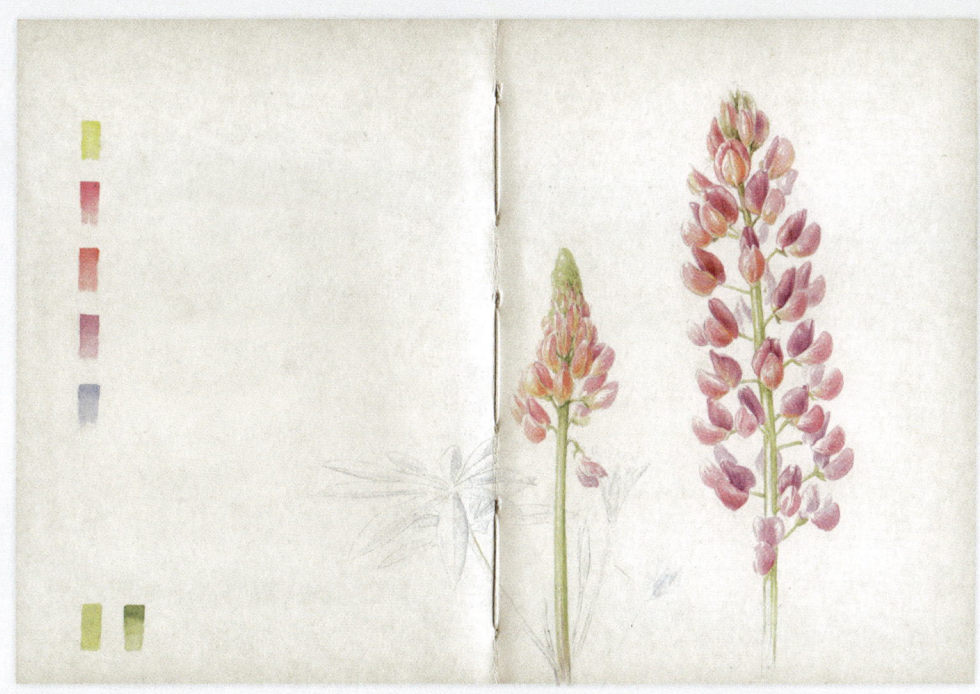

Add a pale green to the stem using a mix of Cobalt Blue, Winsor Lemon, and a very small amount of Permanent Rose. On the rear leaves, add a pale Cobalt Blue wash, ensuring you differentiate between lighter and darker areas to create form.

Add green to the nearest leaves, using the same green mix as used previously. The rear leaf remains blue to create the impression of distance and separation between nearer and more distant parts.

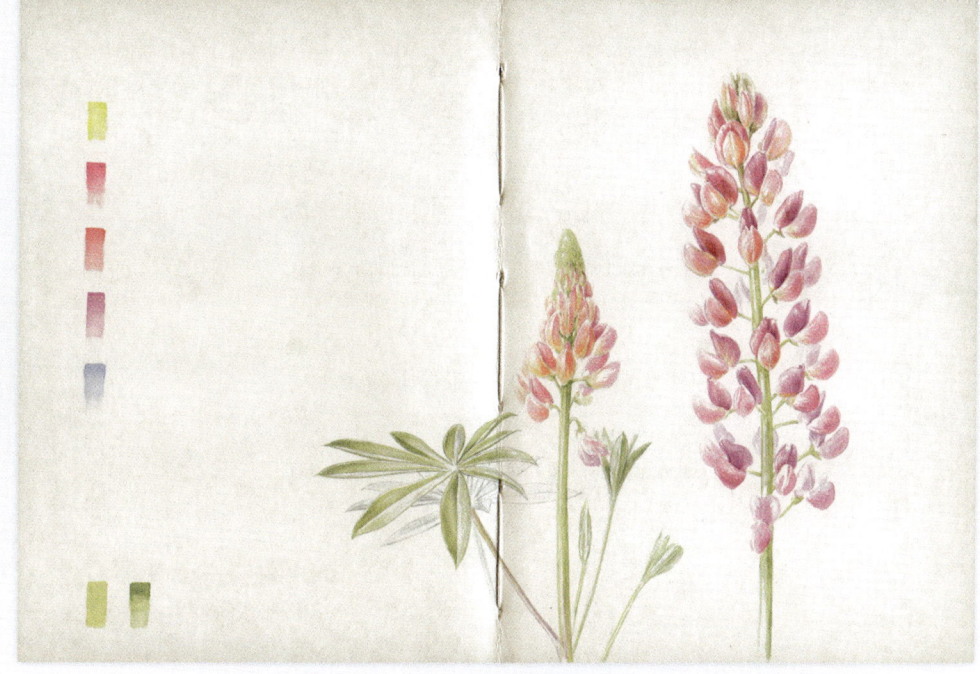

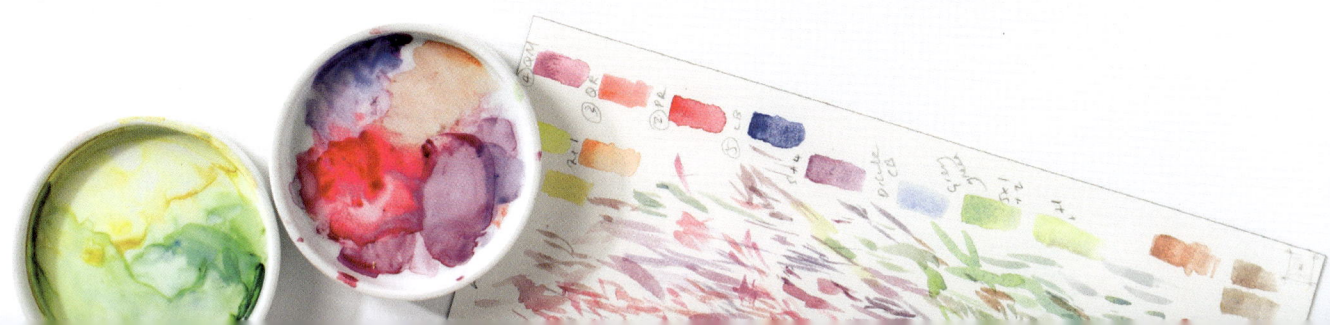

Now turn your attention to the second page, which will have the developing seed-pod stem and a large leaf sitting behind them. I wanted to include this leaf to tell more of the plant story and to show its shape and size in full. Using graphite is a very effective way of showing additional parts in this way, and because you have already shown one smaller leaf in colour, this is a suitable approach of doing so. Also, time is limited with sketch pages, and this fills large areas in quickly while serving the purpose of providing additional information about the plant.

You can now add watercolour to the fruiting stem. You don't have to worry about painting the large leaf behind it, which could be problematic as well as time-consuming.

I sketched the remainder of the plant parts using an HB pencil. This included the rear leaf and the stem with the developing seed pods. The rear leaf can be a line drawing or can have a small amount of tone added, but I kept it as line until I painted the seed-pod stem.

I use this graphite approach regularly. Sometimes I render the leaf with graphite and other times only line drawing is used. Occasionally, I paint part of the leaf because older leaves tend to be darker than young ones. Using a mixture of approaches and media is a very useful strategy for organizing many overlapping parts of a plant on a spread.

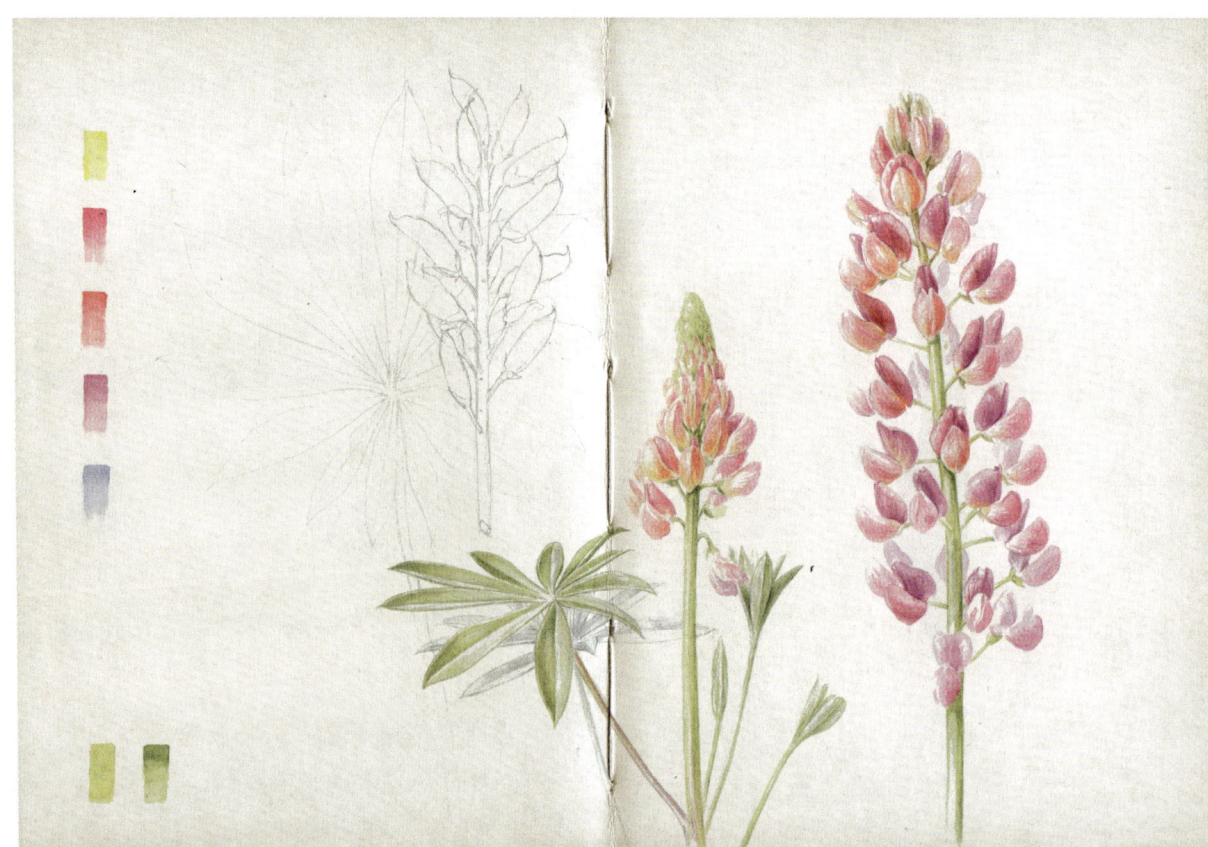

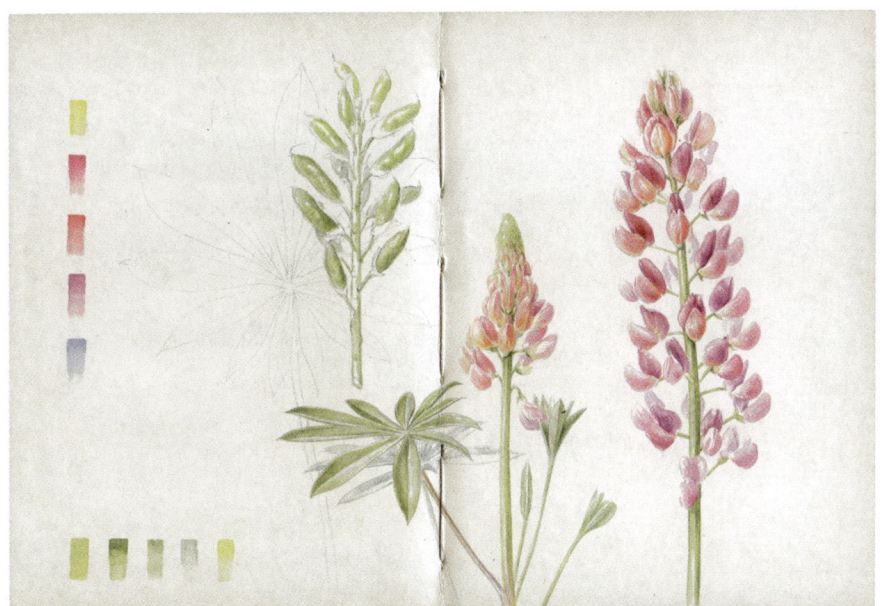

Add a yellow-biased green to the seed pods using a mix of Cobalt Blue, Winsor Lemon, Winsor Yellow, and a small amount of Permanent Rose. Pods are roughly painted to create the hairy texture, such as in the areas where hairs might catch the light.

←————————

I included a dissection of the flower on the first page as it made for a more interesting page and provided additional information about the plant, and this is especially important when the reproductive parts are concealed inside the flower. The purpose of enlarging the dissection was to make it clearer to see, and it's also easier to paint those tiny parts at a larger size.

It is always best to position dissections in the nearest place to the part of the plant that they relate to – although sometimes it's not possible. For reference, I find that taking a photograph of a dissection is always a good idea as the flower will die very quickly once it's cut. Today, we have incrediblly powerful cameras to help with this sort of work but remember to make sure your dimensions in the initial drawing are correct. You can paint the flower using the same approach as with other flowers, but fine line work is needed, so use a smaller brush with a fine point for the smaller reproductive parts in the dissection. View them with a hand lens to see the details.

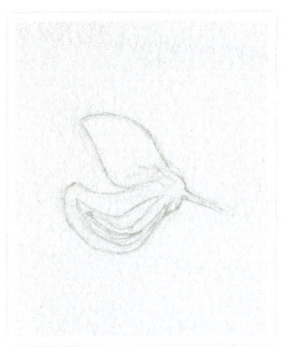

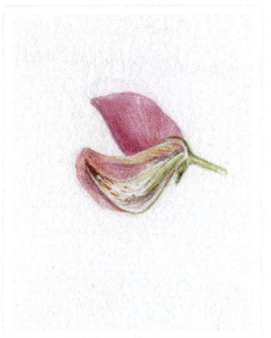

↑ *Using an H-grade pencil, draw the dissection of the flower at x 1.5 or x 2 life-size; this shows half of the flower, revealing the reproductive parts inside that otherwise would not be seen.*

↑ *Paint the dissection using the same colours as in the main illustration.*

I completed the developing fruit stem on the left-hand page with a cut edge at the base. I added the dried brown petals to the base of the pods using the same three-colour mix, but the mix began with Permanent Rose and Winsor Yellow, and Cobalt Blue was added.

I later add a final addition in the form of a mature seed pod, but if you are going to do this be sure to leave space at the planning stage. This is also why you should research the plant at the outset in order to know what other elements could be added later. The pod is dry and splits open to reveal the seeds, and I painted it open and closed.

Returning to the large leaf, add a little tone with some loose hatching to make it stronger. All that remains is to finish any areas that need more work, and then the pages are complete.

I added a dried seed pod in an open position, showing the five developing seeds. I painted the outer surface of the pods with a mix of Permanent Rose, Winsor Lemon, and Cobalt Blue to make the brown mix; inside the pod, I used a yellow-biased version of the colour. You could also include a closed pod, painting a hatching line effect on the outer surface to create the hairy texture. Use an HB graphite pencil to draw the subtle veins onto the large leaf. You can also add a little hatching-style shading to the large rear leaf, to create more depth, although this could also be left as an outline drawing.

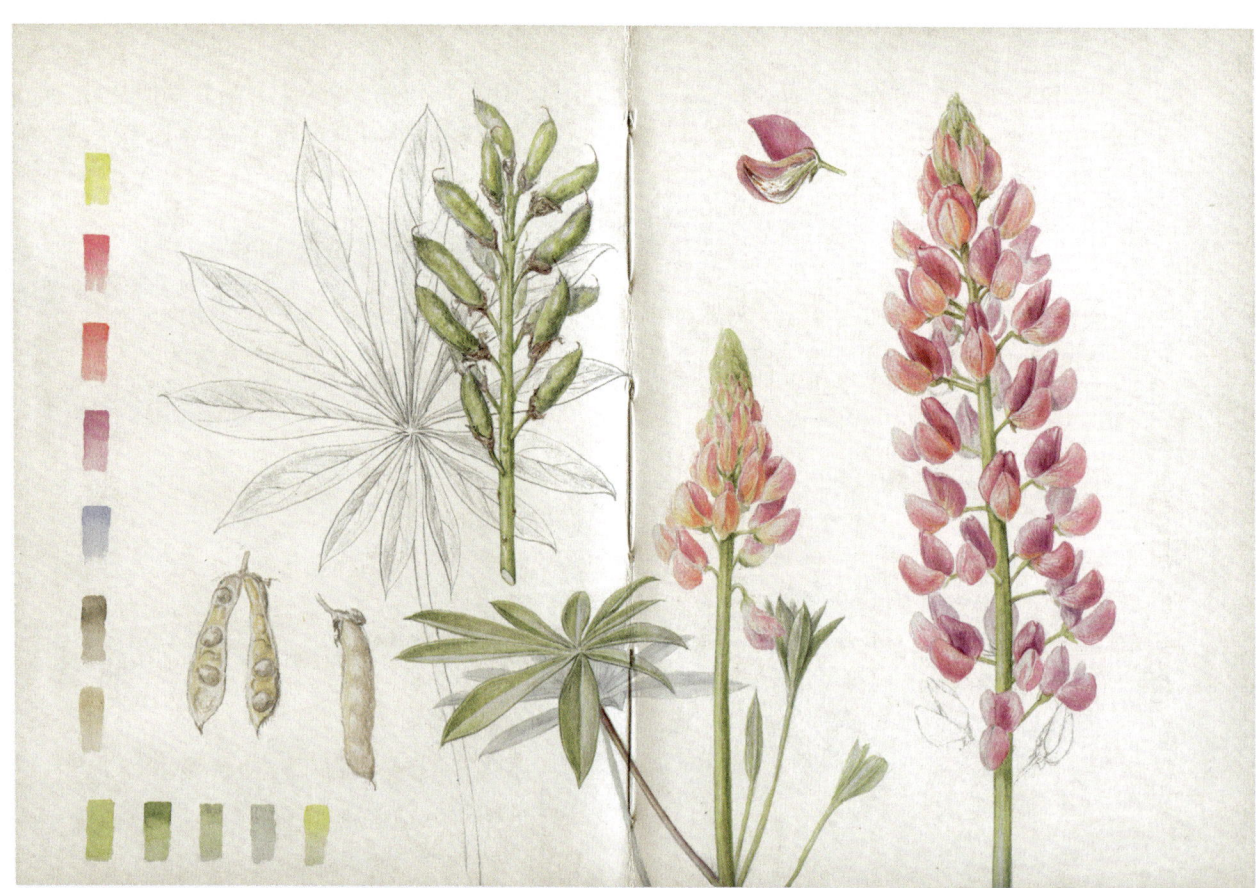

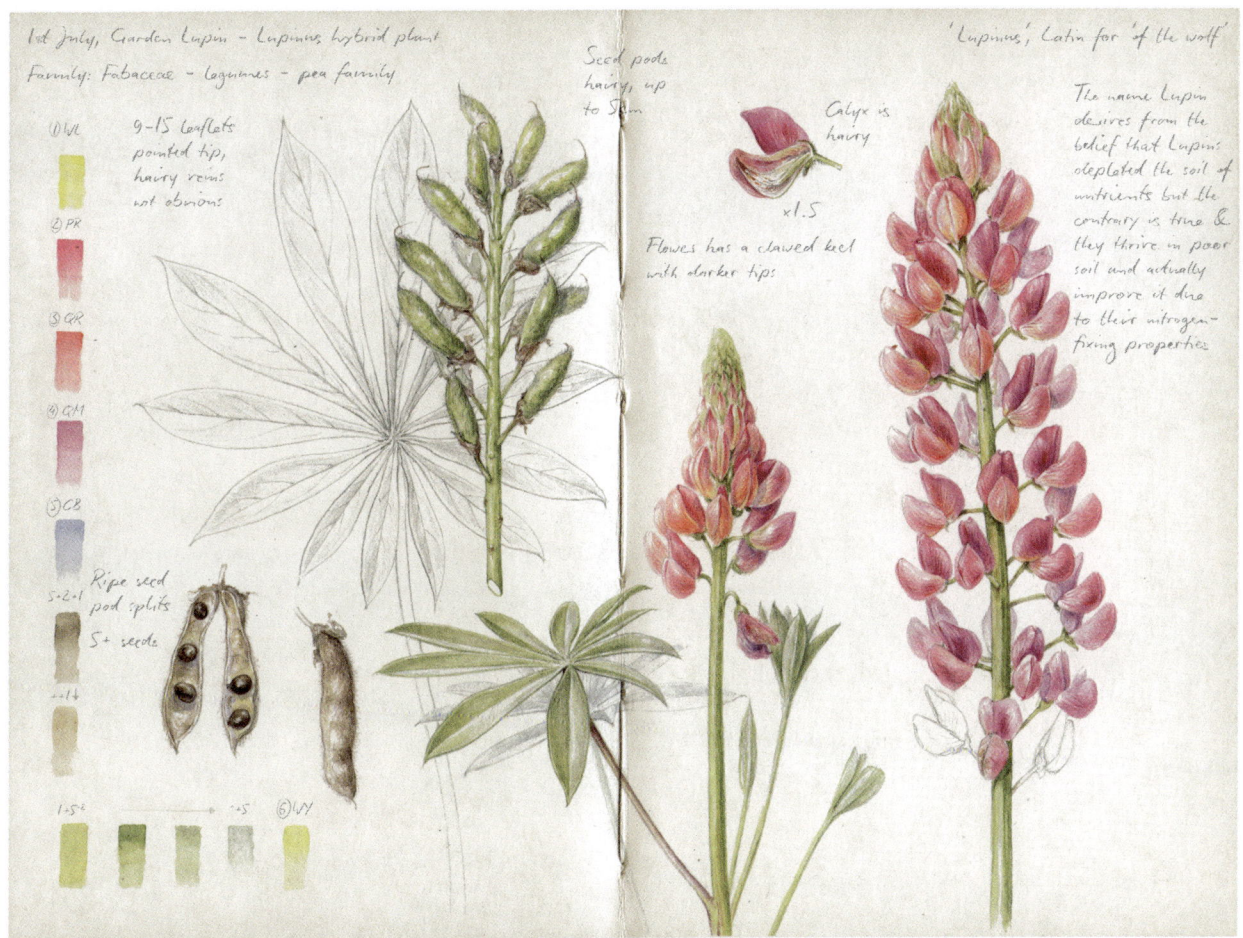

Handwritten notes (on the journal spread):

1st July, Garden Lupin - Lupinus hybrid plant
Family: Fabaceae - legumes - pea family

9-15 leaflets, pointed tip, hairy veins not obvious

Ripe seed pod splits
5+ seeds

Seed pods hairy, up to 5cm

Calyx is hairy
×1.5

Flower has a clawed keel with darker tips

'Lupinus', Latin for 'of the wolf'

The name Lupin derives from the belief that Lupins depleted the soil of nutrients but the contrary is true & they thrive in poor soil and actually improve it due to their nitrogen-fixing properties

Colour swatch labels:
① WL
② PR
③ QR
④ QM
⑤ CB
5·2·1
1·5 → ·5 ⑥ WY

Intensify colour in all parts of the painted elements and add small hairs on the fruit. For the hairs, mix Cobalt Blue, Permanent Rose, and Winsor Lemon to create a pale neutral grey that is painted from the pod outwards onto the white of the paper. Within the pod surface, paint shadows under hairs to give an indication of them. Darken the seeds inside the pods, using the same brown mix but in a more saturated concentration of paint. This completes the spread.

If you are unsure how to deal with multiple elements of a larger plant on a relatively small page, why not experiment with different media and saturations of colour? This can help you fit much more content onto the small page by creating visual distinction between overlaps, making them easier to see.

Conclusion

If you've read this book, you're likely already to be considering starting your own nature sketchbook. I hope that by sharing my process and sketchbook pages with you, I have inspired you to begin and, more importantly, to keep going with your book. Whether you're just starting out or have some experience, I'm confident you'll find that documenting plant stories and nature is a rewarding and enjoyable experience. Perhaps you'll even inspire others to take up the practice as well.

About the Author

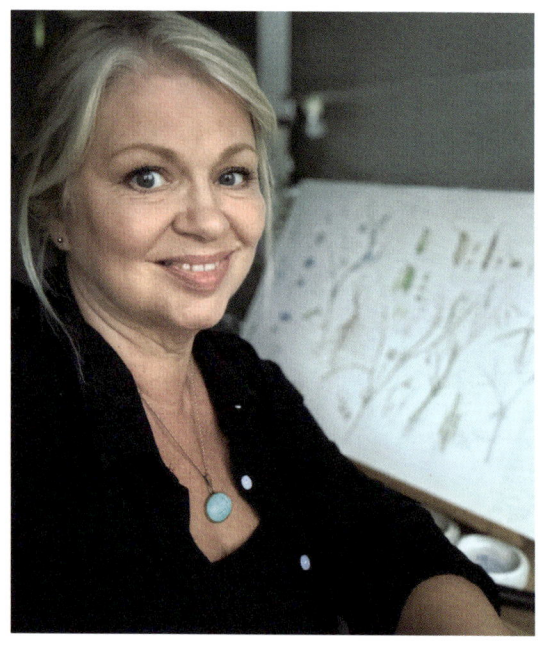

Dianne Sutherland is a British botanical artist and illustrator who initially trained as a ceramics painter with the Royal Albert design studio in Staffordshire. She then worked as a freelance artist and illustrator, spending 20 years in Scotland, where she developed a deeper interest in plants and the environment. To understand her subjects more thoroughly, she pursued a BSc in Plant Biology. In 2012, she moved back to her hometown and leveraged her SciArt background to continue her work as a botanical artist, developing an online programme to teach botanical art to others.

Dianne has a particular passion for recording native British species in her sketchbooks, but she also travels extensively to document plants and the stories behind them. In her more recent works, she diversifies with various other natural history subjects. Her preferred media are watercolour and graphite.

She is a Fellow of the Linnean Society and the Society of Botanical Artists. Her work is included in permanent collections at the Hunt Institute for Botanical Documentation, the Sydney Florilegium, the Singapore Botanic Gardens, and the Royal Botanic Garden Edinburgh Florilegium.

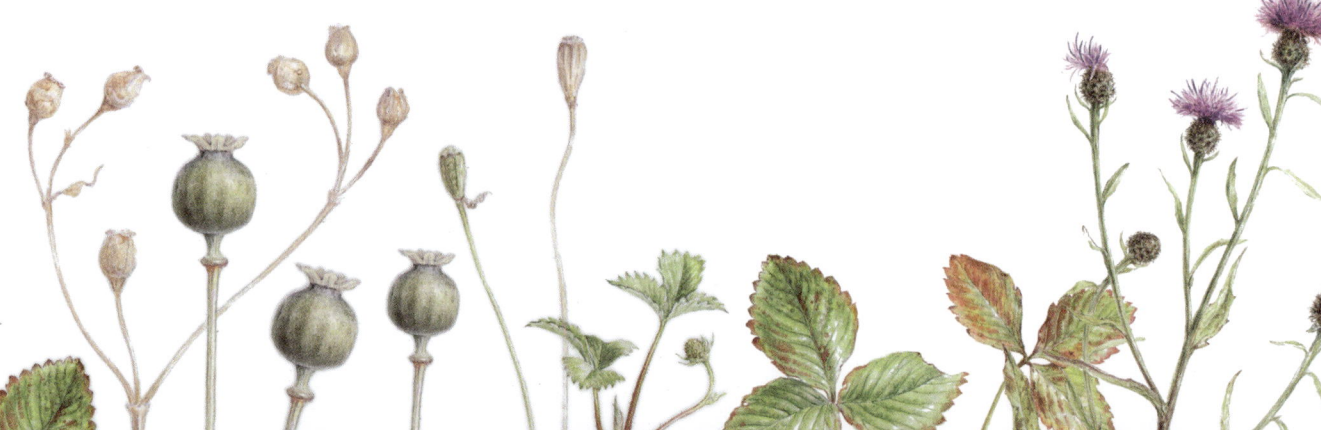

Index

A DAVID AND CHARLES BOOK
© David and Charles, Ltd 2025

David and Charles is an imprint of David and Charles, Ltd
Suite A, Tourism House, Pynes Hill, Exeter, EX2 5WS

Text and Designs © Dianne Sutherland 2025
Layout and Photography © David and Charles, Ltd 2025

First published in the UK and USA in 2025

A catalogue record for this book is available from the British Library.

ISBN-13: 9781446314098 paperback
ISBN-13: 9781446314104 EPUB

This book has been printed on paper from approved suppliers and made from pulp from sustainable sources.

Printed in Bosnia and Herzegovina by GPS for:
David and Charles, Ltd
Suite A, Tourism House, Pynes Hill, Exeter, EX2 5WS

10 9 8 7 6 5 4 3

Publishing Director: Ame Verso
Publishing Manager: Jeni Chown
Editor: Victoria Allen
Project Editor: Melanie Robinson and Cheryl Brown
Designer: Sam Staddon
Pre-press Designer: Susan Reansbury
Art Direction: Sarah Rowntree
Photography: Jason Jenkins
Production Manager: Beverley Richardson

Credits: Photo p66 features *Drawings of British Plants* by Stella Ross-Craig, published by G Bell & Sons 1960-63.

David and Charles publishes high-quality books on a wide range of subjects. For more information visit www.davidandcharles.com.

Share your art with us on social media using #dandcbooks and follow us on Facebook and Instagram by searching for @dandcbooks

Layout of the digital edition of this book may vary depending on reader hardware and display settings.